W9-AGY-405
DISCARDED

No One Gardens Alone

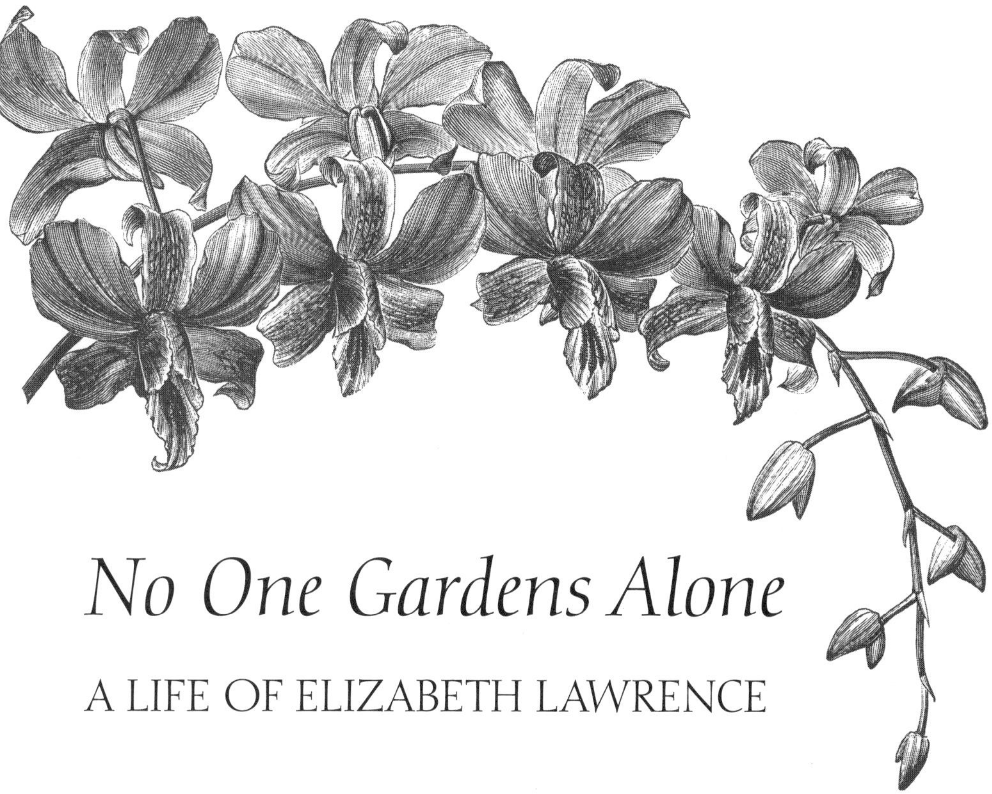

No One Gardens Alone

A LIFE OF ELIZABETH LAWRENCE

EMILY HERRING WILSON

BEACON PRESS

BOSTON

BEACON PRESS
25 Beacon Street
Boston, Massachusetts 02108-2892
www.beacon.org

Beacon Press books are published under the auspices of
the Unitarian Universalist Association of Congregations.

Printed in the United States of America

07 06 05 04 8 7 6 5 4 3 2 1

This book is printed on acid-free paper that meets the uncoated paper ANSI/NISO specifications for permanence as revised in 1992.

Text design by Christopher Kuntze
Composition by Wilsted & Taylor Publishing Services

LIBRARY OF CONGRESS CATALOGING-IN-PUBLICATION DATA

Wilson, Emily Herring.
No one gardens alone : a life of Elizabeth Lawrence / by Emily Herring Wilson.
p. cm.
Includes bibliographical references and index.
ISBN 0-8070-8560-X (cloth : alk. paper)
1. Lawrence, Elizabeth, 1904–1985. 2. Gardeners—North Carolina—Charlotte—Biography.
3. Women gardeners—North Carolina—Charlotte—Biography. I. Title.

SB63.L36W56 2004
712'.092—DC22 2004006384

For Jane Hatcher

"I want you to know how much I have loved life and how necessary it was just the way I played it."

ELIZABETH LAWRENCE TO FRAN WAY (1970S)

"She was *inside* the wonderful garden and she could come through the door under the ivy any time and she felt as if she had found a world all her own."

FRANCES HODGSON BURNETT, *The Secret Garden*

Contents

Prologue

ELIZABETH LAWRENCE is the garden's biographer. She brings the garden to life and makes us feel as if we ourselves are in it. The titles of her books suggest the range of her interests: *A Southern Garden, The Little Bulbs, Gardens in Winter, Lob's Wood, Gardening for Love,* and *A Rock Garden in the South. A Garden of One's Own* is a collection of her garden articles that appeared in journals, and *Through the Garden Gate* includes a selection from her more than seven hundred newspaper columns. Her first book, *A Southern Garden,* published in 1942 and reissued in three editions, is regarded as a classic in garden literature. Each of her books has its own following, both among gardeners who go to Lawrence for information and advice that remains relevant today, and among readers who regard Lawrence as a gifted literary writer who knew poetry as well as she knew plants.

Elizabeth Lawrence had an implicit understanding of how essential her life was to her work, and she wrote from her experiences at home and in the garden. She had the ability to write about herself and her friends in a way that preserves rather than destroys privacy, a gift so rare in our time that we may underestimate its importance. In each of her books, she invites the reader inside: We see the red cardinal in the bamboo by the candle-lit window, where Elizabeth and her mother are having dinner; smell the scent of sweet olive; hear the sound of branches breaking under the weight of ice; and feel woolly thyme and lamb's ears. Our senses are aroused, and, if only for a moment, time stands still. No one knew better than Elizabeth Lawrence how ephemeral a garden is, and she teaches her readers to savor every season because it will not last forever. In this lesson, we learn another way of being, imagined if not lived. In an age of speed, such moments of peace are essential, I must believe, to our well-being.

Elizabeth Lawrence was a woman of a certain time and place. Born at the beginning of the twentieth century, she revered the past. She knew her great-grandparents, grandparents, and parents and their Georgia and West Virginia homes. Her literary forebears were Virgil, Proust, and Jane Austen. But she was not stuck in the past. She wrote her own poetry in the style of Edna St. Vincent Millay, whose verses she read as a student at Barnard College in New York City. Her most insistent credo for gardeners was that they try something new, and she introduced hundreds of exotic plants into their gardens. Even before she died, her reputation was complex. Behind her back, some people called her "St. Elizabeth," a title that may refer to her image as "the Southern gardener." Some found her "shy"; others, "feisty." A cousin remembered her as "rebellious" for having worn knickers when she visited her grandparents in Marietta, Georgia. She was, I believe, mysterious, for she could seem to be all of these. However closely I have tried to understand the private life that I discovered in personal letters, I admit to having felt myself still a visitor to her house and garden. It was, in fact, the appeal of a private life that drew me in, and kept my intentions honest. How could I ever write about such a life, I reasoned, unless I also respected its privacies? I have written her story as I best understood it, knowing that as her biographer, I have known less about her than she knew about the garden. Still, what I found, including what she left for us to find in books and in papers, was compelling. I have had the same intensity of interest in her life that she had in the garden. I believe that readers may share my interests. In my years of reading letters, I found a love story, a remarkable friendship, a notebook of her own poems, and a complexity of personalities—a college girl who had never been kissed finding herself at a party in the 1920s in Greenwich Village; a dutiful granddaughter and daughter who loved to argue; an artist and a scientist who lived a dream life in the garden; a writer who battled with editors; and an old lady, shy and feisty by turns.

Elizabeth Lawrence was an old-fashioned kind of garden writer, collecting scientific information—much of it from records of several thousand plants she had grown in her own gardens—and then personalizing it. Right in the midst of telling us about a plant we have never seen, called by a name we cannot spell or pronounce, she makes us want to go out and find *Iris unguicularis* so that we can enjoy the "whiff" of the first breath of spring.

A half-dozen of Lawrence's admirers represent the breadth of her appeal: Katharine White, editor at *The New Yorker;* Joseph Mitchell, prose writer at *The New Yorker;* Eudora Welty, fiction writer; Stanley Kunitz, poet; Allen Lacy, garden writer; and Elisabeth Woodburn, book dealer. They and other reviewers have placed Elizabeth Lawrence in the top rank of garden writers. Not only in the South but throughout the United States and in England, she has a following among gardeners that is extraordinary—whether they take her books with them into the garden or leave them by a favorite chair.

Looking for Elizabeth Lawrence's place in the history of American garden literature rewards us with the same satisfactions as looking for a plant—finding it is only half the adventure. Along the way, we discover treasures, almost by accident. Isn't that often the experience of the avid gardener? It is certainly one of the lessons we learn from reading Lawrence, who describes how she sometimes found almost beneath her feet the very plant she had been looking for (and sometimes found it in her *own* garden). Lawrence also teaches us where to look—not only down at our feet, but in the gardens of neighbors and friends, in untrammeled woods (if we can find them), in nurseries, in farmers' markets, and on street corners.

And she taught us in her very first book, *A Southern Garden,* that we learn gardening not only by gardening but by reading about gardens. Many of Lawrence's favorite writers belong to what antiquarian book dealer Elisabeth Woodburn called the Golden Age of American horticultural writing—the late nineteenth and the early twentieth century. Many of those were women: Ida Bennett, Neltje Blanchan, Celia Thaxter, Alice Morse Earle, Helena Rutherfurd Ely, Louisa King, and Louise Beebe Wilder. Books by British writers were also some of her favorites, especially those by Mrs. Loudon, Gertrude Jekyll, E. A. Bowles, and Vita Sackville-West. But she did not stop there. She continued to read as many new books as she could, and we find Beverley Nichols, Michael James Jefferson-Brown, Jens Jensen, Russell Page, Rosemary Verey, Josephine Nuese, Allen Lacy, and hundreds of others in her library, now housed at the Cherokee Garden Library at the Atlanta History Center. Hers was a "working library," which she consulted every day as she gardened or wrote about gardening. In writing about garden books, Elizabeth Lawrence further enlarged the landscape of her readers.

As a writer, Elizabeth Lawrence had a particular genius for making us feel as if her backyard garden were the world. Although she earned her reputation as the quintessential Southern gardener because she gardened in North Carolina, she found her way down countless garden paths in countless places, some of which she had seen, many of which she had only read about. She was as much at home in books as she was in gardens, and her love of one enhanced her love of the other. In honor of Homer she persisted in trying to grow the rare asphodel. It came to her attention by way of Pope's translation of the *Odyssey,* and her understanding of it deepened when she did her own translation. She ordered it through a nursery in South Carolina. When it did not survive its first summer, she replaced it with one given to her from a friend's garden in Cincinnati. When that also died, she replaced it with another Cincinnati seedling—by that time she had learned to plant the rare asphodel where the soil is never soggy. It was not a particularly long quest, by Elizabeth's standards.

A traveler of the imagination, Elizabeth Lawrence believed there was no place like home. After graduating from Barnard College and taking a long trip abroad, she returned to North Carolina. The Raleigh garden, which her mother had maintained in her absence, was so beautiful that she decided never again to leave it, at least not for long. She was the first woman to enroll in a new program in landscape architecture at North Carolina State College in Raleigh, and after completing her studies, she embarked upon a career as a garden designer, lecturer, and writer. But it was her garden that was the talk of the town. Her circle of interests included nearby St. Mary's School, which she had loved as a young girl; the Episcopal Church, with the beauty of the Book of Common

Prayer; a mission Sunday school, where she introduced children to music and poetry; and garden clubs, where audiences thought her the most "charming" speaker they had ever had and a "plantswoman" of encyclopedic knowledge.

Small, thin, and fair, Elizabeth Lawrence always seemed too delicate for heavy work, until she lifted rocks; quiet and reticent, she seemed shy, until she argued; kind and well-mannered, she did not tolerate fools gladly. Young or old she always looked like a girl, and to the end of her mother's life (in 1964), she was a dutiful daughter. But her story has surprises, too, as unexpected as those at Misselthwaite Manor in Lawrence's favorite book, *The Secret Garden*. And Elizabeth Lawrence, like Mary Lennox in *The Secret Garden,* found the key that unlocks the garden's surprises. And of course, friends come in through the gate, and we will find them, too.

After her father's death in 1936 and her sister Ann's move to New York City, Elizabeth and her mother ("Bessie") filled up their large old house in Raleigh with friends. During World War II they also entertained soldiers, many of whom had never seen such a garden, or eaten a four-course meal by candlelight, or been encouraged to talk so much about themselves. Elizabeth and Bessie got along well as mother and daughter, as Bessie and her mother "Nana" had. Elizabeth especially loved the old (her great-grandparents, her grandparents, and her mother) and the young (her sister's son and daughter, children of friends, and neighborhood children).

Elizabeth always made good friends, and in Raleigh she was especially lucky. Most important to her were her neighbors, the Bridgers family. A widowed mother and three unmarried adult children made their home a center of good food, conversation, and encouragement. The two daughters—Emily and Ann Preston Bridgers—were successful writers, and they took Elizabeth under their wings. Throughout the 1930s and 1940s, with their help, Elizabeth became the garden writer we know today. Chapters about these friendships and others will show how close relationships enabled Elizabeth Lawrence to grow emotionally stronger. As we read from three generations of private letters, we will begin to trace a family history that informs this biography as much as the garden does. Without getting to know Grandpa-pa and Grandma-ma, Nana and Bessie, we will not be able to understand Elizabeth, nor will we be able to appreciate why Elizabeth and Bessie and Elizabeth's sister Ann and her family chose to live next door to one another until the end of their lives. A "move" is often a chance to start over, and yet when Elizabeth and Bessie moved from Raleigh to Charlotte to be near Ann and her family, a pattern was repeated. At the same time, Elizabeth did experience a certain newness of life, for she had a chance to design a new house (a bungalow) and a new garden (with some of her old favorites).

Although Elizabeth liked to stay at home, in the botanical world she ranged as widely as a seed blown by the wind. Geography and time were no boundaries to her vivid curiosity. A favorite plant was as likely to come from Cape Town, South Africa, as from Marietta, Georgia, where her grandmother gardened. She understood the language of Southern farm ladies ("I gin ter you as gun ter me") as well as Virgil's Latin: *Quid faciat laetas segetes,* "What makes the crops joyous?"

Lawrence was a passionate letter writer, and in a steady flow of correspondence over more than a half-century, as she collected bloom dates for her records, she also collected friends. Although books about gardening were important, she believed that the most valuable source of information was other gardeners who had themselves grown the plants in all places and conditions, and she wrote to them across the country, from Maine to California. And when they wrote back, she put them in her books: Mr. Krippendorf in his old clothes and red bandanna, worn as he roams the woods in Ohio; Caroline Dormon exclaiming, "Come runnin'!"; and Rosa Hicks's listing of plants, written with the stub of a pencil.

"No one can garden alone," Lawrence reminds us, but it is a statement underplanted with paradox. No one was more conscious than she of a person's need to be alone. She had the courage to be private. In our quest to satisfy that need, we may find the gardener in ourselves, a discovery that may or may not require us to plant something (though it could not hurt us if we did).

Prologue

Elizabeth Lawrence is not easy to find. As her biographer, I have taken long, sometimes circuitous paths, which I followed in her books and papers, while laying out a few new ones of my own—always mindful that she was master of the well-planned, but informal, garden. My work is done, and now you are going to meet her: Look for the tall sasanqua hedge sheltering the small gray-shingled house from the street. You have come to the right place if you see the Old Blush rose climbing up the wild cherry tree by the front door. Enter through the garden gate and pass along the curtain of bamboo and down the rock steps. Sherry will be served on the terrace. Afterwards, pick up a pair of secateurs or a digging fork from the basket. Take your time walking down the gravel paths (wide enough for companions), stopping to sit by the pool where some neighborhood children are playing, listening to the birds at the feeder; then continue on your way to the back woods of pines and hellebores, returning by the lower path until you find something—a seedling, a flower, a puzzling leaf, a little piece of ivy—and carefully make it yours. And if you suddenly remember a missed appointment and must hurry away, please smooth over any disturbance, leave the prongs of the fork turned down, and close the gate behind you.

We are being allowed to enter a private life and a private garden only because of the welcoming spirit that Elizabeth Lawrence left in her books and in a thousand (or more) letters, many of which are, in a phrase, in private hands. Family members—especially her niece, Elizabeth Way Rogers, and her nephew, Warren Way III, and his wife, Fran Way—and friends, many of whom I name in the acknowledgments, have made it possible for us to be here. I especially thank them.

I do not believe that we ever fully understand another person; something mysterious will always remain private. Thus, as I have spent many years trying to "know" the life of Elizabeth Lawrence, I have reminded myself, as I remind others, in a paraphrase of Yeats (one of Lawrence's favorite poets): Tread softly, for we tread on her dreams.

CHAPTER ONE

Family History

"I would like to live in the same soil as my ancestors, and walk under their trees, and do what they did, and think their thoughts."

ELIZABETH LAWRENCE TO ANN PRESTON BRIDGERS (1939)

THE EXCITEMENT OF DEPARTURE and the long overnight train ride from New York City to Raleigh, North Carolina, had left Elizabeth in a state of wakefulness. Her graduation from Barnard College had felt like a surprise, and since nobody from her family back home had actually been there to see her receive the diploma, she might have wondered if she had really graduated. Anyone would have a hard time finding her in the class photograph—was she the small one in the back row, at the very end, unsmiling and half-hidden? On the day of her graduation—June 1, 1926—a sudden cold rain had ended the ceremonies, scattering the crowd, and leaving her chilled. Four years in New York City had been a test of her ability to survive in a place that still frightened her if she was alone, but she had made friends and stuck it out. Now she was going home. All night on the train she had written in her journal, waiting for the time when she could raise the shade and see the passing fields and hamlets of the Southern landscape she knew by heart.

Home for breakfast, she had been fretful when her mother reminded her that they were having a tea the next afternoon, but when her father teased her, his warm laughter made her feel better. She looked at both of them with such adoration that her mother jumped up from the table and hurried to the kitchen, returning with a package, which she set in front of Elizabeth. They watched as she opened it—and heard her soft "oh" of delight. Her sister Ann might be welcomed home with pearls, but pruning shears and her mother's stern look softening into a smile were the perfect gifts for Elizabeth. Now it was her turn to jump up from the table, and blowing each of them a kiss, she hurried out of the room, through the kitchen, and out of the house.

It was a picture-perfect early June morning, warm and bright. Elizabeth sat on the back steps and looked around. There was work to be done—gravel for the paths, repairs to the rock walls. The garden pool had been neglected—she might begin there. At the far end, chairs and a table had been set up in the summerhouse. She stood up and moved down the path. The sun felt good on her shoulders, and she pushed back her hair, then stopping at a flower bed and brushing aside the leaves, she discovered a blossom of her grandmother's rose-colored rain lily. She remembered it from her childhood as "the sign and seal of summer," which is how she would describe it in her first book.[1] But that was in the future. It took her as many years to write about it as the lilies required to spread and become a "sea of pink"—and for exotic plants from all parts of the world to find a home in her garden.[2]

Elizabeth Lewis Lawrence was born to Elizabeth Bradenbaugh Lawrence and Samuel Lawrence in his parents' large clapboard house at 237 Whitlock Avenue in Marietta, Georgia. The year was 1904, and on May 27, the day of Elizabeth's birth, tea roses bloomed under the bay window where Grandma-ma Lawrence sat with her sewing. In Parkersburg, West Virginia, her mother's family awaited the good news.[3]

The Lawrence family Bible lay on the dining table in the Marietta home, to be inscribed with the baby's name. The dark-paneled rooms lit by oil lamps filled with shadows, softening the commotion in the house. After dishes had been cleared away and the red and white checkered cloth had been spread across the table, Grandpa-pa took out the Book of Common Prayer and read aloud the service of Evening Prayer, as he had done when Sam had been born in the house. Again, the men went out to sit on the side porch that opened off the dining room through high screen doors, while the women comforted the new mother and baby. Outside, darkness was long in coming, pulled down to a grassy knoll by the heavy branches of an old oak tree so large that three grown men would have had to link hands to measure its trunk. Before she was one year old, Elizabeth was baptized at nearby St. James Episcopal Church in Marietta and photographed in Parkersburg.

And so, home, garden, family, and church were laid as the cornerstones of Elizabeth Lawrence's life, upon which she was to build her own house of memory, made beautiful by Grandma-ma's Safrono roses and Nana's witch hazel, and a thousand flowers of her own.

Dwelling in her family's history became one of Elizabeth's favorite pastimes. She came to know three generations of kin very well because, every summer until they were young adults, she and her sister, Ann, went for long visits to the house on Ann Street in Parkersburg, West Virginia, and to the house on Whitlock Avenue in Marietta. Because Elizabeth spent more time in Parkersburg, including one long winter after college, her most vivid memories began there.

Elizabeth's family on her mother's side came from Wood County, West Virginia, where they had lived before that part of the state split off from Virginia in 1863, in opposition to slavery. The earliest relative the family knew anything about was Captain James Neal, who was of Irish descent (he apparently changed the spelling of the family name —O'Neal). He was, Elizabeth observed, her family's "only Patriot." During the Revolutionary War, Neal raised a company and joined Washington's army at Valley Forge. After the American victory, he became a surveyor, and in 1772–1773 he bought land near present-day Parkersburg, West Virginia. In the fall of 1785, he built a blockhouse on the Little Kanawha River, near its mouth at the Ohio River, which became known as Neal's Station. In 1786, after the death of his first wife, he married Mary Phelps, daughter of a Revolutionary War officer. He and Mary and his single and married children made Neal's Station their permanent residence in 1787. They appear in West Virginia history as the first permanent settlers of Parkersburg.[4] When a monument was erected in memory of Neal and other Revolutionary soldiers, young Elizabeth unveiled it.

Elizabeth's maternal great-grandfather, Joseph Beard Neal, was the grandson of Captain Neal. He was born in Parkersburg in 1830, and in 1854 he married Elizabeth Frances Lewis, also from Wood County. By the time he was thirty, he had established himself in Parkersburg as a druggist, and building upon his success, he had acquired other business interests that had resulted in the accumulation of a good deal of money and property, including a fine house. The Neals' daughter, Ann "Nannie" Beard Neal, was born in 1856, was baptized at Trinity Episcopal Church, and was educated in a private academy in Leesburg, Virginia, and later at a college in Missouri. She had other opportunities to travel, and when she was nineteen years old and visiting friends in Baltimore, she met Jacob Frank Bradenbaugh, who was ten years older. Frank, a businessman, was descended from German immigrants who had arrived in Philadelphia in 1767, and may have soon moved to Baltimore.[5] Apparently, Nannie was much persuaded by the generosity of Frank's affection. In one of his letters, in which he admitted to having done nothing but work, he urged her to write him about the good times that she had been having. Nannie may have surprised everyone when she agreed to marry Frank in 1875, because it meant that she would move from Parkersburg to Frank's hometown of Baltimore. The next year, their daughter, Elizabeth ("Bessie"), was born; and the following year, a son, Frank Elliott Bradenbaugh. For the first six years of their married life, the family lived in Baltimore. By 1881 or 1882, however, apparently Frank's health was so poor that they made plans to move to Parkersburg, where he may have worked for a few years in her father's hardware business. He died young—at age thirty-eight—and for most of the years of Nannie's long life, no one could remember that she had ever been married.

In the summer of 1887, with her family's encouragement, Nannie agreed to go with her Baltimore friends, Sallie and Howard Atterbury, to Europe, where everyone hoped that she would lose her sense of melancholy. Although Nannie and the Atterburys traveled to all the great cities, Nannie was always thinking of home, and she wrote her parents and her children almost every day. Thanking Bessie (who was eleven) for having written to her, she said, "I know of no greater accomplishment than to write a good letter." In a letter to her son, she confessed, "I must fix myself up and try to look younger [she was thirty-one], but that is hard to do when I do not care to be young." In Paris, she remembered the graveyard in Parkersburg. "Wherever I go or wherever I turn that one little spot is always in my mind, but there is nothing I think will ever make me get over the loneliness and sorrow I feel in not having dear Frank to share everything with me."[6] When she returned home, Nannie found some relief from her melancholy by giving herself totally to her family and friends and to the house on Ann Street.

Parkersburg in the early 1900s seems an unlikely place for a future gardener to love. Railroads and barges moved heavy freight; industries produced oil, gas, lumber, and grime; and breweries added a sour mix to the stagnant air. Even the great Ohio River, upon which the region depended for transport, seemed darkly serpentine when it flooded, all the way to downtown churches. Joseph Beard Neal was an ardent Democrat, respected locally as a historian. He had been one of the city's leading businessmen, president of the Novelty Mill Company, partner in building the Ohio River Railroad, and founder of the largest wholesale hardware business in the city. If Elizabeth ever heard the names of some of his flours, she might have loved "Little Dude," "Perfection," and "Sea Foam." Neal's son, Robert, joined him in the hardware business. Joseph Neal's grandson, Frank Elliott Bradenbaugh (Bessie's brother), returned from college to take his place in the family business too, and was elected to the city council, before dying when he was thirty-five. This tradition—men making the money and reputations as civic leaders, and women staying at home—was to influence the direction of Elizabeth's life. Her memories of Parkersburg—carriage rides, picnics on Blennerhassett Island, card games in the library, sitting in the swing with her great-grandfather, callers in the afternoon—were remembrances of things past, but even when she came by train to Parkersburg, Elizabeth felt herself on familiar ground.

Going away and soon returning was a common pattern for many in the Lawrence family. It became a pattern for Elizabeth's life as well, when she rode through the night on the trains bound for home.

The scene in the 1880s when Nannie, with Frank and their children, returned to Parkersburg, was probably much the same as it was in the first two decades of the 1900s when Elizabeth came with her family to spend summers there. As the train approached the edge of the Parkersburg business district and moved slowly over the long, high trestle with its enormous rock supports, passengers had a view of the great Ohio River and the dark ridges of the Allegheny Mountains. Parkersburg's claims on the landscape were in church steeples, turrets of houses and hotels, and dark industries that lay along the water. When the train stopped and the doors were open and the luggage collected, Elizabeth and her sister and their mother and father gathered themselves together and climbed into a carriage for the ride up the hill to 1110 Ann Street, where their grandmother (whom the children called "Nana") and her parents were waiting. The heavy doors opened, and the children, Bessie, and Sam stepped into the tiled foyer and then through another set of heavy doors and were hurried into the parlor to have their wraps removed before the fire. The next day, Elizabeth and Ann stretched their legs by climbing the stairs to the third-floor ballroom, where they made a playhouse; soon, they discovered Uncle Frank's trains stored in the attic. Elizabeth remembered the arrival scene in the middle of the night, when they were met by a driver to "go clopping through the sleeping streets," as "one of the most exquisite moments of childhood."[7]

Ann Street was a neighborhood of many imposing houses, built in the 1800s on small lots on a hill out of reach of the flood-prone Ohio River. Today many of them, including the Neal house, still hold their looks. Their solid foundations and decorative flourishes show the success of the men who built them—men who had made money in oil and railroads, and who by their good works in churches, civic organizations, and city councils established their family names in the history of Parkersburg.

Built sometime between 1870 and 1875, the Neal house reflects the popularity of Victorian architecture. The two-story brick exterior is topped off by a mansard roof, deep enough for double-hung windows matching those on the floor below. Fireplaces throughout the house did not chase away the chill of rooms with twelve-foot ceilings, and gas lights—later electric—still left plenty of shadows, especially late at night when Elizabeth and her grandmother played backgammon in the front parlor. On cool summer mornings, Elizabeth sat on the deep front porch, waiting for the postman, Mr. Cook De Vol, who stopped at every house to talk before bringing the mail to 1110.[8] When a storm threatened, it was her younger sister Ann who had the courage to run upstairs and close the windows on the third floor.

Across the street lived the Sammel family, whose two little girls, Veronica and Betty, became summer playmates of Elizabeth and Ann when they visited Parkersburg. Veronica, called "Bill," was Ann's age. They later shared a New York apartment, and after they married and had children, they remained friends. Across town on a large wooded estate lived the Sammels' three maiden aunts in the antebellum house "Oakland," which their grandfather had built around 1833 on a thousand acres, worked by slaves until the encampment of Union soldiers in the grove. When Bessie and her mother arrived at the aunts' home by carriage, they saw a kind of historic grandeur that Victorian houses could not equal. When Elizabeth and Ann were children in summertime Parkersburg, they sometimes rode out in Mrs. Sammel's fine new automobile. Elizabeth loved the old aunts, as she loved older people generally, and she appreciated their talents: one of them kept house, one of them cooked, and one of them gardened. Later when she was a published author, she sent them copies of her books, which occasioned days of lively discussion among the sisters.[9]

Parkersburg was also the location of Blennerhassett Island. Located in the Ohio River, downstream from Parkersburg, it was a favorite place for excursions. Elizabeth, whose cousins owned part of the island, enjoyed swimming, Sunday School picnics, and walks on the beach to collect angel-wing shells. At the end of a day's outing as they returned in the launch, Elizabeth loved to drag her hands in the water so she could take back the feel of the river. Here on Blennerhassett Island she began to learn the names of plants—black walnut, locust, beech, and hackberry. Some seventy years after she had seen it as a child, she remembered the thicket of pawpaws with ripe fruit.[10]

The island was originally home to Indian tribes, and shards of their culture still remained. In 1797, when they were driven out and new settlers entered the Ohio Valley, the island acquired its present-day name. A rich man and his wife from Ireland, Harman and Margaret Blennerhassett, had purchased the island and built what was intended to be "a paradise," but a misadventure destroyed their dream. Aaron Burr had persuaded the wealthy Harman Blennerhassett to back him in a scheme to start an empire in the Southwest. He was living on the island as a friend of the Blennerhassetts when President Thomas Jefferson ordered his arrest as an accused traitor to his country, and he and Harman Blennerhassett were captured trying to leave the island. When Blennerhassett was released, he and his family had to abandon their island estate.

For a child like Elizabeth Lawrence, such a tale added excitement to her long evenings in the library with Nana, who was a very patriotic American and who reminded her granddaughter that their ancestor had fought with General Washington. Nana also told her of their own family's legend—that Harman Blennerhassett was said to have invited one of their forebears to go in with him in developing the island paradise, but that he had said that he was not willing to risk all without knowing more about it. Many years later when Elizabeth repeated Nana's tale to Eudora Welty, who had written a story based upon the character of Aaron Burr, Lawrence humorously noted that her ancestor's lack of ambition had given her an "inferiority complex."[11]

When Elizabeth visited her father's parents in Marietta, Georgia, she heard a different chapter in American history. During the Civil War, her great-grandparents had fled with many other Marietta families when Sherman's troops had set fire to their houses and occupied the town. Her grandfather, Robert T. de Treville Lawrence, had left college in Charleston to fight for the Confederacy, and after the war was over, he and the family returned to Marietta. He married Anne Eliza Atkinson, whose grandfather, Charles J. McDonald, was a state governor. In 1917, when "Miss Eliza" and Mr. Lawrence celebrated their fiftieth wedding anniversary, young Elizabeth and her sister Ann attended the celebration in Marietta with their parents. At the end of a very long life, Lawrence was president of the board of trustees of the Confederate Soldiers' Home in Atlanta and state pension commissioner. Reporters writing about the colorful octogenarian and well-known public citizen alluded to his energy and his sense of humor. When he was eighty-nine, he successfully challenged state officials to a footrace up the stairs at the capital; when he was ninety, he was photographed demonstrating the right way to eat corn pone.[12] To feel the past merge with the present, Elizabeth had only to sit with Grandpa-pa on the porch of the house that Sherman had burned and he had rebuilt, to pick flowers in the garden with Grandma-ma, and to go to Sunday School at St. James Episcopal Church in the building that her grandfather had helped build with his own hands. Walking to the Square, he could have told her how her parents had first met. It was a story that she would read for herself many years later when she discovered their courtship letters. In Elizabeth's childhood, Marietta still looked pretty much the way it had when Sam Lawrence and Bessie Bradenbaugh had walked to the Square.

By the late 1800s, Marietta, Georgia, located at the foot of Kennesaw Mountain,[13] was a popular health resort in summer and winter for guests wanting to escape the heat or cold of their own climates. They came to "take the waters" from the abundant springs, and to enjoy the comforts of a number of fine hotels. Only twenty miles away, the city of Atlanta was rising, but visitors to Marietta had not chosen it in order to be near ambitious and upstart Atlanta. They sought the healing effects of the natural springs, good food, and good society in a town large enough to offer diversions and small enough to center many of them around the town square. Wagons loaded with cotton filled the streets on a Saturday morning, and by afternoon a band was setting up to provide the evening's entertainment. On Sunday mornings, nearby churches were meeting places not only for worship but for socializing.

A generation after the Civil War, a war in which Grandpa-pa had been a young soldier, enough time had passed that some families in Marietta were living well again. Not that everyone did, of course—poor people, black and white, lived as determined by the old white Marietta families. In 1904, the year Elizabeth Lawrence was born, she was nursed by a woman she still called "Mammy," a relationship of such meaning for Elizabeth that she was to make it the subject of a high-school essay. Throughout the South, towns and cities had rebuilt themselves, and Marietta was a model of how it could be done.

Elizabeth's mother and father had met in Marietta in the winter of 1897, when her mother and her grandmother had taken rooms at a local hotel. Mrs. Bradenbaugh was a widow traveling with her twenty-one-year-old daughter, who hoped that a winter away from the harsh climate of West Virginia would improve her mother's health. Nannie had chronic insomnia, and perhaps in Marietta, free of her cares, she could sleep. Perhaps drinking spring water filled with iron would also give her a new sense of well-being. Her daughter would do anything to make her happier. Things had been going well, though Nannie was not an optimist. Her son, Frank Jr., had graduated with a degree in mechanical engineering from Lehigh University, and Bessie had finished her education in the arts at the McDonald-Ellis school for young ladies in Washington, D.C. Bessie was a devoted daughter and an agreeable traveling companion, and the choice to spend the winter in Marietta was proving to be wise. Nannie was proud of her mother's and father's Virginia roots; she and Bessie liked the South.

Mrs. and Miss Bradenbaugh may have arrived on the train from

Elizabeth's parents: Elizabeth Bradenbaugh Lawrence and Samuel Lawrence, probably in 1903, soon after they had married. Bessie and Sam present themselves as self-confidently to the photographer as they did to one another in their long courtship by letters. (By permission of Warren Way and Elizabeth Rogers.)

Parkersburg in time for the holiday season and spent their first Sunday morning at St. James Episcopal Church, where Sam Lawrence's father was a member of the vestry. Thus, when a traditional invitation went out from the "young men of Marietta" to attend a Christmas party at one of the resort hotels, Bessie probably already knew some of the young men from church. Her mother, ever one to watch closely to make sure that Bessie was in company with people she approved of, had nothing to worry about—or if she did, she had only to look sternly to summon Bessie to her side. One of the "historical and characteristic southern scenes" that the hotels promised in advertisements was about to unfold.

A few minutes before eight o'clock, the appointed hour, Sam Lawrence and the oldest of his three brothers, Alex, set forth to walk from their house to the party.[14] Although both already had graduated from the University of Georgia and had begun their professions—Alex in law in Savannah, and Sam in civil engineering in Atlanta—neither had yet married. Alex was twenty-eight, Sam, twenty-three, and they loved to come home to Marietta to see their family and friends. As they walked on a cold December night, they passed houses festooned with greenery and lit by candlelight, and the two young men on the way to a party were unknowingly about to meet the women they would marry.

Bessie was at an age when most unmarried girls were beginning to worry whether or not they were going to remain spinsters. But she was not like many of her contemporaries, who wanted to become dependent wives. She expressed her own opinions and kept her own busy calendar. Like her mother, she was interested in *everything*. The problem was that she was so closely tied to her mother, grandmother, grandfather, and her friends that the thought of having anyone take their place was troubling. Her own spirited self, her deference to her mother's needs, and her wariness of admitting any outsider into her affections made her an outspoken, but perhaps inwardly uncertain, young woman. The fun of being at a party and the fear of neglecting her mother may have been warring just below the surface of her social composure the evening she made a good and lasting impression upon Sam Lawrence.

Sam was a tall, handsome man, a great favorite in the Lawrence family, flirtatious and charming. Years later, a nephew remembered Uncle Sam's happy countenance in front of a mirror as he shaved, singing about Old Dan Tucker, who "brushed his hair with a wagon wheel"; a niece remembered that Uncle Sam always sent her five dollars for Christmas. Since his graduation from the University of Georgia at Athens, he had been working hard constructing spur tracks to new cotton mills. He moved from place to place as he was assigned to railroad projects, and he had missed his life back in Marietta. It was time to settle down.

Sam Lawrence did not sweep Elizabeth (as he called her at first) off her feet when they met in Marietta. She was *the* dutiful daughter with a good head on her shoulders, who was traveling with her widowed mother. Maybe she did take some particular care in dressing for the party to meet Marietta's eligible young bachelors, but she could have said that she had done it to please her dear mother. She was bound to her mother's needs, first and foremost, because they had been together since her father's death in 1884. Bessie, who was eight when he died, and her brother Frank, who was six, had sought to take their father's place, even as young children, and there was nothing that they wouldn't do for their mother. Bessie and her mother did everything together, and when they were separated, it usually was because Mrs. Bradenbaugh had lent her out to be spoiled by her friends. The charming and persistent attentions of Sam Lawrence therefore introduced a new presence into the life of Bessie Bradenbaugh, who, like her mother, seemed willing to be old before her time.

Sam and Bessie began writing infrequent letters sometime after they met in Marietta. Most of his letters are missing, but several hundred of her letters were preserved by the family. Her mother had taught her the importance of writing a good letter. Her earliest ones began, "Dear Mr. Lawrence," and were signed, "Very sincerely your friend Elizabeth

Bradenbaugh." She continued in this way for several years, until the fall of 1901, when she wrote from California, where she and her mother were attending an Episcopal Church general convention. "You will probably be surprised to hear that I am in San Francisco," she wrote, and added, "if anything I do could surprise you." Perhaps Bessie was herself surprised, for in no other letter does she seem so exuberant. In Banff the scenery was "beyond words." Alone on the train's observation deck at night, she thought of "nothing but Peace." She attended church in Portland, and in the afternoon she saw Mt. Hood and Mt. St. Helena. A friend took them to dinner at the "Pooh Dog" restaurant in San Francisco. "I am taking for granted you are interested in all this and have written quite a volume," Bessie, who often found it difficult to fill two pages, concluded. "I enjoyed hearing about your mining camp and I hope you will write me more about it."[15]

The difference between a hotel dining room in Banff and a tent near a north Georgia railroad town could not have been drawn more sharply—fair warning to Sam Lawrence that he had set his sights on a girl whose only experience in camping had depended upon young men carrying her basket. He was not dismayed. In Bessie's next letter, written from San Antonio, she told him their change of plans; she had decided that they would go home by way of Marietta. Perhaps the romance of Western travel had aroused a feeling about Mr. Lawrence that she had not consciously recognized. Although she said that she hoped that his sister Amanda would be in Marietta for her to see, she may have been disingenuous. Sam Lawrence was perceptive enough to read between the lines and to wonder if it was he who was being given another chance to meet Miss Bradenbaugh (and her mother).

The second visit was everything he had hoped for. After Bessie returned home to Parkersburg, Sam wrote and asked her to marry him. She hesitated, and he had to make his case again and again. He was confident that he and Bessie would make a good marriage. Finally, by Christmas 1901, Sam again asked Bessie to marry him, but her response was tentative, indeed. "I could not know you as I have for five years without feeling a great admiration and respect for you and they are both very necessary to me as well as love for I could not marry any one that I could not look up to and love. I do feel sure that I could trust you in every way. On the other hand, I feel very much afraid that you are loving an idea."

That was not her final answer, however. Bessie's letter on January 4, 1902, written in Parkersburg, indicated that Sam had written two more letters, and they were persuasive. She said at once, "I am going to say Yes. Are you very glad? I hope you are, for it is a great deal for me to say," adding, "I do beg of you do not idealize me too much for when you know me very well you will find how many faults I have." The letter then turns back to the subject of Parkersburg—she had had to do a lot of the work because they were looking for a new cook, and she was afraid that her mother would do more than she ought and make herself ill again. She hoped that Sam had avoided getting a cold and that he would remember to take his cod liver oil. She was sorry that he had been alone at Christmas. "My grandmother sends her love to you," she concluded. "Good night, God bless and keep you, Elizabeth."

Several weeks later, Mrs. Bradenbaugh wrote to Sam: "I could not find it in my heart to make any serious objection to anyone to whom Elizabeth has given her heart as wholly as I think she has to you. . . . This being the case I must put myself aside and pray that God will bless your love for each other now and always." Sam had reason to feel relieved, but she attached conditions to her acceptance: "I must beg that you both must be very confidential with me so I may have a little share in your happiness." She came to her final point, which perhaps was the main one. "I think there is no objection to young people starting life in a modest way, and I have realized that the greatest things of life are those that money cannot buy. I must tell you though that Elizabeth is a delicate girl, with far more energy and capability than physical strength. She would not be equal to the accumulated cares and responsibilities that come into the lives of some married women, and I am certain you would only have to know these things, to shield and protect her from them."

Bessie apparently followed her mother's letter with one of her own.

"I am so glad you are fond of my family and especially of mother for I want you to love each other very much. I love you each in a different way and neither could take the place of the other. I know she will be very fond of you when she gets used to the idea of my belonging to someone else."

During the years of writing to Bessie, Sam Lawrence had been on the move, helping to build railroads, working his way from one rough railroad camp to another in southern Virginia and northern Georgia. Sometimes business took him to Richmond or to Atlanta, close enough to enable him to get back to Marietta to see his parents, but more often he was living in places so remote that Bessie could not find them on any map. Sometimes he walked twenty miles in the snow to get to a post office, where he hoped a letter from Bessie would be waiting for him. Sometimes he rode horseback and slept in a tent. Cold winters and hot summers were daunting, the food was bad, he didn't have a good bed, he was lonely; sometimes he was the only white man in a camp. He frequently caught colds and had to doctor himself. A toothache was a misery worse than a fever. But Sam Lawrence was young, handsome, and ambitious. And he liked to write letters.

The only extant letter from Sam discovered in the Lawrence papers is a good one. It was written in August 1899. "My dear Miss Elizabeth," he began, thanking her for photographs she had sent him, apologizing for his delay in answering, and explaining, "It is certainly an unsatisfactory life to be all the time running from pillar to post, never feeling that any particular place is your home." He asked, "Don't you sympathize with me?" and concluded, "How delightful it must be to be a woman having your own way about everything and never knowing what it is to be inconvenienced or worried." Sam Lawrence's blunt and often humorous manner of speaking should not have worried Mrs. Bradenbaugh, who quickly learned that he posed no threat to her close relationship with her daughter.

The letters exchanged between Bessie and Sam over the next year show that she was also accepting of his needs—to do the work he was trained to do and to live where he had to live. It became apparent that he was not going to settle in the seaport of Norfolk, Virginia, or any other city—as he had once thought—but in small railroad towns in Georgia or North Carolina. Bessie was not discouraged. Letters worked their magic so well that when she agreed to marry Sam, she said that all she wanted was their "own little house," that she was willing to find contentment in "the simplest kind." But the most dramatic evidence of the change in Bessie is reflected in what she wrote after their engagement had been announced: "Everyone thinks I must love you very much because I am willing to go so far from home." A few more letters leading up to the marriage will show us how she came to that happy conclusion.

Bessie wrote about her family and friends: her old grandparents, her mother, and her brother Frank, all living together in the house her grandfather had built; aunts, cousins, and neighbors; girls she went to boarding school with in Washington. Any time she left 1110 Ann Street, and she traveled often, someone was home counting the days until she returned. If Sam loved her, he also must love Grandma and Grandpa, her mother, Frank, Mac, Kathryn, the Gordons, the Atterburys, Bishop and Mrs. Peterkin, Annie Murdoch, old bachelors who came for lunch, and old ladies who came to call—dozens of others.

"I long to be out of doors all of the time when the weather is good," Bessie exclaimed. Some of her longest letters contain descriptions of picnics on the Ohio and overnight camping trips on the island, where she learned to swim, took a part in impromptu plays, and endured teasing about staying in her tent to write to Mr. Lawrence. "I am a summer girl," she exclaimed, reveling in walks and boat rides and stargazing. She was a keen weather watcher, reporting on the gloom of a rainy day, the splendor of fall colors, the excitement of snow, the dread of winter's hanging on too long, and the river's rising. She was, she told Sam, seldom "blue," and if she was, well, she busied herself with some distraction. The arrival of boxes of spring flowers from Marietta, sent at Sam's request by his sister Amanda, was cause for great excitement in Parkersburg, where the house on Ann Street was filled with the smell of jasmine, and the overflow of blossoms shared with neighbors. In early July when her garden was filled with sweet peas, Bessie shared them with neighbors and longed to send a box to Amanda, but could not, knowing "they do not keep."

After their engagement, on the first of January in 1902, Sam reminded Bessie that she had fallen in love with him during her second visit to Marietta. She insisted that he was mistaken. She remembered exactly what she had said to her mother as they were taking a walk before packing their bags for the trip home. She thought of Sam Lawrence as "one of her best friends"; he was not her "beau," a word she confessed she did not care for, but it seemed to fit. In her letters to Sam, mostly written the year before they married the next January, events were reported and questions asked and answered.

"We live in an undemonstrative family," Bessie wrote Sam, six months into their engagement, responding apparently to his oft-expressed doubt that she loved him as much as he loved her. He would have to take her word for it. She was going to marry him, but it would take a while to set the date. She needed to make certain that her mother had adjusted to the idea. When the date was set, it was to be on the day of her grandparents' forty-ninth wedding anniversary—January 19—in the same place where they had married, Trinity Episcopal Church in Parkersburg. When a friend suggested that they should wait another year to be married on her grandparents' fiftieth anniversary, Bessie wrote Sam that maybe they should—but she was not serious. Bessie knew that she had kept lonely Sam Lawrence waiting long enough.

Then in the fall of 1902—four months away from their marriage in January—Bessie's tone changed again. At eight o'clock one morning, she received a telegram from Sam saying that his only sister, Amanda, who had not yet married and was still living at home, had died suddenly. Bessie abandons her usual restraint as she tries to absorb the "great shock"; her "heart aches," and she declares, "I am yours and you have a right to call me for anything I can do for you." The shock also seemed to have made her more expressive about the limits of her relationship to her mother, who "has been as much like a sister as possible but an older person cannot be just the same. I hope I can be a great deal to your Mother. I am used to dividing myself around and being daughter to different people so it will be quite natural." Now she was writing less often of life in Parkersburg and more often of the forthcoming marriage, ending one letter, "Good night, dear Boy. God bless you. With a heartful of love, as ever your devoted Bessie."

On January 19, 1903, at Trinity Episcopal Church in Parkersburg, West Virginia, Elizabeth Clement Bradenbaugh married Samuel Lawrence. The next morning the newspaper carried a long story about the grandeur of the occasion. It was "an imposing ceremony and a brilliant social event," owing to the "popularity of the bride and the importance of her family, which is one of the oldest and largest in this section of the State." Over a thousand invitations had been sent out, and the church was overflowing. The wedding party made its entrance into the church with six ushers and a best man (Sam's brother Alex), five bridesmaids, and a maid of honor. Miss Bradenbaugh was given in marriage by her brother, Frank Elliott Bradenbaugh. A reception afterwards given by Bessie's mother and grandparents in the house on Ann Street merited a separate story, for it had opened the social season "in a most auspicious manner." There were lavish bowls of salvia and Michaelmas daisies. Those assisting in the reception were "most zealous in dispensing the hospitalities." In short, Sam Lawrence had made it into Bessie's family and society. Before she left to make her home "in a faraway Southern state," the newspaper story continued, it was to be remembered that there were few girls anywhere who had "preserved such a careful balance between the heavy demands of society and the obligations of duty."

CHAPTER TWO

Childhood 1904–1916

"Hearken; Behold, there went out a sower to sow."

THE PARABLE OF THE SOWER, MARK 4:3

FOR THE FIRST YEAR of the Lawrences' marriage, Sam's work continued to take him from one railroad town to another. Bessie stayed with his parents in Marietta at least some of the time, which she had promised him she would do if she did not like nearby Cedartown, Georgia, where he had been living. She spent part of the summer of 1903 back in Parkersburg, where she hosted luncheons for friends at the new country club. After Christmas, she was with her mother and Sam in Marietta, where they all attended the D.A.R. Colonial Ball at the Chancellor Hotel.[1] Sometime after Elizabeth's birth in the Lawrence house in Marietta on May 27, 1904, Sam and Bessie and the new baby moved to Hamlet, North Carolina, a railroad hub in the south central part of the state. Although Bessie took Elizabeth home for visits to Parkersburg (and Nana came to see them in Hamlet), the Lawrences were settled, at least for a few years.

Hamlet was named by its founder, John Shortridge, an Englishman who had migrated south before the Civil War and who stayed when he saw that new businesses would be needed for the region's recovery. In 1873 the place in which he had chosen to live exactly fit the definition of a small cluster of houses, and "Hamlet" it was called—and still is called.[2] According to the 1900 Hamlet census, there were more than six hundred people in the village; a decade later, it had more than tripled in size.

In 1877, only four years after the founding of Hamlet as a railroad town, the first train had pulled into the village. The next year, there was a merchandise store. In 1896 it had its first electric plant, built on a stream near the main street. The town became a crossroads for freight and passenger service, and for a growing textile industry both there and in nearby Rockingham. A depot with striking Queen Anne architecture was photographed by visitors. Up the street from the depot was a YMCA where travelers could rent rooms. In 1900, the same year the station had been built by the Seaboard Airline Railroad, the impressively large Seaboard Hotel opened. W. R. Bonsal was one of the owners. He had built the first water system, owned one of the first automobiles in town, and lived in the biggest house. When Bonsal invited Sam Lawrence to join him in a partnership to quarry and sell gravel and sand, Lawrence accepted the offer. It would remain a successful venture until the Great Depression, providing Sam Lawrence with the work he enjoyed and his family with some very happy years. Everything that he and Bessie had hoped for seemed to be coming true.

Bonsal may have arranged for the Lawrences to live in a house next door to his own, on a large lot near the center of the village. Bessie perhaps was not unduly impressed with the way the Bonsals lived, because she was used to a big house herself, but apparently the Bonsals' style of living was noted. Elizabeth remembered her mother saying that Mr. Bonsal never spoke directly to a servant—a sign, Bessie thought, of sophistication.[3] Mrs. Bonsal was from Lenox, Massachusetts, and she and her children spent only a few winter months in the small North Carolina town, with long summers in Lenox and in Newport, Rhode Island. Bessie was apparently her only friend in Hamlet, except for houseguests who stayed over on their way to Florida. She and Bessie had tea together every afternoon, and they organized a congregation and raised money to build a small Episcopal church in Hamlet. The family chauffeur took Mrs. Bonsal and their children for long drives. There remained an aura of mutual respect between the Bonsals and the Lawrences even after Mr. Lawrence's bad health and the Depression had wiped out his ability to remain a viable business partner.

Bonsal had what Lawrence lacked—capital. And when Bonsal had moved to Hamlet in 1898 to direct his company's aggressive plans to build railroads in the South, establishing Hamlet as the hub for the Seaboard Airline Railroad, what he needed was a reliable engineer. Five spurs connected travelers to Richmond, Wilmington, Atlanta, Birmingham, Savannah, Charleston, and Columbia. The Bonsal Company in its earliest days furnished all the crossties and switches for the Seaboard and sold bridge timbers and telephone and telegraph poles; by the early 1900s it was contracting to build sections of the railroad lines, an enterprise tied to the dynamic development of North Carolina. Bonsal had found a very good man and a well-trained engineer in Sam Lawrence, and he sent him to supervise major projects. In the winter of 1906, when the company undertook the construction in Raleigh of one of the largest railroad yards in the South, it was "Chief Engineer Lawrence" who was put in charge.[4]

Hamlet had some of the necessary resources for a good life: a doctor, the handsome bachelor Dr. H. F. Kinsman (who had moved down from Connecticut); a book club; a park with flower beds, benches, and hammocks—a favorite place for church picnics, when members were photographed wearing their Sunday best. The train station was grand. When Nana came from Parkersburg to visit, Bessie and Sam were proud to meet her at the station, and Bessie talked enough to distract her mother's attention from what looked like a frontier town. If they hurried, Sam and Bessie could get Nana home before the men got off work and headed for the saloons. The Seaboard Hotel with its ornamental turrets, located on a street that was nothing more than a sandy lane, may have made the "hamlet" look like a lady wearing a fancy hat and no shoes. And Nana *was* a stickler for appearances. When she came to visit, Nana was happy to be invited to go for a drive in the Bonsal automobile—and to feel that Bessie and Sam had such good neighbors. Apparently, Bessie had a black woman to help her with Elizabeth, and to help with the second baby, born March 31, 1908, and named Ann de Treville (after the Lawrence side of the family).

Years later, Elizabeth Lawrence still had memories of Hamlet. She remembered that her mother did not think well of the public school in a "rough" railroad town and taught her at home. Elizabeth had saved a letter that she had written to Nana, telling her that her mother had helped raise funds to build a church. (After their mother's death in 1964, Elizabeth and her sister Ann gave stained-glass windows to the church, All Saints Church, in memory of their parents.) She remembered the Bonsals' automobile and her mother's having been invited for drives with Mrs. Bonsal and her children. She also remembered:

> But they never asked me, and I was never asked to play with them. Only at Christmas I was asked to [see] their tree. It touched the ceiling, and had real candles that were lighted. I used to watch the little Bonsals riding by on their ponies. They had smart riding habits, and had been taught to ride as if to hounds. They were handsome children, and very strong, like their Yankee mother, and not at all like their father. I took great pleasure in them, as if they were children in a book. But I do not remember envying them, or ever wondering that they were next door, and I played alone always, and they played alone always. And we were almost the same age.[5]

Sometime during the fall of 1910, Lawrence, apparently dispatched by Mr. Bonsal to secure contracts for the railroad business, moved his family from Hamlet to Richmond, Virginia. The move was meant to be only temporary, so the family lived in a boarding house near downtown. Richmond was a New South city, being transformed by industrial growth and civic pride, but with its Confederate monuments and minstrel shows, it consciously promoted an Old South image. The Lawrences were among the new arrivals who, leaving the train station and crossing the James River, were dazzled by the lights of the city. When Sam Lawrence sat down at the table in Mrs. Jones's boarding house and read the *Richmond Times,* he formed his own opinions: it was a good place for a railroad man to secure contracts.

Living in a boarding house with two young children—Elizabeth was six, Ann two—Bessie had little time to get involved in organizations. She took her daughters to some of Richmond's beautiful parks, and she went shopping with her mother when Nana came from Parkersburg, but she cultivated few if any acquaintances among Richmond's "Old South" society. Riding the streetcar and walking were popular pastimes for mothers and children. Bessie's walks in the handsome neighborhood where the boarding house was located would have taken her past many beautiful places, including fine row houses and the nearby Woman's Club. Houses with cast-iron fences around small yards, mansard roofs, deep porches, ornamental moldings, and chimneys emerging from the tops of high roofs looked like some of the houses in Parkersburg. A few blocks east of the boarding house were the public buildings and activities of Capitol Square. In the spring of 1915, when Bessie and her mother and Elizabeth came back to Richmond—several years after the Lawrences had moved to Garysburg—they stayed at the elegant Jefferson Hotel, about four blocks west of the boarding house where they had lived. Apparently the only person Mrs. Lawrence went to visit was Mrs. Jones.

By 1912 Sam had learned a lot from being in business with Mr. Bonsal, and he was ready to take charge of his own operation. He moved his family to another North Carolina railroad hamlet—Garysburg, in the northeastern part of the state. Continuing his partnership with Bonsal, he opened Lawrence Stone and Gravel Company. For the next four years his employees would think of him as a rich man.[6] Life in Garysburg was good for the family. Bessie had already made the adjustment to a small town in Hamlet, and she was ready to go to Garysburg, where she could fulfill the dream of a "small house" that she had spoken of in letters to Sam during their engagement.

Garysburg, bordering on the state of Virginia to the north and the Roanoke River to the south, was smaller than Hamlet, and it was smaller than the nearby villages of Weldon and Roanoke Rapids. A new stone railroad bridge had recently been constructed over the Roanoke River to Weldon, which also had a new railroad station. Many passengers found themselves passing through Garysburg, but Garysburg had landowners who made it seem like an important place. A few of the most prominent men had gone to Raleigh as legislators and judges. Women like Bessie were interested in the village and beyond; taking the train to have lunch and shop in Richmond was the thing to do. Garysburg was insulated, without being isolated.[7]

There was a constant coming and going of friends in Garysburg. Sam had to stay near home more often to manage his operation, which meant that he also could come home for lunch. Bessie and Sam had been married for a decade and, approaching their late thirties, they felt both mature enough to be parents and young enough to have fun. Best of all, for Elizabeth, there was a garden to be planted.

Life in Garysburg in what Elizabeth was to remember as "a sweet old house with no heat but fire places & a stove in the hall, & no bathroom"[8] was surprisingly good. Sam Lawrence knew the biggest landowner in that part of northeast North Carolina, Willie Jones Long. While traveling on railroad business before he married, Lawrence had slept so often in the front bedroom of the Longs' plantation house that it was called "Mr. Lawrence's room." After Sam and Bessie with their two young girls moved to Garysburg, the Lawrences and the Longs were like one family. Sam was doing well supplying sand and gravel to the Seaboard railroad, making him one of the area's leading businessmen. He was a fit companion for Long in every way—educated and charming.

The Long family, which owned thousands of acres of land in Northampton and Halifax counties, was notable in North Carolina history. Before the Civil War, the Long family had owned slaves; afterwards, they had tenant families to put in cotton, peanuts, corn, and soybeans in fields that stretched as far as the eye could see. When the Roanoke River flooded, fields were underwater, and transport was by boat. From the porch of the big house, family and friends could sit (and still can) and watch the approach of visitors down the tree-lined sandy lane. The Lawrences knew the vista well.

Sunday was special at Longview (named for the view, rather than the family), when all the family members got together for the children to play, and for the Long women and the black cooks to prepare dinner, which was served at 2:00 p.m. It was a household dominated by "Gran," or "Miss Betty" (Betty Mason Long). "Nobody messed with

Elizabeth with her mother, Bessie, and her only sibling, Ann, about 1910. For more than a half-century Elizabeth and Bessie remained as close as they were in this picture. Ann was always the more independent. (By permission of Warren Way and Elizabeth Rogers.)

my grandmother," Willie Jr. was to remember many years later. "She thought all the men were perfect and the women weren't worth much." In fact, the Long sons thought that the women were exceptional, especially their mother, Caroline Clarkson Moncure Long.[9] The Long women and the Lawrence women got along well. They all liked gardens, especially Gran, whose own garden rambled, with flowers falling over the walkways—a style that became Elizabeth Lawrence's own in her later gardens. Gran also cut flowers for the house, and when visitors came through the front door they were often greeted by one of her colorful bouquets. It is Gran's garden (though often mistaken for her own grandmother's) that Lawrence wrote a poem about for *A Southern Garden*.[10]

> As long as my grandmother lived,
> The sweet white violets that grew
> On either side of the garden path
> Bloomed every spring, and when in bloom
> Made sweet the garden and the lane,
> And scented all the avenue;
> While in the house, from room to room,
> Their fragrance traveled with the breeze.
> They thrived until they died, and then
> Survived her death another spring.
> And after that nobody knew
> The words she said to make them bloom,
> When walking up and down the path
> She poked among them with her cane.

Close to where the Lawrences lived in Garysburg, there was a post office, a mercantile store, a doctor's office, a bank, a telephone company, a small hotel, and a new public school with electric lights and an auditorium for meetings and performances. Everything was within walking distance. Elizabeth and her sister walked with their friend Byrd Suiter to Sunday School at the Methodist Church, where Byrd's mother was their teacher. In summer the women of the church often held plays, cast with locals, and ice cream and cake were sold after the performance. One playbill promised a "moonlight night. Come and bring your family."

Roads in Garysburg were dusty in summer and rutted in winter, but a few families had automobiles—Whippets and Packards—and loved to take their friends for a drive. Mr. Lawrence walked down to the station to meet the train bringing the newspapers—the Norfolk *Virginian-Pilot* and the Raleigh *News & Observer*. The railroad brought everything, including the children from Weldon, who walked the railroad bridge to school in Garysburg.

The four years in Garysburg were idyllic for Elizabeth. In Hamlet she had watched the Bonsal children riding their pony, and when the Lawrences moved to Garysburg, her father bought her one, which she knew how to take care of and saddle. Riding through the woods and down to the creekbeds, where she could pick wildflowers, was one of her favorite activities. One morning she rose early to pick forty poppies. On Sunday she made herself a bouquet of violets to wear to church. In Garysburg there were Chinaberry trees in dooryards, and children strung the beadlike seeds—like the monks of earlier times, as she was to read later. When Elizabeth was thirty she wrote an essay about childhood for her friend and writing mentor, Ann Preston Bridgers. In it she celebrated "uninterrupted mornings." When she was past fifty, she still had hold of an image of growing up in the country, a "fortunate child . . . allowed to ramble, or go off on my own pony as far as I liked, and all alone." Then she was ready to admit, "it unfits one for life."[11]

Elizabeth's early education had been mostly conducted at home. In Garysburg, that changed. The Garysburg Graded School was in sight of her house. Miss Bessie Williams was her teacher as well as a friend of her mother's. In one of her early journals, she wrote: "Byrd spent the night with us last night and we had a play. Mrs. Joyner came over this afternoon and we dyed some Easter eggs." Elizabeth and Ann saw their friend Byrd and a half-dozen other girls their ages every day; Mr. and Mrs. Lawrence and Mr. and Mrs. Joyner played cards. The Lawrences went down to the train station, where Sam made a fire in the stove to knock the chill off the morning, and they waited for the train that would bring Bessie's mother from Parkersburg or Sam's mother from Marietta. Passenger service in Garysburg and Weldon also carried them to Norfolk, Richmond, and Washington. On weekends and holidays, Elizabeth read most of the morning, and again before she went to sleep at night. On every page of her journal, she recorded that there were friends who had come over to play, often to spend the night. Parents and children played card games together; Rook was a favorite. They all turned out for baseball games. Plummy, the cook, came to prepare breakfast. On Sunday their father drove Elizabeth and Ann in a buggy over to Grace Episcopal Church in Weldon.[12]

Garysburg men and women attended many of the same events—card games in homes, programs in the school auditorium. But they also enjoyed their separate activities. Bessie's women friends came to visit every day; her special favorite was Mary Joyner, the wife of Garysburg's leading citizen, William Henry Joyner, who served as mayor for nineteen years, and was later in the North Carolina Legislature. Bessie probably attended a "Rose Afternoon," sponsored by the Ladies' Aid Society, when her friend Mrs. Suiter read a poem about a rose, Mrs. Harrison sang "The Last Rose of Summer," and they all guessed the number of petals in a bowl. They also became avid supporters of the state's School Betterment Society, and helped to pay for gaslights at the Garysburg Graded School by making and selling ice cream. At home mothers took their children to pick cherries and taught their girls to knit; Elizabeth made a scarf for the Belgians.[13] Sam Lawrence went fishing with Willie Long, and sometimes they would take the wives and children, who also loved to fish.

In June of 1913, some of the villagers spent most of the day at the school, beginning with a morning dedication of the new building, followed by a barbecue dinner at 2:30 p.m., and a commencement exercise in the evening. Nine-year-old Elizabeth Lawrence had a part in a one-act comedy, part of a commencement program that also included recitations and the singing of "America" and the state song, "The Old North State."[14]

Elizabeth Lawrence considered childhood the most important stage in a person's life. In 1943, when she was asked to write a statement about herself for a horticultural journal, she remembered her Garysburg years:

> When I was a little girl, my mother took great pains to interest me in learning to know the birds and wildflowers and in planting a garden. I thought that roots and bulbs and seeds were as wonderful as flowers, and the Latin names on seed packages as full of enchantment as the counting-out rhymes that children chant in the spring. I remember the first time I planted seeds. My mother asked me if I knew the Parable of the Sower. I said I did not, and she took me into the house and read it to me. Once the relation between poetry and the soil is established in the mind, all growing things are endowed with more than material beauty.[15]

If Lawrence's autobiographical statement, written at age thirty-nine, sets out her mature gardening philosophy, the journal she kept as a child in Garysburg shows her promise. She was always an early riser (often at 6:00 a.m.), a weather watcher, and a record keeper. "When I woke up this morning," she noted in early April of 1915, "I found snow on the ground. There was ice too. It has snowed all day but the snow began to melt and what is falling now don't seem to be sticking." The next day, Easter Sunday, the snow was "melting fast." Several days later, she noticed every change—it was a "very pretty morning and very warm," later "very cloudy," and in the afternoon, it rained for half an hour. She picked wildflowers, poppies, and—near the creek—flags and water lilies. In the vegetable garden, she picked lettuce, onions, and what she called "my" radishes. On April 24, she set out pansy plants; a week later, she helped her mother transplant some snapdragons. She made a birdbath, nailed a box on a post in the garden and filled it with corn and oats. But when she found a sparrow's nest in the birdhouse, she tore it out, apparently with no remorse. When her goldfish died, she buried "him" in a box with a glass top, for viewing. At night, she read *The Secret Garden* and Nana's copy of *Elizabeth and Her German Garden*.

The Garysburg years were also a time when Elizabeth realized that home was a good place to be, and women were the ones to keep the home going. Every day her mother's friends came over with fruits and flowers, to talk, to sew, and to visit. Sam's mother from Marietta, Georgia, and Bessie's from Parkersburg, West Virginia, came often enough that they easily took their places in the circle. When Elizabeth put down her book and went outside to play Green Rover, she could hear their voices in the background.

The Garysburg years were also perhaps Sam Lawrence's best, when he was a successful businessman, healthy and happy. He could go out before breakfast to pick peas with his wife and pretty little girls. Besides family, every day he could see his best friend, Willie Long, and they could go fishing as often as they wanted to. In the evenings, he and Bessie could play bridge with the Joyners. Anybody who saw him talking with workers at his sand and gravel pits or driving his buckboard down a country road would have said that Sam Lawrence was a lucky man. All too soon Lawrence's luck—and with it, his health—would suffer like that of other businessmen who were trying to take care of their families and workers during the Great Depression. Even Willie Long, with all of his thousands of acres, was to go broke. But in 1912 when Sam moved his family into the little house in Garysburg, times were good.

CHAPTER THREE

Raleigh 1916–1922

"There isn't anything in the world that Elizabeth doesn't want to know."

ST. MARY'S SCHOOL YEARBOOK, 1922

In 1916 Bessie and Sam Lawrence, having decided that they wanted their daughters—ages twelve and eight—to attend St. Mary's School in Raleigh, closed the door on Garysburg and moved the family from the rural northeast to the state capital. Sam set up the central office for Lawrence Sand and Gravel Company[1] in Raleigh, in continued partnership with W. R. Bonsal, and returned as necessary to check on things at the Garysburg facility; in later years, Elizabeth would drive him back, and they would spend the night at Longview.

Elizabeth's father could have described Raleigh as being like the mercantile store in Garysburg—a place where country people gathered. The "country" feeling of Raleigh would be almost as true when Bessie and Elizabeth Lawrence left in 1948 as when the Lawrences moved there in 1916: families in their Sunday best, coming to Capital Square to look at the public buildings and monuments; earnest men and women waiting in line for a government job; farmers bringing produce and plants to sell at the market; mothers in department stores, studying their lists to see what they could afford to buy for the children's school clothes; and once a year, families flocking to the state fair, where livestock and exhibits were straight off the farm. In 1916, girls no older than Elizabeth were learning how to can tomatoes from a home demonstration agent; by 1917, when Elizabeth went to study literature and art at St. Mary's, the private Episcopal church school, more than one hundred girls had sold enough canned tomatoes to help pay their fees to study home economics at the state's women's college in Greensboro.[2]

The Lawrences were not a farm family, but they had lived happily in modest houses in small villages, attending country churches, and meeting country people. Bessie and Elizabeth had learned to plant "by the signs" and to find old plants in country graveyards. Sam Lawrence often said that what Bessie wanted was a farm in town—she loved everything about the country except being in it. Unpaved alleys with an overhang of trees ran along the backs of houses in their new neighborhood and reminded Elizabeth of Garysburg.

Most Raleigh residents—black and white—were still closely attached by family relations to a rural homeplace. (North Carolina had a majority rural population for much of the twentieth century.) Even college professors and students at North Carolina State College of Agriculture and Engineering studied real life, unlike the gentleman scholars at Chapel Hill who read Latin. State legislators crossing the Square walked like men used to striding about their own farms and holding court on Saturdays in the backs of trucks and in small-town restaurants. Raleigh was the seat of government, but government had deep rural roots. Old politicians had more power than enterprising newcomers. And church schools were an important part of the picture. There were three schools for white women—Meredith, Peace, and St. Mary's; two schools for black men and women—Shaw and St. Augustine's; as well as the state land-grant college, North Carolina State. There were two good newspapers—the *Raleigh Times* and the *News & Observer*. Men at home shook out the N & O and said aloud to their children, who had heard it before, "Think I'll see what's going on in the Nuisance and Disturber." (Sam Lawrence read the newspaper, too, but after he had read the *Atlantic* magazine.)

The growing middle class had a strong work ethic and a sense of responsibility to help better the community. In 1904, the year that Elizabeth was born, Raleigh clubwomen had undertaken to improve things by joining the nationwide City Beautiful movement, which sponsored the planting of trees, the widening of streets, and the erection of monuments. The wickedness of urban life, as depicted in newspaper reports of prostitutes and vagrants, could be cleaned up if women's organizations would function as "municipal housekeepers." The Raleigh Woman's Club had been founded on the belief that "the City is the next thing to the home."[3]

Once the Lawrences had moved into their house at 115 Park Avenue, near St. Mary's School, Sam Lawrence went to his office, the girls were enrolled at St. Mary's, and Bessie Lawrence liked the sound of a club movement for "self-improvement and social betterment." She became a Red Cross volunteer, and went on to serve through two world wars. The Lawrences became members of Christ Episcopal Church, across the street from Capital Square. Sam served on the vestry and Bessie joined the women's auxiliary. She also took the girls to special services at St. Saviour's, a mission sponsored by Christ Church, with children from working-class families like those she had taught in a Sunday School in Parkersburg. Bessie rolled up her sleeves and went to work. A Red Cross uniform rather than a ball gown was her most characteristic dress. She also entertained often at home. Among the most frequent guests at the Lawrences were St. Mary's faculty members, several of whom became such good friends as to seem to belong to the family. Thirty years after leaving St. Mary's, Frances Bottum, who taught science classes there, wrote that she felt she would never again have the sense of "belonging" that she had had "sipping sherry or orange juice on the deep sofa by [the] fire."[4] In 1924 Sam Lawrence founded the Sandwich Club, and invited his friends to meet once a month in homes to discuss lofty topics, laced with wit. His favorite subject was the world federalist movement.

This good life was certainly not shared by everyone, nor did the economic disparities mean that the Lawrences or many other middle-class Raleigh families tried to change the system in which poverty and segregation were entrenched. Black housekeepers worked in many homes in the neighborhood where the Lawrences lived, and Bessie usually had at least one servant. In West Virginia, Bessie's family had sometimes

The Lawrence family in 1917 in Marietta, Georgia, at the golden wedding celebration of Elizabeth's paternal grandparents, Robert de Treville Lawrence and Anna Eliza Atkinson Lawrence. Elizabeth stands behind her grandmother; Ann is seated to the right, between two older cousins. Bessie and Sam Lawrence are standing with Elizabeth behind Sam's parents. (Courtesy of Robert de Treville Lawrence III.)

taken in a young Irish or German woman as a boarder to cook and help with the housework; a black woman who had washed Bessie's hair she called her "friend." The family's remembrance of black women who had looked after the children in Marietta, Hamlet, and Garysburg was long-lasting. For many years Bessie wrote letters and sent packages to Sarah Christian in Marietta, who wrote to her and "Miss Elizabeth" and "Miss Ann," even dictating her letters when she was old and ill. In Raleigh, Bessie and Sam Lawrence took a particular interest in Dallie P. Harris, a black man who helped them in various ways, including driving them in their new Buick. After he left Raleigh, they assisted with his medical education, and when he graduated from Meharry College in Nashville in 1930, he wrote to tell them about his success. The Lawrences were particularly respectful of individuals, but they considered racial segregation a way of life in the South and sought to help rectify some of its inequalities through personal charity.

In 1916 Elizabeth, who had turned twelve in May, was enrolled in the fall term at St. Mary's as a boarding student, but after a month or so, she came back to live at home. Her senior year she boarded again, but it did not seem to matter where she lived; she and her friends could easily walk between St. Mary's and the Lawrence house, only a few blocks away. This setting had what Elizabeth needed: a house with a library and a garden, a church, and a neighborhood of friends with gardens.

St. Mary's, founded by the Episcopal Diocese in 1842 as "a school for young ladies," was by 1916 a venerable institution set back in a grove off Hillsboro Street, where it had survived through a period of tumultuous history. It had continued to function during the Civil War when the city was surrendered to General William T. Sherman, who set up headquarters a mile or so away in the Governor's mansion. After the War, the founder, the Reverend Aldert Smedes, had appealed to Episcopalians throughout the state to help in any way they could to enable students "once the possessors of affluence, now the victims of poverty" to enroll.[5] Although St. Mary's leaders often struggled over the years to find money to improve the school, parents who could afford tuition for private education were decidedly more affluent than most parents whose children went to public schools. Whatever the school's finances showed in good times and bad, St. Mary's was like many private Southern girls' schools in having a lovely campus and offering gracious hospitality.

The "look" of St. Mary's was romanticized in an 1846 painting of a confirmation of St. Mary's students by Bishop Levi Ives. Four young girls are kneeling, their heads bowed, as the towering bishop places his delicate hands on the head of one of them.[6] When Elizabeth was fifteen she wrote in her journal that she was considering becoming a missionary, but that was the last mention she made of a possible call to service. She did not often talk about faith, nor apparently did anyone else in her family, though the Lawrences were very "churched," as Episcopalians describe their close ties. Her young niece and namesake, Elizabeth, called "Fuzz," once accused her of not caring about anything but beauty. "You never think of God," she observed, and Aunt, though delighted with her niece's teasing, did not explain her beliefs even then.[7]

On the first day of school, Bessie walked Elizabeth and Ann to St. Mary's, where for the next decade Bessie was such a favorite with the girls that they made her an honorary member of the class. Her photograph appears in the yearbook, with the description, "Energetic, Benevolent, Loyal." The gathering of the "family" of students and faculty was so congenial that Mr. and Mrs. Lawrence were convinced that they had done the right thing in moving to Raleigh so that they could enroll their daughters at St. Mary's.

The school comprised the primary grades and four years of high school, at a time when most public schools in North Carolina offered no more than a total of six years of schooling. Episcopalians took pride in the reputation of St. Mary's for high standards and a classical curriculum; by 1918, during the administration of George Lay, the curriculum had been broadened to include the first two years of college courses. Lay was a "father figure"—all five of his daughters graduated from St. Mary's. He was gruff, though he meant to be funny, and sometimes people were offended, which hurt him a great deal. Elizabeth understood even as a student that he enjoyed "little skirmishes." Once, "He tried me out," she remembered, "and I said, putting my finger tips to my breast bone, 'Oh, Mr. Lay. You have cut me to the quick.' And he said, 'Is that where you keep the quick? I have always wondered.' "[8]

In 1918 Lay was succeeded by the Reverend Warren Wade Way, who continued to strengthen the curriculum so that students completing two years of college courses at St. Mary's could transfer to a four-year college. Among those who did were his daughter Evelyn and Elizabeth's sister, Ann. Way became a good friend of Sam Lawrence's and was invited to become a member of the Sandwich Club.

Elizabeth Lawrence thrived at St. Mary's. She loved to dance with the other girls in the parlor after dinner, and to explore the fields of the campus with her botany teacher, looking for rare plants. It was a wonderful place for a future gardener. In her senior year, Elizabeth's poem about the sundial in her garden was published in the school bulletin. Dr. Lay's daughter Elizabeth was to remember the fragrance of wisteria, magnolias, and musk roses, the taste of wild strawberries, "the lilac carpets of pansy violets, the purity of Mother's calla lilies brought from her greenhouse to the Chapel altar, the freshness of her pots and vases of blooms on the tables in the dining room."[9] Elizabeth's science teacher, Frances Bottum, showed her students where to find pitcher plants and a rare alga that grew along the streams on the back campus, and took them on walks into the country to a lake where they caught wood frogs, "that went off like alarm clocks in one's bedroom terrarium of a night."[10] Faculty members were always encouraged to challenge their students academically, and although Elizabeth Lawrence struggled to rise above a B or a C in her grades, she made a strong impression on her teachers and classmates. The staff of the school yearbook vividly characterized her:

> Elizabeth puts the spice into Mr. Way's philosophy class. She's our chief discusser, arguer and questioner. There isn't anything in the world that Elizabeth doesn't want to know. She's as bad as a little brother—which is perfectly right and proper, because she comes very near being one of those infant prodigies that Miss Morgan is most vehemently not in favor of. We don't know which we envy Elizabeth most, her cleverness, her rose leaf complexion, her solo dancing, or her guileless smile.

Photographs of Elizabeth Lawrence from her St. Mary's years show a pretty girl—small and fair, with short blonde hair and a mischievous smile. There was something enchanting about her, and she used this quality to her advantage in making friends, usually one at a time. She and a classmate, Mary Wiatt Yarborough, were to remain lifelong friends. Mary, one of seven children, was born in Louisburg, North Carolina. Like Elizabeth she had loved growing up in a small rural

North Carolina community, though, unlike Elizabeth, she came from a large family. Mary Wiatt attended school in her hometown of Louisburg until her mother, having determined that her children were going to be well educated, somehow found enough money to send her off to boarding school in Raleigh. Mary Wiatt began in the fall of 1918, when she was fourteen years old. One of the first girls she met was Elizabeth Lawrence. They immediately chose nicknames—Elizabeth became "Libba" and Mary Wiatt, "Tommie." They were the youngest in their class and were natural allies. Mary Wiatt was invited to overnights and parties at Elizabeth's house, where the family also got to know her well. Elizabeth met Mary Wiatt's brothers and sisters. "Libba" would always remember her as "brilliant Mary Wiatt." They loved to talk, to laugh, and to argue, especially when no one else was around. Years later, when Mary Wiatt married and had a child, Laura, Elizabeth was the child's godmother.[11]

Elizabeth loved St. Mary's, and she always considered her Barnard College education inferior to the one she received at St. Mary's. One of the major differences between her experiences at the two schools was the personal attention that she was given at St. Mary's. Her teachers knew her family, and attended the Episcopal church; many visited in her home, and when she failed an exam, one of them allowed her to take it over. Elizabeth's social life was easy. She went to parties—apparently not with boys, though some girls dated—and she played basketball and bridge; friends went home with her for supper, to study Caesar, to help her clean up her room and wash the family dog, Pitapat, and often to spend the night. The house was usually full of visiting family and friends. The girls ate in the kitchen, while Mr. and Mrs. Lawrence and their guests had a formal dinner in the dining room. Elizabeth had three best friends, but she was "crushed on"[12] one, "Polly," and wrote her name all over the last page of her botany textbook. In 1919 she confided to her journal: "Thursday, Jan. 9, 9:55 p.m. This is the end of a perfect day! No—not quite perfect, not any day is perfect since Polly forgot me. The girls say I'm fickle and that I have gone back on Polly, and love P best, but it isn't so!!! Polly is the only really truly crush I ever had, or ever will have." After Polly left school, the mention of her name still aroused Elizabeth's feelings of having been abandoned; when her friends wrote in chalk on the sidewalk that she was crushed on Rebecca, Elizabeth raced around campus to rub it out. On May 27, she wrote, "Today is my birthday and it has been a happy one. I am fifteen and I don't like it at all. I hate to grow up."

In late August 1920—Elizabeth had turned sixteen that summer—as she and her classmates were still enjoying their vacations, something historic was about to occur in Raleigh on Capital Square, across from Christ Church. Crowds were assembling outside the capitol building because the North Carolina legislature was going to move to a vote on the question of woman suffrage and the Nineteenth Amendment, which had been submitted to the states for ratification. The amendment required only one more affirmative state vote to be passed into law, and suffragists and antisuffragists had been working for months—many of them for years—for their opposing sides. According to historian Glenda Gilmore, "state legislators found the capital city in an uproar."[13]

Mrs. Lawrence and her daughters would have had a good view of what was happening, but if she took Elizabeth and Ann to join the crowd waiting for the first messenger to run out of the capital with the news of the legislature's decision, no one recorded the event. There is evidence, however, that after women received the vote, Bessie Lawrence used it. In the presidential election of 1928, Elizabeth predicted that her mother would vote "wet" for Al Smith and her father "dry" for Herbert Hoover. From the time that Bessie and Elizabeth voted for FDR in 1932, they both were unwavering Democrats.

Much was at stake for both sides in the debate about the Nineteenth Amendment. The suffragists and the antis were out in large numbers because if North Carolina voted affirmatively, the amendment would then have the support of the requisite number of states (thirty-six) to become law. By the summer of 1920 the woman question had been around—nationally and regionally—for so long that positions had hardened, and the question of who got to vote was inflamed by the issue of race. With Jim Crow, Southern states had become hotbeds of racism, and in North Carolina, Josephus Daniels, editor and publisher of Raleigh's *News & Observer,* and U.S. senator Furnifold Simmons from New Bern had used the media to support white supremacy. Even though North Carolina governor Thomas Bickett admitted that the time had come for women to gain the vote, his less than enthusiastic voice was often drowned out by a storm of opposition.

Among the women who were most prominent in the suffrage debate on both sides were graduates from St. Mary's. The first president of the North Carolina Equal Suffrage Association, founded in 1904, was an alumna, Helen Morris Lewis. One of the leading antisuffragists was a St. Mary's graduate, Mary Hilliard Hinton. Although Martha Stoop, who wrote the history of St. Mary's, believes that most St. Mary's alumnae and students did not favor woman suffrage, over the years the question was discussed on campus, and students were aware of the prominent leadership roles that graduates of their school were taking.

When the vote finally could not be put off any longer, the legislature voted twenty-five to twenty-three to postpone consideration until the next year. There was no woman in the city better known for her political views than Nell Battle Lewis, a St. Mary's graduate, whose liberalism at the time was not typical of her social class. Years after the North Carolina legislature had acted, she remembered, "It was quite a sensation to be a young southern woman just slapped in the face by her state."[14] But North Carolina did not have the last word. When the amendment went on to Tennessee, Tennessee voted Yes, and the amendment passed. Women could vote.

Most North Carolinians probably agreed with Episcopal bishop Joseph Blount Cheshire Jr., the first native North Carolinian to become bishop, and a great friend of St. Mary's, who said in 1919 that he was "strongly opposed in sentiment and in judgment to woman suffrage in both civil and ecclesiastical matters." Suffrage was, he insisted, "opposed to the very fundamental conception of the very important and sacred function of women in the scheme of human life."[15]

On Tuesday morning, January 23, 1922, Elizabeth graduated from St. Mary's. Graduation exercises were held in the auditorium. After a prayer by Bishop Cheshire, the singing of the school song, and brief salutatory remarks by a classmate, Elizabeth was introduced and rose to read an essay, which had been selected as the winner in a school literary competition. Her essay was entitled "Cullud Folks" and was based on her own childhood memories. She began, speaking out of deep conviction, "I love 'cullud' folks—those happy, carefree people who have always been my friends and whom I dislike to consider a problem."[16]

These words that had the power to soothe that particular audience in 1922 still have the power to disturb audiences today. As an eighteen-year-old graduating senior, Elizabeth was retelling a familiar story. She had absorbed with unquestioning devotion her class and racial legacy—in her own words, the "exquisitely tender romances of the South." This phrase should give us our first clue about her sources: she was influenced by what had already been written. In her essay, she quoted liberally from published books, including an Uncle Remus tale, "Story of the War," by Joel Chandler Harris. She then turned to personal anecdotes, one about an old colored man named "Ten Cent Bill," who lived at the Soldiers' Home in Atlanta; another about her own "Mammy Ca'line"; and a long narrative about "darkies" who worked in railroad camps.

She acknowledged that although "much had been written about that picturesque darky, the slave of ante-bellum days," he was still "ever fresh and interesting." Admiring his "childlike simplicity," his "wistful longing" for the old life and the "kind masters," she then gave examples from literature and anecdotes. She did not say where she had heard the story about Ten Cent Bill or the scenes from railroad camps, except to allude to "a young civil engineer" who had been to the camps. But the sources she used are unmistakable: a pamphlet about "10 Cent Bill" was written and published in 1920 by her grandfather Lawrence, and her own father, Sam Lawrence, was the young civil engineer.

Elizabeth's essay began with a defense of the South's treatment of blacks and ended with her own experiences, her love for "Mammy Ca'line" in Marietta, and her recent visit to St. Augustine's, an Episcopal school for blacks in Raleigh. Dean Charles Boyer had taken her to observe some of the classes, and she used her learned language to describe him as "a friendly, white-haired Negro" with "a kindly smile and genial manners." She concluded her oration by returning to her theme—the "friendly feeling" she had toward "the happy, singing nature of the Negro . . . tucked away with the tender memories of my old Mammy."

Among the other winners in the spring writing competition were Lucy Lay's "Darky Love Song," in Negro dialect, and Sarah Harrell's story of how an "old Mammy" saved a Rebel soldier from being discovered by a Yankee. The young, affluent white girls of St. Mary's were limited in their experiences to those of their families, and in their language to what they had heard and read. Elizabeth's essay was, after all, written when she was eighteen, and she seems never to have mentioned it in later years. It lacked critical thinking and originality.[17] What is ironic, however, is how much her high-school essay reflects what she declared some ten years later when she said that she wanted "to live in the same soil" as her ancestors and to "think their thoughts."

Elizabeth and Mary Wiatt were among the four members of a class of twenty-two who would go on to college, and they were accepted at two of the best colleges in the country—Elizabeth at Barnard and Mary Wiatt at Smith. When Grace St. John, her English teacher, urged Elizabeth to consider her own alma mater, Barnard College, Elizabeth protested that she would never be able to get in because she had not made high grades. Miss St. John had heard that Barnard was going to use some kind of "psychological test" for high-school graduates.[18] It was to be given in Asheville, and when Elizabeth found out that Mary Wiatt was taking her test for Smith at the same place, she decided to sign up for the Barnard test and to go with her.

As an old woman, Elizabeth still remembered what had happened:

> A delightful woman clocked me. As she handed out each set of questions, I read them aloud & when we could stop laughing I checked the

answers. . . . One of the questions was how would you go about finding a baseball lost in a rectangular meadow [presumably, a question which required some math skills]. I said I would look for it. I have never been more surprised than when they wrote that I was accepted. I thought that as I had nothing to do, not being in love or without any thing better, I might as well go.[19]

CHAPTER FOUR

Barnard College 1922–1926

She's a little girl all day/But at night she steals away.

BARNARD COLLEGE YEARBOOK, 1926

IN SEPTEMBER of 1922 Elizabeth's parents had made all the arrangements to take Elizabeth to school in New York, and the three of them boarded the train in Raleigh, loaded down with Elizabeth's books and "grips," and a new cloak that Bessie had bought for her. Elizabeth had surprised herself when she agreed to take an entrance examination for Barnard College, and she was even more surprised when she was accepted. Now there was no turning back, and it was a comfort to have her parents with her. They were proud that she was going to Barnard, and considered four years in New York "an education in itself." But Grandpa-pa Lawrence had warned that she would never get married if she got educated, and Nana warned that "all the education in the world wouldn't do me any good if it made me a Unitarian."[1] Grace St. John hoped that the St. Mary's student she had recommended to Barnard would like it and do well, which had been her own experience as a Barnard student in the Class of 1916. Elizabeth had not had much time to think about what might happen. She had recently returned from a long train trip to the West Coast, traveling with some of her mother's Parkersburg friends; they had written postcards to Bessie exclaiming over what a charming companion she was.

In the 1920s, America was in the grip of dramatic changes, and nowhere were they more in evidence than in New York. The Jazz Age was in full swing; Louise Brooks took the stage as a flamboyant flapper, lighting up the silent screen in 1926; F. Scott Fitzgerald immortalized beautiful young men and women in fiction (and lived the parts with his wife, Zelda); and Sinclair Lewis debunked the myth of the innocence of small-town America. Women bobbed their hair, used make-up, rolled their stockings below their knees; some were a little "fast," others downright reckless. It didn't take much for couples drinking Prohibition whiskey out of a hip flask to move from "petting" to something more sexually adventurous, especially at parties in Greenwich Village, the Bohemian capital of the age. According to Dorothy Parker, the flapper's golden rule was "plain enough—/Just get them young and treat them rough." Women could do what men did—smoke, drink, dance, make love, and come home at four in the morning.

Even poetry was undergoing dramatic changes. While e. e. cummings experimented with the look of poetry, it was the mesmerizing look of a poet herself that made audiences stamp their feet. Edna St. Vincent Millay dared to do more than write sensual verses—she flaunted her sensuality in dress (scarlet robes), voice (low and sultry), and behavior (flings with lovers, both women and men). She was the most Byronic figure in American literature—in love with despair and desire. Even a staid committee of judges could not resist her: in the spring of 1923 she became the first woman to win a Pulitzer Prize for poetry.[2]

"Vincent," as she was called, had escaped what she considered her provincial life in Camden, Maine, by making it clear to her family and friends that she had ambition and talent. In the early 1900s a young girl writing and behaving with such boldness was astonishing. The traditional image of a woman poet was that of a nineteenth-century "recluse"—Emily Dickinson. Things were about to change. In 1913 a wealthy woman patron brought Vincent to New York and enrolled her for a semester at Barnard College, to make up her deficiencies so that she could be admitted to Vassar—and from there launch herself upon the world. Vincent exclaimed, "Well, here I am in New York! at last!" She had been to a concert, ridden the subway, and shopped on Fifth Avenue, adding, "I have been so very good that I haven't yet been sent home."[3] Barnard professors took the behavior of their students in stride: at the end of World War I, eight hundred Barnard students had snake-danced down Morningside Heights to celebrate the signing of the Armistice.[4]

Barnard College 1922–1926

When Elizabeth Lawrence arrived from North Carolina, she was closer to living the life of Emily Dickinson than that of Vincent Millay. She was also excited by poetry, but verses written while she was looking out her dormitory window and describing what she saw below did not reveal anything personal about her. Her parents and grandparents did not have to worry about her being sent home for bad behavior: Elizabeth tried to be as "good" as Vincent had tried to be "bad." But the excitement of being in New York that had thrilled Vincent Millay also had an effect upon Elizabeth Lawrence, an innocent girl, ripe for enthrallment, and perhaps quite scared.

Elizabeth apparently had been reading Millay's poems before she got to Barnard, and knew that Vincent had been a student there. Later, Elizabeth was to explain the attraction this way: "Edna Millay will always be a poet to me. Because she wrote in my time, and because I clipped her verses before I knew her name—and then I saw that a number of them I liked were written by the same person; and then I found that every one but me knew who that person was. The first poem I clipped was 'Afternoon on a Hill.' You can see how welcome its simplicity would be to me, brought up on English poets of the 19th century, and never having heard of Housman or Verlaine."[5] At Barnard, Elizabeth was taught that Shakespeare's sonnets may have been written to a man, and when she read them again, she thought it possible. Homosexual implications in poetry, including Housman's and Millay's, did not offend her. Elizabeth was an innocent, but she was not narrow or judgmental, and on at least one occasion she surprised herself with her own sophistication.

In spite of Elizabeth's fears of the city, which she later admitted to, she ventured forth to enjoy some of its possibilities. She heard Paderewski play the *Emperor Concerto* at Carnegie Hall, and sat with a classmate in a first-row seat in the peanut gallery at the Metropolitan Opera. On Washington's birthday in her freshman year, she met a friend from Raleigh, Christine Busbee (who was teaching in New York), for lunch at the Vanity Fair Tea Room on Fortieth Street and afterwards they went to hear Martinelli sing in *Aida*. Every morning Elizabeth walked to the nearby Cathedral of St. John the Divine for the early service of Holy Communion in one of the small chapels. Her literary tastes were broadened by the books she read and the plays she saw. She made two especially good friends: Ellen Bracelen, who lived on Park Avenue, and Jean Lowry, who was a Barnard student and as adventuresome as Vincent Millay. And yet, after Elizabeth graduated in 1926, she maintained no further contact with Barnard, and people who knew her best never heard her talk about college. In later years, she insisted that she had "hated" Barnard and New York, but by then her fears of the city and her sense of failure in certain courses had grown in her imagination. At the time she was a student, however, for a seemingly shy girl from the South, she was surprisingly "at home" in the city.[6]

Barnard College was founded as a college for women in 1889, in affiliation with Columbia University. Virginia Gildersleeve, who earned her undergraduate degree from Barnard in 1899, received her Ph.D. from Columbia in 1908, and was made Dean and Professor of English at Barnard in 1911, was one of the most distinguished academic women in the country and a leader in international affairs by 1922, when Lawrence arrived. Until her retirement in 1947, she *was* the lengthened shadow of Barnard College. For thirty-six years she commanded her charges to take advantage of every minute of their education. She would remind them of the exacting standards to which they would be held at Barnard College, for if they succeeded, they would be ready to embark upon careers in society. In 1918, Gildersleeve had discouraged students from leaving school to join the war effort; "trained brains" were needed most. According to her, the world awaited Barnard's graduates, and, indeed, many would distinguish themselves. (Two of Lawrence's near contemporaries were Margaret Mead (class of 1923) and Zora Neale Hurston (class of 1928). Dorothy Height, who went on to graduate from New York University and to head the National Council of Negro Women, was refused admission to Barnard in 1928 because its quota of two black students was already "filled."[7]

When Elizabeth arrived with her parents at the handsome iron gate marking the entrance to Barnard College, she knew she was in a new world. Behind her was the impressive library on the campus of Columbia University, before her the high columns of Barnard's Students Hall (in 1926 it was renamed Barnard Hall). Between the two campuses, Broadway carried more cars and people than she had ever seen. Still, she had some familiarity with New York from having heard from Uncle Jim about his studies at General Theological Seminary, his summers as a parish priest, and his favorite store—Tiffany's, where he bought his silver drinking cups. Her teacher, Grace St. John, could have told her how to take the subway down to Greenwich Village, where St. John was to live after she left North Carolina. At St. Mary's, Elizabeth had learned how to move about a small campus and to make new friends. Now all she and her parents needed to do was follow the other students through the gate and head toward Brooks Hall, the dormitory where she would reside. When she moved into her room, she found a letter from St. John waiting for her, saying that she had written to one of her former Barnard professors to let him know that Elizabeth was to be a member of the freshman class. St. John had asked him if Barnard would exempt Elizabeth from an English course on the basis of her work at St. Mary's, and he had replied that she would have to make formal application to a committee herself. St. John knew how difficult that would be for Elizabeth. "Oh, Betty!" she commiserated. She closed her letter by saying, "Now see everything and do everything for me." Perhaps before her parents left, they suggested that they take Elizabeth for a little more shopping—this may have been when she acquired a turtle she named Geronimo (which she carried with her when she went back on the train to North Carolina). And then her parents said goodbye; later, back at the Hotel Pennsylvania, where they had all stayed when they first arrived, her father wrote her a letter to tell her how much he loved her.[8]

Elizabeth's "Brooks Hall sister," Peggy Melosh, from Jersey City, New Jersey, showed Elizabeth the boardwalk to the college's cloisters, the marble staircase in Milbank Hall, and the walk on Riverside Drive. Sometime during the first week, Elizabeth met Dean Gildersleeve, who the older girls noted had bobbed her hair. At dinner the dean told them about her summer in France and England, where she shared a cottage with the noted English scholar Caroline Spurgeon. (Spurgeon later came to live part of the year with Gildersleeve in the Deanery.) New York was a big place, but the campus was small. Elizabeth began to move around more freely. After a few weeks of classes, Sam Lawrence wrote Elizabeth to urge her not to study too hard and to feel free to make her own decisions: "I feel you have now reached the age of discretion."[9]

Many of the best graduates of New York City public high schools were day students at Barnard who had won competitive scholarships; Lawrence had been admitted on the basis of the new test (she had scored 82.3). Apparently, she was the first St. Mary's graduate to attend Barnard, and the admissions director probably had relied heavily on Grace St. John's recommendation to trust that Elizabeth could do the work. The Lawrences were paying all her fees, which amounted to about one thousand dollars a year—an amount that, together with payment for her transportation and clothes, was out of reach for most North Carolina families. In 1922 Mr. Lawrence's sand and gravel business was going well. The family was not extravagant in any way, but he always wrote to tell Elizabeth to let him know if she needed more money. (She was not one of those students who got jobs to help pay for their school expenses—making three to four dollars an hour if they were lucky enough to work in a department store, a dollar fifty an hour for babysitting.)

To the large number of day students, the girls in Brooks Hall appeared to be "rich" (especially those from the South), and they seemed to keep to themselves. Elizabeth Lazer (Hormon), a member of the class of 1926, was a more typical Barnard student—she had graduated in a class of three thousand students from a large public high school in New York City. For her, Barnard was "a place where you found yourself." More than seventy years after their graduation, Hormon thought that she remembered Lawrence as one of the Southern girls who lived in Brooks Hall. Except for being "different" because she lived on campus, Elizabeth looked like the other students, who had shortened their hair, lengthened their skirts, and donned Bramley sweaters and saddle shoes—and, of course, rolled their stockings. When the president of Columbia University sent word that Barnard girls were to wear bras, they laughed—and flaunted their freedom to wear teddies.[10]

In addition to dress, there were other uniformities in the college experience. Freshmen were hazed by sophomores—made to wear their middies backwards and to pay a ten-cent radiator tax. The highlight of the first two years was always the annual Greek Games, since 1903 an elaborate competition between freshmen and sophomores, held in April. Students competed in discus throwing, hurdling, hoop rolling, and chariot racing. The arts were represented in elaborate dances and original poetry. Elizabeth's mother may have been in the audience for these dances, with other parents, when she came to New York to see Elizabeth in the spring of her first year at Barnard. And she probably brought a box of daffodils that she had cut from their garden, hoping that they would still be fresh, and not in the forlorn state of others that had been sent through the mail.[11]

There was much to do in the city, and Barnard students mostly went out together. It was hard to meet boys, unless a girl spent a good deal of time on the Columbia campus. Apparently, Elizabeth did not. Once she went for a weekend at the Academy at West Point, but she did not give any further details about it in her letter home. On the rare occasion when she was invited home by one of her classmates who lived on Long Island, she had to receive permission from her parents, and Nana wrote to remind her to accept invitations only from the right kind of people. Elizabeth, as was true at St. Mary's, made a few good friends she was always to remember, and at Barnard she got to know one of the most beautiful and brilliant women in her class—Jean Lowry. Jean, from Lexington, Kentucky, was completely at home in the city, where her married sister and brother-in-law lived, and her mother visited often. She was confident and ambitious, and brought an element of daring into Elizabeth's life: they cut classes and went to movies at the Nemo at Broadway and 110th. At the end of their junior year, Jean was placed on probation, but when the notice came from the college, she had already left for Paris. Mrs. Lowry wrote Elizabeth to tell her that at least "her darling baby" had not been expelled. Mrs. Lowry also expressed the hope that she and "Libba" (as they called her) and Jean (and "maybe your mother, too") would go to Paris together someday. She was, Zetta Lowry told her, "Jean's dearest friend." But they never did take the trip. Jean married an American journalist, traveled to Russia with him, recklessly abused her health, and died when she was forty-five. When Elizabeth heard the news, she spoke of Jean to her family and a few close friends, remembering how vividly alive she had been at Barnard, and grieving that love was "no protection" for Mrs. Lowry's "darling baby."[12]

At St. Mary's, Elizabeth had never made the high grades that teachers expected of her, but most of them knew her (and her family) and found nothing lacking in her background. No one at Barnard knew her that well—the classes were larger, and the work more demanding—and at first she had difficulty making grades above a C. At the end of her first year she was suspended for having failed French. It was one of the most humiliating experiences of her life, and she was especially upset because she took great pride in being able to read and translate French poetry. Apparently, she had to leave Brooks Hall and could not continue at Barnard for the fall semester of 1923, and she may have moved in with Jean's mother, who was living on West 114th Street. When she was readmitted and came back to campus to begin the January term, she slipped quietly back among her classmates. There was a lovely snow that winter, students were glad to see each other, and they hurried to unpack so that they could take a walk along scenic Riverside Drive.

Elizabeth settled down, and by the end of the term she had made her first A—in Comparative Literature—together with four Cs, including two in French. She was still on probation spring term of her sophomore year, when she compiled more Cs, in courses she would have wanted to excel in—Classical Civilization, English, and Fine Arts. As often happens after the first two years, however, Elizabeth began to master college work as a junior and senior, making As in Anthropology and Music, and Bs in English and Fine Arts. She continued to struggle in French, but the struggle apparently only made her try harder: for more than a half-century she was to translate French verses.

What is remarkable is that Elizabeth did not leave Barnard and return home but stuck it out. Years later, Elizabeth said that New York City still frightened her. She had not found any teacher at Barnard as helpful as Mr. Stone at St. Mary's, who, when she had failed, had given her a reexamination. (She believed that he liked her for having answered a question in class "dreamily.") "Barnard had no place for dreamers," she was to explain as a reason for her "hatred" of Barnard. "But do not suppose that scholarship was unappreciated at St. Mary's," she insisted. "It was and it was rewarded. I was careless, and I was marked accordingly. But I was constant and uncommon."[13] If any of her Barnard teachers commended her, she never said, at least not in the few letters in which she mentions her college years.

Elizabeth's difficulties at Barnard nevertheless brought her a piece of good luck. In making up her deficiency in order to be readmitted to Barnard, she enrolled in classes at Columbia Extension. In addition to studying French, she took a writing course with Professor Samuel Lee Wolfe, which she vividly remembered a half-century later. "Mr. Wolfe said, 'Miss Lawrence, haven't you anything to write about but your childhood?' " Elizabeth explained, "At that point, a sophomore at Barnard, [childhood's] ending was the only thing I felt keenly about."[14] A chance to defend herself was seldom wasted on Elizabeth (who liked to argue), and it is possible that Mr. Wolfe's question, rather than discouraging her, made her determined to write about what mattered to her. Indeed, some ten years later, at the beginning of her career, she wrote a long reflection on childhood.

Elizabeth's classwork at Columbia Extension was not only a test of her determination to remain at Barnard; it had a great personal reward as well. Here she met the friend of a lifetime—Ellen Bracelen, whose mother had recently died, and whose father asked that she not go away to college but that she continue to live with him at home. Ellen consented and enrolled in classes at Columbia Extension. Mr. Bracelen was vice president and general counsel of American Telephone & Telegraph

Company, and he was able to provide his daughter with great comfort. In addition, he was a man of charm and intellect. As frequent guests, Elizabeth, and later her sister, Ann, loved being at the dinner table when he was in an expansive mood. He laughed and he talked to Ellen's friends, and they loved him dearly. Perhaps Elizabeth told him about the lecture she heard at Barnard, raising the question, "Can every man earn a living under capitalism?" Many liberal-leaning Barnard women thought not. Mr. Bracelen loved to talk politics with Elizabeth, and they had lively discussions, especially in the early years of Franklin Roosevelt's New Deal.[15]

Elizabeth and Ellen were a wonderful match—they were smart, they read literature, and they loved to argue. That a young girl from the South and a young girl who had grown up in New York became best friends was one of the loveliest happenstances in Elizabeth's life. Just as Mr. and Mrs. Lawrence had hoped, four years in New York City was itself an education, and Elizabeth did not have anyone who stimulated her desire to learn as much as Ellen did.

Although Elizabeth often struggled through her courses, her extracurricular activities were a major outlet for her energies, and perhaps her frustrations. She had loved acting and dancing at St. Mary's, and she fell right into the same kinds of activities at Barnard. At some of the most intense periods in her life, Elizabeth dreamed that she was dancing. Barnard had its own Brinkerhoff Theatre and a much loved drama teacher, Minor Latham, whose tenure would be as long as Dean Gildersleeve's, and for whom the theater was later renamed. Miss Latham wore knickerbockers and ran her fingers through her hair. She talked in a way that many of the girls had never heard—"Oh, for God's sake, girls," she admonished, "Go out and live!"[16] For Miss Latham's students, New York City was part of Barnard's campus. She not only taught students to read plays ("she made them come alive") but she encouraged them to pay a dollar to stand in the balcony of New York theaters to see Eva Le Gallienne, Helen Hayes, Katharine Cornell, and the Barrymores; and she taught them to write their own plays. After she had returned to Raleigh,

Elizabeth became a volunteer with the Little Theatre, which her friend Ann Bridgers helped found.

There were two distinct groups of Barnard students—those interested in the arts and those interested in government. Elizabeth belonged to the former, being more creative than political. The fact that she loved to argue put her in the position of arguing over verse translations. Dean Gildersleeve had little patience with women who wanted to become artists. Politics excited—even radicalized—many students; the Red Scare had inflamed the nerves of their parents, and the Sacco-Vanzetti case kept alive a passionate debate about justice and the rights of minorities, even after the 1927 execution. Apparently Elizabeth Lawrence had not taken an active interest in the question of women's suffrage when it was debated in North Carolina. At Barnard in the spring of her junior year, she was exposed to a vigorous debate on the merits of the Equal Rights Amendment. Proponents insisted on "freedom at all costs," and opponents from the Woman's Trade Union League argued that the ERA would abolish laws protecting women. Although most Barnard students were ardent suffragists, one of their most revered trustees, Annie Nathan Meyer, who championed the cause of women's education, prided herself on being an antisuffrage feminist. What decidedly made Barnard different from St. Mary's was the diversity of opinions and the opportunity to think whatever one wanted to: in New York City, everything was possible.

Elizabeth expressed her creative side in a very safe place: on stage. For the sophomore dance, she was one of fifteen mischievous children, stealing off at nightfall to play by themselves, and captured by sorcerers and magicians. They are rescued by Hecate, and the children, "happy in their release, return to their homes." Later in 1924, Elizabeth and other students in Miss Latham's drama class presented three miracle plays in Brinkerhoff Theatre. Elizabeth took the role of Eve in *The Temptation,* and was expelled from the Garden of Eden. In the fall of her junior year, she danced as an animated doll in the Athletic Association Circus and had a part in a play by W. B. Yeats. In her senior year she performed with

Miss Latham's playwriting class; the reviewer noted, "Libba Lawrence as the young wife, Josee, acted well at all times, and sometimes quite brilliantly."

Another of Elizabeth's favorite activities was attending the teas held every afternoon at four o'clock. The long refectory table in Brooks Hall was loaded with sandwiches and cookies, and often Dean Gildersleeve, faculty, and guests joined the students. After Vachel Lindsay's reading, he came to tea, and students thought his shy "half-smile" was enchanting. Elizabeth had pasted copies of some of Lindsay's poems in her scrapbook, bought at the Columbia University Bookstore, and she continued to fill it with poems for many years.

Graduation weekend for the class of 1926 began on Friday afternoon, May 28, with a tea dance in Brooks Hall. In the evening there was the traditional "step ceremony" at Milbank Hall, followed by the senior show in Brinkerhoff, which was presented again the next day. The baccalaureate service was held on Sunday afternoon in St. Paul's chapel, where the sermon was preached by the university chaplain. In late afternoon the seniors and their guests returned to Brooks Hall for tea. Monday night there was a senior ball, and the next day, on the first of June, Class Day was held in the gymnasium—the graduates in caps and gowns took part in a musical comedy, and a chorus danced the Charleston. The 230 members of Barnard's class of 1926 joined graduates from Columbia in a ceremony held outdoors in South Court on the Columbia campus. It began to rain during the procession, and the program was cut short, but the Barnard graduates were in high spirits, singing, "Twenty-six shall march together/To the unknown good ahead." (As a class they had helped launch the National Student Federation to encourage participation in world affairs.)

Barnard's graduation was over, Dean Gildersleeve was off to London, Oxford, Paris, and Amsterdam, and the students dispersed. Elizabeth took her time saying her goodbyes and packing her things (including about a hundred books) for the train ride home, which had become so

Elizabeth Lawrence, Class of 1926, Barnard College.
"She's a little girl all day/But at night she steals away."
(Courtesy of Barnard College Archives.)

familiar in the past four years. Apparently, no one in her family had come for the ceremonies—Ann was graduating from St. Mary's at the time. From Parkersburg, Nana wrote Elizabeth that she should enjoy her last days and that she was thinking of her.

Elizabeth had not much to look forward to, having made no plans for getting a job, though she had talked with Jean Lowry about traveling overseas. Jean had won a Carnegie Scholarship to study abroad.

Others went on to medical and graduate school, became social workers, high-school and college teachers, organizers, journalists, secretaries, statisticians, and artists. The next year, Barnard College and six other colleges for women became the Seven Sisters, and in 1928, all the professional schools of Columbia University were opened to women.

At the first assembly for the opening of school, when Elizabeth began her junior year, Dean Gildersleeve had delivered her traditional address on "The keeping open of the mind's own windows." Her girls always expected her to tell them what to do, whether they followed her advice or not. One of her favorite themes was the expectation that each student would give something back to the college. A month or so before they were to graduate, members of the class of 1926 were reminded by Dean Gildersleeve: "Everybody should have a career, whether she needs it financially or not."

It is difficult to say how Elizabeth Lawrence felt about such a message because she apparently did not take a public stance about anything, even when she had strong feelings. She had survived the test of having lived four years away from home, and she had graduated with her class from one of the premier women's colleges. She had become best friends with two brilliant young women—Ellen Bracelen and Jean Lowry—who had taken her in hand to show her some of the sights of the city. She had ridden subways, crossed Broadway to classes on the Columbia campus, walked along Riverside Drive, and shopped on Fifth Avenue. And after long rides home and short holidays with her parents and sister in Raleigh, and her grandmother in Parkersburg, she had gotten back on the train and returned to finish another semester at Barnard. Her father's letters do not suggest that she suffered, except for this question: "Have you ever wondered what you would have done if Mrs. Lowry had not taken you in?"[17] If he is alluding to the time when Elizabeth was suspended from Barnard, it is a question that suggests how nearly she may have come to giving up.

When Elizabeth wrote about Barnard some fifty years later, in an essay for her archivist, Carol Wells, she was not admiring: "They turned out then, & still do, robots (perhaps they call them robotesses or robot persons)." It seems ironic that while other Barnard students were enjoying the freedom to express themselves, Elizabeth felt that she had had to give up freedom. What happened during her college years to make her feel this way?

Elizabeth had been admired by her St. Mary's classmates as the one who argued with her teachers. Arguments, mostly about literature, were the delights of her friendship with Ellen. Being one in a class of some two hundred students, mostly girls who had performed well in large public high schools in New York City, was more daunting than being in a class of twenty-two girls, almost exclusively from the South. Perhaps Elizabeth was afraid to speak up at Barnard (where her soft Southern accent might have been noticed). Since no Barnard teacher took her under her wing, as Grace St. John had done at St. Mary's, Elizabeth was nurtured only by controlling women—her grandmother and her mother. Students who remember college years fondly are usually those who enjoy talking about either their adventures or their successes. Elizabeth fell into neither camp. The image that at least some of her Barnard classmates had of her was captured in the caption under her yearbook picture: "She's a little girl all day/But at night she steals away."

"A little girl" is a characterization that later friends would still have recognized in the mature Elizabeth. But there was the other mysterious side alluded to in the yearbook that only the girls in Brooks Hall could have seen (and few others ever heard about). A decade after she had graduated from Barnard, Elizabeth wrote about where she had been going when she stole away.[18]

CHAPTER FIVE

Peter and Elizabeth

"Love itself shall slumber on."

PERCY BYSSHE SHELLEY

In February of 1926 at the annual Kit-Kat Ball in Greenwich Village, costumed guests were keeping warm by drinking gin and making love. Arriving late, Elizabeth Lawrence, dressed as a nymph, had already been reduced almost to tears when guests at an earlier party had taken scissors and shortened her skirt. Her date, dressed as a toy soldier, had not been able to hold his liquor and had been sick all over himself and her—they'd had to be sponged off in the bathroom. When the party moved to the Village, she found herself in an even more compromising situation when a man dressed as a pirate complained loudly that she would not kiss him. She was nervous for a lot of reasons, including the fact that she had never been kissed. A young man, older than the toy soldier and dressed as a Florentine page, stepped forward to show him how it was done, lightly dipping down to brush her lips like a hummingbird that had changed its mind at the last second. The nymph and the Florentine page had not met, but she had heard that he had a reputation with women. He turned away from his date—she looked like one of those women in a Picasso painting—and led Elizabeth away from the dance floor to a quiet balcony, where they talked the rest of the night, as if they had known each other always. He lived up to his reputation as a man of enchantment. By the end of the evening, he had asked her to come to see him in his apartment, and she had said that she would.[1]

This scene, as described in an essay by Elizabeth Lawrence more than a decade later, when she was living back at home in North Carolina, would come as a surprise to most of those who knew her. Libba, as most of her college friends called her, was twenty-one years old and a Barnard senior, more a nymph of ancient Greece than a 1920s flapper; she had worn the tunic first at the college's Greek Games. The Florentine page was a New York sportswriter named Peter Burnaugh, thirty-two years old and already an authority in his field, covering important horse races in America and in France. He was not a handsome man—in fact, she thought him "very ugly"—but he was the most charming man she had ever met.

Almost every Thursday for the rest of the spring until she graduated in May, Elizabeth went to Peter's apartment in Washington Square.

Elizabeth Lawrence was by nature a very private person. Like most private people, she guarded her privacy by different means of concealment. She did not talk much about herself except to a few close friends, and she did not believe in psychoanalysis. Although she was reserved, she was not self-effacing, and as a schoolgirl when she discovered the excitement of playacting, she discovered a way of presenting herself. The role of nymph was a contrivance for the Kit-Kat Ball, but it was a role she acted at other times in her life (later friends thought her "elfin"). Like the stereotypical image of the Southern lady, it was well made for deception.

The story of Peter Burnaugh perhaps was Elizabeth's best-kept secret. By the time she wrote of it some ten years later, she had her emotions under control, and she had begun to think of herself as a writer, whose inner life might offer good material. It was intended to be read only by her older friend and tutor, Ann Preston Bridgers, who was, importantly, a successful writer. Since Elizabeth had already told Ann about Peter, the manuscript about him seems to have been intended for some purpose other than the need to unburden herself. It is important, then, to consider why she wrote the story. Was Elizabeth trying to offer her own more mature analysis of something very upsetting that had happened to her as an immature college student? Had she come to a turning point in her life, in which she saw the future as a reliving (or retelling) of the past? And if a turning point, was it the point at which she explained to herself why she had not married? Was she, perhaps for the first time, laying claim to her own exercise of the imaginative energies she felt so intensely in her readings of favorite writers as different as Marcel Proust and Edna St. Vincent Millay? Was she learning to revise a life as well as a manuscript?

Whatever Elizabeth's motives (perhaps known and unknown to her), this unpublished manuscript is unlike anything else she wrote. It may offer clues as to why she chose to live at home, in the garden.

Elizabeth's letters to Ann Preston Bridgers are the most personally revealing of her many correspondences. In 1934, which may be when she wrote the story about Peter Burnaugh, Elizabeth had written many long letters to Ann—who was often out of town working on her own manuscripts. In fact, Elizabeth found it easier to write about herself when Ann was not in the neighborhood. In the letter to Ann accompanying the manuscript, Elizabeth said that it was spring, "when the shop windows are filled with ruffled organdy collars, and the sky is filled with fleecy white clouds." She explained that she could not concentrate on writing a garden article until she had written "what is in my mind." A twenty-eight-page manuscript was enclosed, and it contained this epigraph: "And so thy thoughts, when thou art gone,/Love itself shall slumber on." These lines from Shelley's poem "To —" were indeed mysterious. The story in the manuscript is told here, mostly in her own words.

Peter Burnaugh was a man with "an inordinate curiosity, and a large ego." She had heard him talked about by one of her closest Barnard friends, Jean Lowry, who dated many men. Jean had arranged Elizabeth's date for the Kit-Kat Ball, but after Elizabeth and her date arrived, Peter had found her on his own. When they met, she refused to tell him what she had already heard about him. "If I had wanted him to be interested in me," Elizabeth wrote, "I could not have found a better way," adding, "But I did not think of that. It was simply because what the Lowrys had said was that he slept with a different woman every night." "Sleeping with" was a phrase she had heard only once before in her life, when someone had told a dirty joke in her presence.

When Elizabeth arrived at the first party, according to the manuscript, "The men all looked at me as if I hadn't any clothes on." She went on, "And I hadn't much.... Trying not to look embarrassed, I said: 'It *is* rather long isn't it?'.... several people jumped up and produced scissors and fell upon me. I was almost in tears and the costume was definitely shorter by the time I had persuaded them that I was joking." In acting the role of ingenue, Elizabeth may not have realized that she was flirting with danger.

The woman Peter had come with was "one of the most dreadful looking women." Elizabeth had never seen such "love-making" as she witnessed among the others who were there. Then, at this point in her story, she broke away from the narrative and matter-of-factly reported that the party was to be for her the "first and last" of its kind. She moved the narrative forward to the winter after her graduation from Barnard, when she was staying with her maternal grandmother in Parkersburg. In Nana's house, she had received an invitation to the annual Kit-Kat, and she had hastily torn it up. When her grandmother found it, "She laid me out." Nana did not think that they were "proper people." They were "Bohemians!"

Nana was well known to Elizabeth's reader, Ann Bridgers, who had certainly heard about Nana and may even have met her in 1929, when at the end of her long life Nana had come to live with the Lawrences in Raleigh. Ann, who had an apartment in New York, had many "Bohemian," even "leftist," friends—how she must have laughed when Elizabeth first told her what Nana had said. Now she was reading it in Elizabeth's manuscript, where it had been placed early in the narrative, a writer's foreshadowing of what was to come.

Elizabeth then shifted her narrative back to Peter and the scene at the Kit-Kat Ball. "He asked if I would come to see him at his apartment, and I said I would. He said whenever I was free I was just to call him and come. I said I would not do that, that I never telephoned men. He said he never telephoned women, so we had better decide on a day right then, and we decided on Thursday. For the rest of the spring I went almost every Thursday."

The matter-of-fact reporting, the summarized dialogue, the absence of interior thought suggest that Elizabeth had her story under control, never giving in to the flood of feelings she loved reading about in poems. And yet, she described a scene that did not conceal desire and conflict. Imagine a young girl who never telephoned men agreeing to come to the apartment of a man she had only just met. What will come of it?

> On Thursday I was free in the afternoon. I hurried back from the last morning class, hurried through lunch, and dressed in a hurry. As I went out the door, Peggy called, 'Has Peter come for you? I didn't hear the phone.' 'No,' I told her, very much mortified, 'He is not coming for me.' Even though I would not call him up, I knew better than to expect Peter (who was thirty-two, and had forgot—if he ever knew them—the college proprieties) to come from Washington Square to Brooks Hall to fetch me in broad daylight. It is probably the only spark of sophistication I ever showed, and I still marvel at myself.
>
> When I rang his bell Peter opened the door and said, 'You have come just at the right time.' After that I was always in terror of coming at the wrong time. I wondered how I was expected to know. But he always said that I came just at the right time. We sat down in the living room and began to talk where we had left off. Somehow, I cannot remember how, we were discussing kissing, and I found myself saying (what I had never said to anyone before, because it mortified me so much) that I had never kissed any one. Peter said, 'Have you ever been in love? and I said I had. 'And what happened?' he asked, taking the past tense for granted. I hesitated a moment (for that was a sore point, too) and he said quickly, 'Don't tell me. I know. You saw his lack of intelligence.'

This episode ends with Peter asking her to have dinner with him, and Elizabeth accepting. Dialogue has moved the story forward, and a confessional voice emerges ("what I had never said to anyone before"), but again, more is suggested than actually told. In fact, while Peter's words are direct ("Have you ever been in love?" "And what happened?"), Elizabeth's responses are more distant ("I said I had."). Whom had she been in love with? She does not directly deny or confirm Peter's "taking the past tense for granted," but she seems to assent to his inference that the love is over and that she loved someone who intellectually was no match for her—something she could not have said directly (Elizabeth was often self-deprecating). There is a strikingly passive quality to the role of the narrator.

As their meetings continued, Elizabeth described what she loved about the afternoons and evenings. She always felt as if they had "endless time. I always went right after lunch, and I usually stayed to dinner. No one ever came, no one ever called on the telephone. We were never interrupted. And we never did anything or went anywhere. We just sat and talked all afternoon." When Peter played some records by a French café singer and asked her what she thought of them, she did not say what she was thinking—"that it was the most sensuous and disturbing music that I ever heard, or ever shall hear. I don't suppose I even knew then, that I thought that." But she added, "Long afterward I heard in my mind that low, husky voice singing in French, and knew what I thought of it." Writing herself into the past, Elizabeth wrote the past into the future, a more challenging technique for a writer. At the same time, she moved closer to her own feelings ("Long afterward I heard in my mind"), while still stopping short of saying what she thought of the "sensuous and disturbing music." She did say what it was about Peter that she liked: he knew how to put her at her ease, making her feel "clever . . . not forever wondering if I had said the wrong thing, or if he would attach to what I had said a meaning that I had not intended." And he was gentle in teasing her when she had to admit that she had liked a painting she had insisted she would not like. In all these ways, Peter seemed the perfect person—"essentially a shy man," though "suave and self-possessed"—for Elizabeth to have loved.

But the story was far from told. No more than a third of the way through her narrative, the illusion of compatibility begins to falter. Elizabeth and Peter discovered how different they were when they began talking about their respective families.

The conversation began casually enough when he asked her if she had always read, or if she had got that interest from college. When she said that she had always read, "and so had my family," Peter "looked as if he could not bear it when people had always read." She continued, "I said the thing I was most grateful to my family for was that they read me the children's classics when I was very little." Each of them believed that children should not be talked down to by adults. And it was Peter who, when he was nine, had "made a list of all the things grown people do that children don't like, so he could refresh his memory when he had a little boy—in case he forgot."

But the discussion of childhood led Peter further away from Elizabeth's own experiences. Apparently when his family was living in Kentucky, his father had made him dress in long trousers and a high silk hat and drive a little cart while his father sold patent medicines. "And Peter never forgave him. He had to take him to live with him [in New York City] when he was old, but he never forgave him." This story must have disturbed Elizabeth, who had grown up in a household where she willingly looked after the old people.

Elizabeth's narrative continues with an allusion to her sister Ann's having visited her in New York during her spring holidays from St. Mary's School in Raleigh. Elizabeth had introduced her to Peter, and afterwards, he had asked Elizabeth, "Do you like Ann?" When she said that she did, very much, "he looked disappointed. He said that it was stupid to like your family just because they were your family, and (without giving me a chance to say that I would like Ann even if she were no kin to me) began to tell me with a rush about his family. He said he hated all of them but his Mother. . . . He did not ever want to see any of them again."

"I could not see why he wouldn't allow other people to like their families," she continued. And then she added a very telling observation, "I could not help thinking, often, how fortunate it was that there was no occasion for him to meet my family." The narrative then returns to the earlier theme: "Once when I was repeating to Nana something clever that Peter had said, she looked at me sharply and asked, 'Who is Peter?' I said he was a friend of the Lowrys, and a sports writer on a New York paper. She said. 'Those Lowrys! Sports Writer! I feel sure he is no proper person for you to know.' " And she did not even know what Elizabeth knew—that Peter did not go to church.

At this point in the narrative, Nana's decisive authority reminds Elizabeth of her own indecision. Once when she regretted having turned down an invitation to go out with Peter, she left her dormitory room and walked up and down Riverside Drive, "so miserable" that she went to a drugstore and called him. "And when he answered I hadn't any thing to say. He said he took a blonde in my place." Elizabeth asked if she had enjoyed it, to which Peter responded, "he seemed to," infuriating Elizabeth. "I was so angry with him for saying anything so cheap, and with myself for falling for it, that I put down the phone and cried." Then, abruptly, she adds, "But I thought it was no more than I deserved."

Her remembered disappointment, however, is immediately followed in the story by the great pleasure of a time when she went to his apartment to study while he was writing an article. When he finished, they sat together talking about what she had been reading, and they talked until midnight.

In confessing how hurt she was in having missed being with Peter and how happy she was to be with him again, Elizabeth makes a sudden narrative slip. "I watched Peter at the typewriter," she relates. "He wrote very seriously, the way you do, and with his whole mind. And he looked different with glasses on. . . . so very dependable."

"The way you do" is an intrusive reminder that Elizabeth was writing this story for Ann Bridgers. And in comparing Peter with Ann, Elizabeth found the essential quality that must have reassured her that she had done the right thing in coming to his apartment: he was "so very dependable."

Elizabeth then created a scene that has some of the same surprises as the night at the Kit-Kat: "Mrs. Lowry said it was unwise for me to go so much to Peter's apartment, and asked me to stop. But I could not promise, and she said, 'Well, Libba, you must be very circumspect.' I assured her that I was. 'Doesn't he ever try to make love to you, Libba?' Jean asked incredulously. 'No,' I told her. 'I suppose you would be insulted if he did?' I told her no." Later when Elizabeth told Peter about the conversation, they looked at one another and laughed. "He had a warm spontaneous laugh, and I liked to provoke him to laughter, but I could not do it often.... I do not think he was naturally grave, but somehow a little sad."

They developed a certain kind of intimacy—she said she hated his colored shirts, he reminded her to pin up her hair. "And once he stared at me so hard I thought my nose must be shiny and I took out a compact and put some powder on it. Then he laughed so heartily that I was delighted, and I wished I knew why, so I could make him do it again."

The last time Elizabeth and Peter were together before she graduated provided the turning point for Elizabeth's story. He had offered to give up his morning if she would go with him to the Belmont races, something he said he had never done before, and she accepted his invitation. The scene echoes the one when she first met him at the Kit-Kat, with something of the same mixture of vulgarity and innocence. The friends they joined drank from their flasks, concentrated on betting, and ignored her. "The women were the kind I most detest in New York.... I felt like a school girl in my new spring outfit from Best's." She ordered ginger ale. But when she and Peter walked through a little copse to their seats, Peter looked up at a sparrow in a tree and "asked shyly, the way children ask you things," if she liked birds.

On the train going home, Peter wanted to know if she was hot or tired, or hungry.

> "I guess he felt a little guilty. I was all of them at once." And then he said, "What do you think makes me so concerned about you? Do you think I am falling in love?"
>
> I laughed and said no, I did not think he was falling in love.
>
> "You would know the signs?" he insisted anxiously.
>
> I said yes, I would know the signs.
>
> And he looked relieved.

Another time in Peter's apartment, Elizabeth sat in the window reading. "And Peter came to me without speaking and stood with his arm around me, reading over my shoulder. And I sat very still and did not breathe, the way you do when you listen to music and know that any minute it is going to stop."

Turning away from that moment, Elizabeth writes about the next winter, when she went back to New York for a visit with Ellen Flood. "I thought when I got there," she remembered, "that I would write Peter a note, and say I was at Ellen's, and ask if I might come to see him. I spent a lot of time thinking how to word it, feeling suddenly self-conscious." As it turned out, Peter had been calling to find out when Elizabeth was arriving, and they were to see one another at a cocktail party.

> [When she saw him, Peter] had a girl with him. . . . someone who wrote for a new magazine called *The New Yorker,* and signed herself "Lipstick." He went about slowly, talking to people, and it was a long time before he got to me, and then he said. "Awfully good of you to send me that telegram to let me know you were here."
>
> There was a pause, after which he continued, "You're looking very pretty, Libba," and turned and walked away.
>
> I felt as if I had been slapped. Peter had never called me Libba before; he thought it was a silly name so he did not call me anything. And I knew that an obvious compliment from him was no compliment, but the opposite.
>
> For the rest of the afternoon he and Lipstick sat in one chair, and not a very big one, and talked to one another. I sat and talked to Jean's beau until I could not sit still any longer, and then I got up and started around the room with the cocktail shaker. My hand shook and I spilled some, and some people who remembered me from [the Kit-Kat party] began to tease me about the green dress. They were pretty lit and they laughed every time I spilled the gin, so I began to spill it deliberately.
>
> Then I turned and Peter was standing behind me, looking at me.
>
> "I don't like this," I said.
>
> And he said, "I don't like it either."

He asked how he could get hold of her, and she said, "Peter, you are drunk."

Later, she realized that he had thought the same of her.

"Just before I went back to Nana's," Elizabeth continued, "I suddenly couldn't bear it, and I called Peter up."

> He said, "Oh, so you have decided to be nice."
> I said I had never meant to be anything else.
> I said I was downtown, and could I come by on my way home to Ellen's.
> He said he was just going out.
> And I said, "Oh," and started to put up the phone.
> "Wait, wait," he said. "Give me Ellen's number and I will call you."

When he did call, Elizabeth was out, and Ellen made arrangements for them to meet him for tea—much against his will, Ellen said afterwards.

"He certainly behaved as if he had come against his will," Elizabeth remembered.

> He and Ellen exchanged nasty remarks with zest, and I sat miserable between them, drinking cups of tea. Ellen said afterward that they were like two dogs over a bone.
> Ellen kept saying, "Don't you hurt her."
> And he kept saying: "I'm not going to hurt her."

Ellen said to Peter that she was sorry he had seen Elizabeth so little. He said that it really did not matter, as she had always spent the time she was with him reading a book.

After tea, Elizabeth and Peter left together, going in the same direction.

> When we were jammed in the subway, he said, above the roar: "You are very difficult. And I have never made such an effort to be nice to a person."
> And I said, "Then I would hate to be your mortal enemy."
> And then he laughed his warm delightful laugh.
> He said, "But you will come to see me before you leave?"
> And I said I would.
> "Next Thursday afternoon?"
> I said I would come next Thursday afternoon [before returning to West Virginia].

Back in Peter's apartment, Elizabeth found things changed. It looked and felt different, with too many things, including a grand piano, which Peter said belonged to a girl who had stayed there while he was in Paris covering a race. Elizabeth walked about the apartment, touching the things she had remembered, and looking through the bookshelves.

"Peter seemed very tired. And old. I thought he must have got that wizened look when he was a little boy and drove the cart in a high hat and long pants. I thought it must come back every time he was very tired and very sad."

He lay on the couch, and she sat on the floor beside him, where she could see his clear hazel eyes, "unguarded like a child's." Once when she had told him that he had the most beautiful hands she had ever seen, and had blushed saying it, he had said, very gently, "You need not blush. It is always all right to say what you think."

"But it is not always all right to say what you think," Elizabeth had said. "I wish it were."

The "gray drizzling afternoon" wore on, and they talked about books and things they liked to do as children, and they argued about loyalty to family and friends. He insisted that he had only to be loyal to himself.

They stopped talking. And then he said sadly, "I have changed since you saw me."

She said that he had not changed at all.

He said, "Yes, I have changed. You wouldn't like me anymore."

When she told him goodbye, she asked if he was sorry that he had been "horrid" to her.

"Yes," he answered. "I was very silly." And he asked to see her before she went back to West Virginia.

"But I did not see him again," she wrote. "I never saw him again."

Back at Nana's, Elizabeth wrote Peter a long letter—her first, though she had always wanted to write to him—and she said that when she had called to tell him goodbye, he was out. And so she wrote him about Nana and the jessamine that bloomed in the snow, the walks at night by the river, and her talks with friends. Also, that before she had left New York, she had gone to hear *La Bohème,* which she knew he loved.

"A long time afterward, he wrote to me. The most delightful letter I ever had.[2] He said he was going to Paris, very suddenly, the next day, and that he would write to me on the boat, and that he had something to tell me.

"But he did not write again. I wrote him a note on his birthday, and told him about the garden."

In the summer of 1927, when Elizabeth was visiting Mrs. Lowry and Jean in Lexington, Kentucky, Mrs. Lowry told her that Peter Burnaugh was going to be married. Elizabeth did not say in her story for Ann that she was hurt, or shocked. She wrote instead that although she "had never thought very much about marrying Peter," the possibility of his marrying someone else had never occurred to her. She had thought that he was "a definite and permanent part of my life—like my family." But it *was* a shock.

She sat down to write to him, saying that she could not congratulate him on marrying a person she did not know. To Ann, she added, "I had seen her, but I did not know it. He was marrying Lipstick." She told him that she was camping in the mountains with her mother and Jean Lowry and that she got up early before they were awake and walked in the woods "before the dew was off of the ferns and mosses." And when she finished the letter, she walked up the road in the dark, and dropped it in some farmer's mailbox.

In a few days, in Lexington with Jean, Elizabeth received a letter from Peter, which the Lowrys wanted her to read aloud. And she did, reading about how he could not believe he was really getting married, but that wedding presents were arriving, and that his wife-to-be was a "dear." He wanted Elizabeth to know her. "Perhaps he had forgot that I did," she told Ann parenthetically. "Or was not going to remind me."

He asked her if she remembered some lines from a poem by Rupert Brooke:

> Better oblivion hide dead true loves
> Better the night enfold,
> Than men, to eke the praise of new loves,
> Should lie about the old!

And after the poem, there was a postscript, which Elizabeth did not read aloud. He had written, "I always wanted to camp in the mountains and walk in the dew, but I loved your garden even more." Did the fact that Elizabeth read all of the letter, including the poem, but chose not to tell the Lowrys what he had said about her garden, mean that she regarded what she had said about the garden as being more intimate than the poem?

In Lexington Mrs. Lowry read aloud from the local newspaper an account of the wedding. "It sounded very tacky, and we laughed a lot. And I laughed to myself, afterward, thinking of Peter and Lipstick being married in an Episcopal Church. (The only mistake I ever knew Peter to make in writing or speech was to call it the Episcopalian Church.)"

Lawrence's narrative continues without warning of what is to come next:

> A day or two later I came in one night from a party, and went upstairs to talk to Mrs. Lowry. She always read in bed, and when we came in, Jean and her beau, Thornton, would sit on the porch and talk, and I would go up and tell Mrs. Lowry all the things we had done, and what everyone had said. Especially the funny things. This night I was telling her about meeting a man who knew Peter, and repeating what he had said. I was excited, and I did not notice at first her expression; when I did I stopped in the middle of the sentence.
>
> "I just read it in the evening paper," she said. "Peter is dead."

The New York Times reported that Burnaugh had been taken suddenly ill while he was at the Empire City Track in Yonkers to cover the opening day of the races. After he had been taken to the hospital, he had undergone two surgeries in an attempt to save his life. He died July 12, 1927, at age thirty-five. The *Times* had run the story of his death on the sports page, describing him as a "widely known authority on racing." The Lexington *Herald* put the story on its front page, observing that he had been a "brilliant and popular young journalist," who had been former managing editor of the paper. Both newspapers noted that two weeks before his death he had married Betty Stanley of Wichita, Kansas. They had lived at 45 Washington Square.

The funeral was in nearby Carlisle, Kentucky, and although Elizabeth was still in Lexington, she did not attend the funeral with Mrs. Lowry, because Mrs. Lowry did not suggest that she do so. But she did suggest that Elizabeth write to Peter's mother, and she did.

"I said to Mrs. Burnaugh that I hoped she would not think me impertinent to write when I did not know her. But that I did know her, really, because Peter talked to me about her so much. And I told her about the time he picked up a pair of her gloves that she had left for him to take to the cleaners, and held them to his face and said, 'My mother smells so sweet.' "

The last chapter in Lawrence's manuscript was set the next summer—1928. She was twenty-three, and she was embarking on a long trip to Europe. Before leaving New York, she saw Jean Lowry and a man who had known Peter, who talked with her for a long time.

The friend told her that a day or two before Peter was to be married, he had told him that he would rather be with her than any person he had ever known.

The friend told Jean that Elizabeth had seemed indifferent to Peter's death. "He used to come up here and talk about her every time he got drunk. Sometimes I think he was a little in love with her. But she doesn't seem to have any feeling at all." In describing the conversation, Elizabeth was reportorial: this is what he said about me.

Writing the last scene may have been a greater test of that control. As she was leaving for Europe, Jean asked her to take a carton of cigarettes to a woman named Julia, who was living in Paris, and Elizabeth agreed. When she arrived in Paris, she took the cigarettes to Julia's apartment:

> It was a very smart one and a very smart maid came to the door. Julia was out. I left the cigarettes and [a] note. The next day I had a "petit bleu" [a postal card sent by pneumatic tube] from her inviting me to dinner, and being very cordial and grateful for the cigarettes. It was a charming note, and up to that moment I had every intention of seeing Julia, but the minute I opened it I knew that I did not want to. I wrote

her that I was leaving very soon and was sorry not to have an opportunity to have dinner with her. Afterward, I discovered that she had been Peter's mistress for years.... Peter gave her her first car.

How Ann Bridgers responded to Elizabeth's story is a question that cannot be answered, given the absence of any further mention of it in their correspondence. It is possible that Ann did write to say what she thought, but if she did, Elizabeth did not preserve the letter. Elizabeth trusted Ann with her secret—for "secret" it was, the story of Peter Burnaugh. Only a very few people knew about him, and among them, only two are still living. Ellen Bracelen Flood, Elizabeth's college friend, mentioned in the story, had met Peter. Ellen's children, Mary Ellen Flood Reese and Charles Bracelen Flood, also knew about Peter, not only from their mother but because Elizabeth had told each of them separately about a New York newspaper reporter. Mary Ellen and Bracelen had the same impression that Elizabeth had been in love with Burnaugh (whose name they had not known or did not remember). Elizabeth told Mary Ellen that she had "loved a man who had not loved her." Around 1950, more than twenty years after the relationship had ended, Elizabeth still seemed "heart-broken." Although Elizabeth's sister had met Peter in New York during Elizabeth's senior year at Barnard, Ann did not tell her son and daughter about him. Since Ann had dated many men before marrying Warren Way, and was herself a very intuitive woman, she would have been in a position to give Elizabeth advice and comfort. No one can ever know what the two sisters said about Peter, but Ann respected her sister's privacy.

What then are we to make of the discovered manuscript? Perhaps Elizabeth Lawrence wrote it as a "story" for her teacher, who, like Peter, "wrote seriously." Elizabeth was writing articles and poems at the same time. Perhaps Elizabeth was trying to develop her skills as a writer with "And so thy thoughts." Had Ann Preston Bridgers encouraged Elizabeth to continue writing in this vein, probably she would have written other stories. Perhaps Ann knew that Elizabeth could not make money writing stories, and, more important, that she was too private to write so intimately about herself. Moreover, Ann understood privacy: she too did not write about her own life, either in her plays or in letters to Elizabeth. "Privacy is like time," Elizabeth wrote to her. "It is inside."[3] In teaching Elizabeth the necessity of concentrating on her writing, Ann Bridgers must also have helped her to come to terms with her memories of Peter Burnaugh.

The place of Peter Burnaugh in Elizabeth's life became more important to her as she looked back, and more vivid when she wrote about him. Long afterward, she said, she heard sensuous music "in my mind." Some readers of this romance today may consider Peter to have been a cad; others, a worthy friend. Some may even see him as a potential lover or husband. We all might wish to know Elizabeth's true feelings, but it is clear that Peter held a unique place in her life. Even after she heard that he was getting married, she wrote him about what she loved—her garden. Whatever the nature of their relationship, both Elizabeth and Peter knew that the garden would not break her heart.

CHAPTER SIX

A Time for Reflection 1926–1928

"There—delicate and pure white and resting on a cloud of mist that hung above the city—was the Sacré-Coeur."

AFTER GRADUATION, Elizabeth had nowhere to go except home. Apparently having given no more thought to leaving Barnard than she had to entering, and with no one to guide her to the next stage, she turned again toward family. Her friend Jean Lowry had struck out on her own for Europe, and Ellen was continuing to live with her father—but a New York penthouse seemed to Elizabeth like an exotic country itself, and Ellen was soon to marry. Years later, when she was asked to write about herself for a garden journal, she said that after four years in New York she had come home to a North Carolina spring so beautiful that she had decided at once that her career would be in the garden.[1] Decisions are seldom as easily made as they are remembered, but Elizabeth had reason to be glad to be back in the South. When she left New York, temperatures had been in the chilly sixties, and on her first day at home in Raleigh, they were in the eighties—a day for exploring the garden, where a tall purple iris had softly opened. That very day they could have afternoon tea outside in the "Summer House," where the lattices just concealed them in the shade.[2]

In writing about that first spring, Elizabeth Lawrence chose to remember the flowers. In later years, a friend reminded her that after leaving Barnard she had felt "desolate" (apparently, the friend had not known why).[3] Whether Elizabeth was thinking about Peter or worried about what she should do next, she faced the prospect that many an unmarried daughter without means of support is left with: the need to move back home. Then, perhaps for the same reason that she went to college ("with nothing better to do"), she decided—or it was decided for her—that she would go to Parkersburg and live for a while with Nana and her great-grandmother. Later, in remembering this period in her life, she named the seasons: it was spring when she returned to the Raleigh garden, and winter when she went to live in Parkersburg. In both places there was a large old house (cool in summer, cold in winter) and people who were constant in their love.

In saying goodbye to her father, Elizabeth could count on his reassurances and his warm laughter; "Liz" and "Sammy," as they sometimes called each other, were very close. Sam Lawrence was an expressive man, and he always wrote both of his daughters funny, affectionate letters, never failing to say how much he loved their "Mother dear." He would be happy if they turned out to be "one-tenth as good."[4] Bessie, who signed her letters to family "EBL," continued to be as reticent a letter-writer as she had been when she and Sam were courting, but she showed her affection in other ways. It was Elizabeth's mother who probably rode the train to Parkersburg with her, so that she could see her own mother and help move Elizabeth into an upstairs bedroom. Bessie and Nana were both bossy, and the two of them always gave a lot of directives. With her younger daughter off to Europe with a college group for a year's study, Bessie could concentrate all her attention on Elizabeth.

Who knows what Elizabeth really wanted? Probably she did not know herself. She loved Bessie and Nana. Her most explicit statement of what it had been like to look after three generations—great-grandmother, grandmother, and mother—was made to a cousin, whose daughter was trying to decide what to do with her life. Elizabeth said, "I am glad that I belonged to the generation of women who could stay at home and look after the old people."[5]

Going to live with her grandmother and great-grandmother in Parkersburg was not living at home, but it was certainly the closest thing to it. Elizabeth knew what it would be like. Since she was thirteen she had been carrying trays upstairs to her old great-grandmother, whose physical discomforts and mental anxieties were constant now that she was ninety-one years old (and had been widowed for many years). Perhaps Elizabeth was thinking of that winter on Ann Street, when she later wrote these lines: "They never live at all/Who live among the old,/Under the shadow of death,/Waiting for death to fall." But Elizabeth tended to put her gloomy thoughts into poetry and save her charming self for those around her. News was going from house to house in Parkersburg that young Elizabeth was coming, and Nana and her friends could look forward to her company. In the long, dark West Virginia winter—no picnics on Blennerhassett Island, no boat trips down the Ohio River—Elizabeth and Nana talked and read aloud and played games in the library (whist and backgammon), walked downtown to shop, received callers and made calls, went with Mrs. Sammel over to see the three aunts, and wrote letters.

But family love—that tie that binds—also has its price, and Elizabeth may have paid it in many ways. She suffered most of her life from insomnia—and sometimes from melancholia—which she believed she had inherited from Nana. In wishing that, as a child, she had had someone like Ann Preston Bridgers (who was quiet and a tower of strength) to comfort her, Elizabeth admitted, "When my voice rose, Nana's voice rose."[6] It requires little stretch of the imagination to wonder whether Elizabeth's sleeplessness was heightened by the winter in Parkersburg. One thing came of these experiences: Elizabeth herself tamed the darkness by making it her companion. She read and wrote letters, and the nights passed.

Family friends are sometimes around to weigh in with their opinions about what young people should and should not do, and Elizabeth was to remember at least one of Nana's friends who was critical. The widow Mrs. Peterkin, who had been married to the bishop and still lived across the street, told Elizabeth that she should have stayed in New York and taken a job. Furthermore, Elizabeth should pay more attention to her looks.[7] Elizabeth—who was just about five feet tall, weighed less than one hundred pounds, and had fair skin that required no make-up and blonde hair that required no ribbons—was a natural beauty, many people thought.

In Raleigh, North Carolina, Elizabeth and Bessie gardened together from the first spring after Elizabeth came home from Barnard College in New York City until 1948, when they moved to Charlotte. By then, the Lawrence garden had become the talk of the town. (By permission of Warren Way and Elizabeth Rogers.)

And there was also the matter of Nana's contempt for Elizabeth's "Bohemian" friends, expressed when she discovered that invitation to the Kit-Kat Ball. In this regard, however, Elizabeth ignored Nana's opinion when she saw Peter again in New York, though perhaps Nana did not know about it. Back at Nana's, Elizabeth had written to him, and he had written to her. How secretive she must have had to be, to exchange these letters with Peter! Then, after Elizabeth had made it through the winter in Parkersburg, and was visiting the Lowrys in Kentucky, she received the shocking news of his marriage and sudden death.

At the end of the summer of 1927, after her visit to Kentucky, Elizabeth moved home to Raleigh, perhaps keeping to herself the news about Peter. If Elizabeth had wanted someone to talk things over with, she might not have found a better person than her sister. But Ann was traveling in Europe with young friends—including men who were willing to wait around until she could see them—and she no sooner arrived back home than she needed to get ready to go to Chapel Hill for the fall term. By the time Ann had unpacked, repacked, and departed, and Elizabeth had put things back the way she wanted them at home, the story of Peter may have begun to alter the color of her mind.[8] Writing about Peter was off in the future. Meanwhile, she had reached a turning point. Perhaps her sister's get-up-and-go spirit had energized Elizabeth, and seeing Ann home from Europe and off to Chapel Hill, Elizabeth decided to go back to school for the fall term as well—and in late spring, to travel abroad.

Elizabeth applied to North Carolina State College of Agriculture and Engineering in Raleigh (present-day North Carolina State University) and was accepted as a special student in courses that would prepare her for graduate work in landscape gardening. She took two courses in the spring, and despite the fact that it was difficult being the only woman in most classes, she had reason to feel proud of herself. She made an A in botany and a B in architectural drawing. At home, she and Bessie began to share the garden—where they planned and planted and weeded and had lunch with each other and with friends. Her father's business and health were still good. He was enjoying preparing papers for monthly meetings of the Sandwich Club. He and Elizabeth loved to talk to each other about what they were writing. After a difficult year, Elizabeth had begun to regain her confidence. She soon felt adventuresome again, and in the spring when Uncle Jim was visiting the Lawrences in Raleigh, she accepted his invitation to meet him in Europe that summer.

Elizabeth's decision to embark on a long tour of Europe had everyone's approval. Nana herself, encouraged by her mother, had traveled in Europe with her good friends the Atterburys. Elizabeth's Uncle Nat and Aunt Lucy Stewart were living in Barcelona, where he worked at the

American consul's office. Uncle Jim wanted her to cycle with him in the Pyrenees. She would have a young companion, Catherine Irwin, for part of the way, and Europe that summer was a crossroads for other American friends traveling abroad, including the Sammels from Parkersburg, and Miss Sophie and Miss Christine Busbee from Raleigh. Ann had given her the names of people she had met during her year abroad, and urged her sister to call on them. Elizabeth promised to write often to her mother and father and to Nana. Nana's instructions followed her across the Atlantic—"Always present my compliments to Mademoiselle [Ann's former landlady] in the most approved way, and do not forget the flowers."[9] Elizabeth would be glad for all these connections—Uncle Nat and Aunt Lucy, Uncle Jim, Ann's friends, letters from home—since she often would be traveling alone. But she was still thinking about Peter Burnaugh. She was carrying in the pocket of her new travel diary (a gift from her father, embossed in gold letters with her name and address) a piece of paper with several notes, with the dates of newspaper articles. One referred to Peter Burnaugh's marriage to Betty Stanley, one to his death, and two to articles about horses that he had written from Europe for the *New York Telegram*.[10]

After a few hectic days with Ellen Bracelen Flood and a St. Mary's friend, Mary Wiatt Yarborough Chase (now married and living and working in New York), Elizabeth boarded a Cunard ship and was immediately caught up in the adventure of oceanic travel.[11] She did not use any of the time to make notes in her new travel diary, though she did write a letter to Nana on her last day at sea. She began by reassuring her grandmother that the "glee club boys turned out to be all dears." Catherine Irwin, her traveling companion, had brought lots of food, and their cabin had been popular. After four days of cold, wet weather, it had turned "balmy." She did not mind traveling in steerage (it was a "sturdy" ship), which was filled mostly with nice college students. She had looked up "the Peterkin boy," who was sailing at the same time, and he had "dutifully" asked her to dance. The food had not been "half as bad" as her sister had predicted. A concert by the glee club had been good, the stewards and stewardesses "so kind and eager." The next morning the ship would dock at Plymouth, and Catherine and the glee club would go on to London. The next day—Sunday—Elizabeth would disembark at Le Havre. Although she was eager to get to Paris, she hated for the voyage to be over. It had been "so nice and restful... I just sit and look at the sea."

The interlude was good for Elizabeth, who always tended to be distracted by noises and to be overstimulated by conversations. The best parts of her trip would be the times when she was quiet, even as they gave rise to sadness. On the continent, lovely drives through the Brittany countryside (followed by lunch at the famous La Mère Poulard at Mont St. Michel), praying in cathedrals and small chapels, swimming in the calm bay at St. Malo, studying the way light fell upon church frescoes, finding purple foxglove growing in railroad tracks, drinking tea in a café in the old village of Dinan, browsing in bookstalls and bookshops in Paris and on London's Charing Cross Road—these were the occasions that gave her great pleasure. She loved the darkness inside Spanish churches, the quaintness of French towns and English thatched cottages and gardens, fuchsia blooming by the door of a stone cottage, the ruins of Tintagel, which local legend calls King Arthur's Castle.

Elizabeth was a child wandering at will, and on one occasion she "went through a door you weren't supposed to and wandered around in a garden and [like Peter Rabbit] ate gooseberries and lettuce." In another spot in Italy, when she climbed over a fence to get inside a garden, she was terrified by "two fierce Italian guards bearing down on me. I was so frightened I ran back to the wire fence that surrounds the whole garden, and threw my pocketbook and notebook over, and followed in haste, snagging my skirt but getting safely on the other side. I did not stop running until I was sure I wasn't being followed."[12]

Elizabeth intended to write someone in the family every other day, and she usually did. Her letters to "Mother dearest," to her father, and to Nana were passed around; in turn, she picked up their letters to her at American embassies. On one occasion she wrote a "private" letter to her father ("Sweet darling precious Sammy"), and a "public" letter that could be read aloud. In the private letter she told him how much she loved him, adding, "I don't think you know how much." She urged her parents and Nana not to save her letters because she would write in her diary everything that she wanted to remember (fortunately, they did not follow her instructions).

While traveling, Elizabeth purchased old books in stalls in Paris and London, a skirt and cardigan from Misses Yabsley (Makers to the Trade, 10 Vigo Street, London), a dress made by a French dressmaker whom Ann had recommended, and a St. Christopher medal for the Lawrences' car. In addition, she collected the names of a dozen or more plants that she hoped she and Nana could find in catalogues when she returned, including "a darling tiny yellow water lily" that she and Uncle Jim had seen in the Jardin des Plantes in Paris. She also enjoyed eating lunch in small gardens, a pattern she would continue almost every day of the year back home in her own garden in North Carolina. More beautiful to her than Canterbury Cathedral were the town, the old trees, the gardens, and even a tea tray in front of the fire at the inn. (Eating at a table in front of a fire became one of Elizabeth's favorite ways of entertaining her friends and family.) Time spent having coffee on a private balcony looking out on the Grand Canal in Venice—screened in by oleanders, honeysuckle vines, and star jasmine—also stamped upon her memory a growing excitement about color amidst an atmosphere of seclusion. Outside, the world beckoned, and she listened to the jazz orchestra playing on the terrace when she went to the Lido for tea.

Traveling with Uncle Jim was "quite a lark." They shared the same interests in the arts, often comparing their translations of French and Latin verses. Jim was, and would remain, a handsome bachelor, "very sweet and very funny." The second week in August they met at his hotel in Paris, where he had invited young people he had met to join them at his dining table—and later he took them all out for liqueurs at the Café de la Paix. Elizabeth tasted Cointreau for the first time, and liked it. Uncle Jim and Elizabeth bicycled for a week in early August, going to Verdun, where he had been an American chaplain during World War I; and then they took a train to Barcelona. There Elizabeth and Uncle Jim especially enjoyed being entertained by Elizabeth's Aunt Lucy and

Uncle Nat in their palatial apartment, where Elizabeth's sister had stayed at Christmas. Childless themselves, they enjoyed spoiling Elizabeth, and Aunt Lucy brought her breakfast in bed. After she left, Uncle Nat wrote her that his wife almost wept when she got up in the morning "and [couldn't] go to greet you. We wished that you had remained with the two old people all winter." Uncle Nat had also endeared himself to Elizabeth by his expressions of affection for her father—"the finest fellow I have ever known."

Il pleure dans mon coeur/Comme il pleut sur la ville.
(It weeps in my heart/As it rains on the town.)

VERLAINE

The differences between what Elizabeth wrote in letters home and in her diary reveal how much she withheld from her family. In a letter to Nana, she wrote, "I had such a lovely day all by myself. I went to Chartres. It's much nicer to do things you like as long as you like, and go where you like and come where you like. . . . you can just sit forever and look at the beautiful glass and think—and pray." In her diary she wrote, "The façade of Chartres is not beautiful—they who say so lie." Although the rose window was "perfect, as few things in the world are perfect," how easily "a perfect thing is a little spoiled" (she quarreled with aspects of the architecture). The worst of her dark mood was brought on by her days and nights in Paris: "I don't like Paris. Paris is a place to be happy in and I came feeling desperately sad. Paris is a place to think of others and I came wrapped up in myself. Paris is a place to be with people whose presence is like mine—and I came here alone. No wonder the statues seemed like tombstones, no wonder the city was disenchanted. You take from a place what you bring to it and how could you take gladness when you brought only tears."

In her diary, she wrote about how much she liked being alone, but in her letters, she wrote "what I like about travel is the people." In her letters, she loved Paris; in her diary, she hated Paris.

More expressive than we have found her in any of her letters, Elizabeth asked in her diary, "Why is it that you think so smoothly and simply—and when you start to write it down, the most complicated and tortured sentences and ideas appear?" She then wrote, apparently from memory, the first stanza of a poem by the French poet Verlaine: "It weeps in my heart as it rains on the town./What is this languor that penetrates my heart?"

This diary entry was followed by a rambling discourse on the elusiveness of beauty. Then, suddenly, Elizabeth wrote, "Oh, Libba, I love you so much!"

What was she thinking of? Whom was she thinking of?

On Elizabeth's last day in Paris, she looked for something beautiful, and found it for herself. She describes the experience in her manuscript about Peter Burnaugh. The experience does not appear in her letters or her diary, but constitutes a kind of epilogue to her European journey. It is one of the most moving passages she ever wrote.

> Pete had told me once when we were talking about beautiful things, that the Sacré-Coeur hung above Paris as if it rested on a cloud, if you saw it from the right place.
>
> I went all over Paris looking for the right place and at last when I had given up in despair, I looked up from my book as I came back late one afternoon from Chartres (the train had just passed Versailles) and there—delicate and pure white and resting on a cloud of mist that hung above the city—was the Sacré-Coeur. It hung there like a vision, and I sometimes wonder if it was seen or imagined.

By September 18, Uncle Jim had left Europe to return home, and Elizabeth moved on. With a week left in England to see Oxford and to meet one of her mother's friends in London, she wrote Nana that she would be ready to come home after the journey, "and I can hardly wait to be with you again." To "My darling Father," she said, "I like home better than Spain or Portugal," and she proposed that the two of them go to Switzerland together. Unfortunately, that trip never took place, and many years were to pass before Elizabeth traveled abroad again.

CHAPTER SEVEN

Return to Raleigh 1928

Please have confidence in me.

AFTER FIVE MONTHS of traveling abroad, Elizabeth Lawrence came home to Raleigh in the fall of 1928, stored her big suitcases, and did not take them out again for another forty years. Spring flowers had been in bloom when she returned from Barnard, but now it was that time of year when leaves covered the ground. It was her favorite season, only a few weeks away from the feast of St. Martin (the 11th of November), which marked the beginning of winter.

"There are two awakenings in the garden," Elizabeth was to observe: "one in spring, and one in autumn. But it is autumn, when frost puts an end to the old year's bloom, that the garden year really begins."[1]

It was good to be home. She had missed Sammy and Bessie and Ann and Nana (and Michael, the dog). She wanted to drive her father to work, and to read nursery catalogues with her mother. She hoped to persuade her parents to let Ann go to New York to look for a job after she finished at the University of North Carolina; soon after Elizabeth was back in North Carolina, the sisters met in Chapel Hill. At a Sunday service at the Chapel of the Cross, Ann whispered that she was now an "atheist," then closed her eyes to pray.[2] Perhaps she was trying out on her sister her intention to be "the real Ann" after her adventuresome trip abroad, but Elizabeth knew that Ann was too loved and loving (and funny) to offend the family. When Elizabeth came home from the weekend in Chapel Hill, she must have convinced Bessie and Sammy that they could trust their younger daughter to be on her own. Elizabeth turned her attention toward Parkersburg, where she was anxious to visit Nana, and to kiss her great-grandmother for, she feared, the last time.

Home had many attractions for Elizabeth. The splendor of Notre Dame had not diminished the beauty of Christ Church, nor had fields seen from a passing train seemed more beautiful than the Garysburg countryside. An old Frenchwoman had reminded her of Nana; Frenchmen relaxing on the banks of the Seine were like black men on the sidewalks of Southern towns. In England she had loved lunch in a garden and supper in front of the fire at a country inn. Bessie could make homemade shortcake and serve a high tea that everyone thought was decidedly English. Her father, disappointed that she had met someone in London who had not liked Woodrow Wilson—and disappointed that Elizabeth had failed to change his mind—was not disposed to admire the British. However, a soft curtain of midsummer's darkness made her think of nights in France. And what she would never see the likes of again—the *Winged Victory* in the Louvre—had stirred her in a way that nothing else had.

In Raleigh, winter came, and then the white hyacinth, snowflakes, and violets—and with the warmth of spring and the heat of summer, Elizabeth began to dream a garden. She would have hundreds of different kinds of plants—and a hundred more the next year—and know what they were called and why, and where they came from, and how they grew. How slowly, but clearly, the thought was forming: the garden was a world. With the images of buildings and gardens of Europe mingling in her imagination with those of home, she was more certain now of how she would lead her life.

Before Elizabeth left for Europe, she had done excellent work in botany and architectural drawing as a special student at North Carolina State College. She did not immediately resume her studies, probably because her mother needed her to go with her to Parkersburg to help Nana with Elizabeth's great-grandmother. But in March she enrolled again for the spring term, taking three more courses, apparently to make up for her deficiencies in the sciences. Again, she excelled in horticulture and botany, and was admitted as a graduate student in the new three-year program in landscape architecture. Her writing courses at Barnard were more than sufficient to exempt her from the English composition requirement. Students were to receive training necessary for "the landscape constructor as well as the landscape horticulturist or gardener," but "the landscape artist or designer" would need to pursue further studies elsewhere.

The North Carolina State curriculum was rigorous, requiring some thirty courses, concentrating in engineering and agriculture, followed by courses in civil engineering and architecture, and leading to courses in design and landscape architecture. There were three Ds recorded on her transcript—in Engineering Drawing, Arboriculture (a course in the culture of woody plants), and General Chemistry—but she finished her last term with distinction—As in Landscape Design, Plant Design, and Advanced Plant Pathology. Her favorite courses were taught by Dr. B. W. Wells, head of the Department of Botany and Plant Pathology, who took his students to see the lush savannas in coastal North Carolina. On such trips Wells collected materials for a book, *Natural Gardens of North Carolina,* to be published in 1932 by the University of North Carolina Press, with the assistance of the North Carolina Garden Club. The collection of data, the network of notable gardeners in the club movement, and the university press—each showed Elizabeth Lawrence how a book comes about.

Lawrence and Wells would remain good friends after she graduated, but, perhaps as the only woman in the graduate program, she had felt intimidated by the male students, most of whom were apparently older and ready to get into business as quickly as possible. Yet she had graduated from St. Mary's and Barnard (both arguably more prestigious than many schools her contemporaries had attended), and she completed tough courses at one of the premier land-grant institutions in the country. Given the fact that so few women then were studying science, and that there were no other women in her architectural program, she deserved to brag a bit. All she seems to have said was that it had been difficult being the only woman in the program. And although Elizabeth Lawrence's name was printed in the commencement program as one of three students receiving the degree Bachelor of Science in Landscape Architecture, she probably was not there to receive it on Tuesday morning, the 7th of June, 1932. The good news was that she had her first job: she went to work as an assistant to Miss Isabel Busbee, an excellent gardener, self-taught designer, and near neighbor (and St. Mary's graduate, class of 1899). What probably meant more to Elizabeth than seeing her name in print in the commencement program was to see it in print in the 1932 Raleigh City Directory, along with Busbee's, for the practice of landscape design. Each listed her home address as her place of business.

The years of Elizabeth's graduate work had also been difficult because of the state of the general economy. In the fall of 1929, as Ann was in her senior year at the University of North Carolina at Chapel Hill and Elizabeth was beginning her graduate work, the stock market crashed, and the Great Depression was on. By 1932 the Lawrences were suffering along with other middle-class families, and Sam lost his business. In early January 1932, Zetta and Jean Lowry wrote to say how distressed they were to hear that the family had lost a good deal of money in a bank failure.[3] According to family history, Sam Lawrence began to worry himself to death trying to figure out how to pay off his workers. He sold off his share of properties that he and Bessie owned with the Bonsals in Garysburg and in South Carolina—as final an admission of defeat as he could imagine. For the next several years, family and friends saw the robust figure of Sam Lawrence weaken dramatically, and from his first stroke sometime in 1934 until his death in 1936, he was an invalid. Bessie Lawrence's inheritances, when her grandmother died in 1929 and her mother in 1933, were enough to look after the family's basic needs, and without any noticeable changes in their comfort. There was a male servant to help look after Sam Lawrence, and even in the worst of times, Bessie managed to hire someone to assist her in the kitchen. Sam Lawrence wanted his wife and daughters to continue with their lives.

"There are two kinds of people in the world," Elizabeth observed, "those who want to get out and do things, and those who want to stay

In this photograph made by Bayard Wootten, a distinguished North Carolina portrait artist, Elizabeth Lawrence stands on the steps of her Raleigh garden with her spaniel, Mr. Cayce. (North Carolina Collection: University of North Carolina Library at Chapel Hill.)

at home and garden."[4] Ann was always the more outgoing of the sisters, and during the height of the Depression, she went to New York and found—and kept—a job, working at Macy's. For her part, Elizabeth kept the home fires burning, which also was not easy (in a large, old house). Looking after the house also meant looking after the old people. When Nana's mother died in Parkersburg, a few weeks after the market crash, Elizabeth and Bessie had to pack up books, sell the house, and move Nana to Raleigh. In her upstairs bedroom in the house on Park Avenue, Nana held court, interested in everyone and everything, requiring from others a good deal of running back and forth, up and down the stairs, to keep the household revolving around her. When Elizabeth came in from school, she relieved Bessie by carrying the supper tray up, and by reading to Nana—not from what was on her mind (her course notes), but from Ann's letters, which were full of excitement. Elizabeth worried about Ann, who was uncertain from one week to the next about which man and which Macy's department she preferred, and Ann worried about Elizabeth, who was looking after the family. Then on November 28, 1933, Nana died (a date Elizabeth wrote on one of the index cards she used to record bloom dates in the garden), and the funeral in Parkersburg marked the end of the family's ties to West Virginia.

But the worst was yet to come: in 1934 Sam Lawrence had a debilitating stroke, which left his charm but took away his clear speech. Elizabeth drove her mother to see him at the Duke hospital in Durham, and when he came home, they had to set up a hospital bed downstairs in Elizabeth's studio, with someone to help look after him. One of the Long children—Tom's daughter Margaret—boarded with the Lawrences while she was a student at St. Mary's, and she was good at entertaining Mr. Lawrence. For his part, Sam was like Nana: he never lost interest in life. When he died—on July 16, 1936—Elizabeth lost her soulful parent. During these few years, more change had occurred in Elizabeth Lawrence's life than any she had known, but she had discovered sunshine in the shadows: she had found a friend who did her more good than anyone she would ever know.

Return to Raleigh 1928

In the early spring of 1928, Ann Preston Bridgers, coauthor with George Abbott of the acclaimed Broadway play *Coquette* (starring Helen Hayes), was living in Paris, and she sent a letter home to her family members in Raleigh to ask for their emotional support. The household included her mother, Mrs. Ann Bridgers, who was widowed, and her sister Emily and her brother Robert, who, like Ann, were—and would remain—unmarried. The third daughter, Elizabeth, called "Babs," had married Jonathan Daniels, who succeeded his father, Josephus Daniels, as editor of the Raleigh *News & Observer*. Ann Bridgers had left New York for an indefinite stay in Europe to escape the public's attention and the sudden fame brought on by her stage success, but she confessed that she needed her family: "Thank God you are all dissatisfied and seeking for something or I never could have made the pull. Independence is a strange illusion. We are no more independent from the members of our family than we are independent from our stomachs. . . . . We are like one strand in a rope bound tightly together and unless we pull in the same direction, we only destroy each other. Please have confidence in me and help me."[5] Ann Bridgers was not feeling vulnerable because she was living apart from her family (she spent long periods away from home), but because she had felt unnerved working with *Coquette's* difficult producer, Jed Harris. On the other side of the Atlantic, she had recovered her sense of freedom—and, with it, her desire to write.

If members of her family came out to read the letter on the front porch of their large frame house on Hillsboro Street, and if Elizabeth Lawrence was walking in the neighborhood, she probably stopped to talk—and heard that Ann was in Paris, which would have been of special interest to her, since Elizabeth would be leaving for Paris herself in a few months. Although Elizabeth might not yet have met Ann, she certainly would have read about her in articles in the *News & Observer*. Raleigh took a great deal of hometown pride in Ann Bridgers's Broadway success. Moreover, the Bridgers house was becoming a gathering place for intellectuals and artists. Here writers would meet (calling themselves the Strugglers), readers would discuss books, and actors would talk about the need for a community theater. Whether her daughters were or were not at home (Ann and Emily, also a writer, both took a small New York apartment from time to time), Mrs. Bridgers and Robert were always ready to receive guests. It was a house with a good cook—Mrs. Bridgers herself. In a few years, it would be a house with a garden: Elizabeth Lawrence would plant it.

Mrs. Bridgers (whom the family called "Tancie" or "Aunt Annie") was a tower of strength to everyone who knew her.[6] Her husband died young, and while the estate was being settled, she found herself with four young children to support, and she did something very unconventional for a woman of her class. She opened a boarding house in the small Georgia railroad town where they were then living. When her guests objected to the black cooks singing in the kitchen, Mrs. Bridgers explained that they could sing if they wanted to. Her initiative shocked her late husband's family—which included members of state government and directors of the Atlantic Coast Line Railroad. When Emily developed polio as a very young child, Mrs. Bridgers became an ardent Christian Scientist; her faith helped fortify her belief that Emily would recover—and she did. (Emily walked with crutches, and only in her later years would she agree to use a wheelchair). Mrs. Bridgers moved the family to Boston so that she could study healing at the Mother Church, and with her husband's insurance money, she sent her daughters to Smith College so that they would have the education she had never had, and be able to support themselves. Robert was not as studious and soon dropped out of school. A few years after graduation, Ann went with a group from Smith College to work overseas in a YMCA canteen during World War I, and Robert served with the American Field Service Ambulance Corps. Mrs. Bridgers bought the house on Hillsboro Street (near the Christian Science Church), and there she voluntarily nursed soldiers while they recovered from the flu. Emily helped earn money by writing newspaper and magazine articles, clerking in state government offices, and, in later years, preparing study guides for extension courses offered through the University at Chapel Hill. While Ann was in Europe, Emily managed her business affairs, dealing with New York agents and book publishers. When they were apart, Ann, Emily, and Jonathan Daniels (who was writing a novel) circulated their manuscripts and critiqued one another's work. "Babs" even wrote some scenes for Ann. Emily was a masterful editor, and Ann counted on her honest opinion to help improve her scripts. In turn, Ann was honest with Emily. Once when Emily had written a critical review of a local performance in Raleigh, Ann had cautioned her that there was no need to sound condescending. The Bridgers women were liberal thinkers (Robert, less so)—prepared to respond lovingly and critically to one another and to the world, just as their mother had hoped.

The Bridgers family, however, which had experienced the death of a young husband and father and Emily's polio, was not done with misfortune. Elizabeth Bridgers Daniels, after the birth of a daughter, Adelaide (who later changed her name to her mother's), became pregnant with a second child, but something went wrong, and in December of 1929, she died in childbirth. Jonathan Daniels, who recently had been awarded a Guggenheim fellowship in creative writing to travel in Europe, was, as he said in a letter, "lost without Babs' love," and he turned to her family for comfort for himself and his two-year-old daughter. With characteristic pluck, the family pulled together again, and Mrs. Bridgers, Ann, and Emily traveled with Jonathan to help look after Elizabeth (née Adelaide) so that he could write. Although Daniels was to remarry later, Elizabeth remained closest to her grandmother and to Ann and Emily. "Tancie," as Emily described her, was "like a great solid tree you could hold onto. You could count absolutely on her love." Elizabeth, who was nurtured as a writer by Ann and Emily and became a well-known author of detective novels (using her married name, Elizabeth Daniels Squire), remembered them all in the same way that Ann had described the family in her 1928 letter: "fiercely independent and fiercely interdependent."

In the winter of 1929, Elizabeth Lawrence was living at home and attending State College, when the news of Elizabeth Bridgers Daniels's death shocked the neighborhood and the city. Lawrence was to remember having once met Elizabeth Daniels at the house on Hillsboro Street —and that Daniels mentioned knowing that Elizabeth was a poet. After Daniels' death, when Elizabeth and Bessie went to call on Mrs. Bridgers, they were to remember with heart-breaking poignancy Mrs. Bridgers' sweet and beautiful granddaughter. Ann had been called home from Europe when her sister died, and Elizabeth Lawrence may have met her for the first time then.

But it was not until 1933, when Ann made Raleigh her permanent home (while continuing to leave it for periods of time to write in other places), that she became Elizabeth's closest friend and mentor. It was not a match of kindred spirits (Ann's instincts were universal, Elizabeth's personal), but it was a match of complementary spirits. They loved and respected each other. Elizabeth was attracted to Ann because she was a successful writer, and because she was such a loving human being. The model was clear: Ann's passions were her family and her writing—neither interfering with the other. She was absolutely focused on her work, and told Elizabeth that the reason she had not married was "not a question of courage, but of how much of yourself you can rescue from the chaos of life."[7]

Ann was older by thirteen years, and Elizabeth instinctively looked up to older people, but Ann also introduced her to new ideas. In Europe and New York City, Ann had experienced leftist politics, free-speech movements, artistic innovations, community service, and international understanding. She was unequivocal about the necessity for America's entry into World War II in order to stop Nazism and fascism. Elizabeth learned most of what she knew about contemporary history from Ann, who helped her keep up through recommending newspaper and magazine articles, especially after America entered the War. Encouraged by Ann, Elizabeth joined a group of volunteers in Raleigh to work at a "filter center," where they were trained to help keep track of any aircraft that might fly over the city. When she told Ann about how uninformed they all felt, Ann wrote a play set in a filter center, "Possess These Shores," about a group of people who learned to act together as good citizens in defense of their country. Elizabeth wrote dozens of letters to

Ann that discussed plays that Ann was writing; the plays and their epistolary discussions of the moral themes became a sort of "textbook" for Elizabeth's lessons in American democracy. When she read a play Ann was writing called *Henrietta,* about a "noble" black woman, Elizabeth responded with a long letter about race, which demonstrates how much she had learned in the years since her essay at St. Mary's on "Cullud Folks." Now she was prepared to acknowledge that, if blacks and whites "are ever to have an understanding, it will have to be built on life as it is and not as it was, as you say in your play. The former relationship was created by the plantation owners. But it is the Negro who has the genius for [making a new relationship]."[8] In this and other instances, Ann greatly expanded Elizabeth's thinking, and it gave Ann satisfaction to recognize that her plays had been what she intended—educational. Although she never had another national success like *Coquette,* her plays were performed in Raleigh's Little Theatre, which she had been instrumental in founding. In fact, the building of the Little Theatre with W.P.A. funds was an example to Elizabeth, as it was to many Raleigh citizens, of how their government could enrich communities.

Elizabeth Lawrence was not very politically minded, and she was more conservative than Ann, but she loved to talk, and Ann listened well. "There is nothing like the revelation of a reticent person once started," Elizabeth admitted. At home, in the garden, at Ann's cabin in the mountains, Elizabeth talked and talked. Whenever Ann was away, Elizabeth wrote her a great many long letters, full of anecdotes and vignettes that she hoped would amuse her, and ideas and critiques of Ann's new plays that she hoped would please her. Ann was grateful for Elizabeth's enthusiastic help and wrote that she was "a satisfactory audience of one."[9]

Ann and Emily Bridgers were great nurturers of writers, and a decade before Elizabeth published her first book, she must have said to them implicitly, "Please have confidence in me."

CHAPTER EIGHT

Remembering

The pattern of childhood is the pattern of existence.

HAVING ANN BRIDGERS to talk to seems to have unlocked years of silence in Elizabeth, and now that she was acquiring an ease in writing, she wanted to write about herself. She knew just where to begin: childhood was always the subject closest to her emotions. And so sometime in her mid-thirties, she reflected on several childhood memories that had troubled and shaped her, in an essay that she called "Piper, pipe a song," a phrase from a poem in William Blake's *Songs of Innocence.* It was eleven pages long, in clean typescript, which was unusual for any of her manuscripts, suggesting that she had revised it carefully. Apparently, there was only one copy, and she sent it to Ann.[1]

Blake's introduction to *Songs of Innocence* contains a dialogue between the poet, or piper, and a child. The piper's songs of "pleasant glee" make the child weep with joy. The child responds, "Piper, sit thee down and write/In a book, that all may read." And so the piper writes his "happy songs/Every child may joy to hear."

Her mother may have read this poem to Elizabeth when Elizabeth was a child, but certainly by the time she was a student at St. Mary's School, and later at Barnard College, she had been introduced to the poetry of William Blake. At the same time that she was writing the essay, she was teaching Sunday School to the children of working-class families at St. Saviour's Episcopal mission church in Raleigh, and she may have read "Piper" to them.

Lawrence began her essay with a scene from her own childhood. "When we were very little my father used to take us in his lap and say, 'There were two little girls named Elizabeth and Ann. In the winter they lived with their daddy, but in the summer he would put them on a train, and they would kiss him goodbye, and the train would take them away, and their daddy would be left all alone on the platform.'

"Before the tears were dry we would beg, 'Tell us again. Daddy, tell us again.' "

This memory probably dates to around 1912, when Elizabeth was eight and Ann four, and they were living in Garysburg. Each summer Bessie Lawrence took her daughters on the train to see their father's relatives in Marietta, Georgia, and her own relatives in Parkersburg, West Virginia. After the opening scene about the little girls and their father, Lawrence observed:

> The pattern of childhood is the pattern of existence. It is formed in the very early years, and it is repeated thereafter until the end of life. After five or six there are no new emotions. All emotions feed upon earlier emotions, all experiences repeat former experiences, and all relationships are variations of those that have been known before. When enough years have been accomplished for the pattern to be apparent, there is a moment of revelation. The vaguely felt design that the hours and days and years have made becomes clearly visible. But even when visible it cannot be broken. The life of the child is relived in the man as inevitably as the history of the race is repeated in each generation.

Here is as clear an expression of Lawrence's philosophy of life as we may find. It explains the essentials of why she made the choices she did. Everything depends on "the very early years," which, in her case, were the years in which she lived in a closely knit family of mother, father, sister, and grandparents. Among the latter, her maternal grandmother Nana was the most important older person in her early life; in time, her mother would take Nana's place. The design that hours and days and years had made was a design with home and an older woman at the center. Written from the child's perspective, it does not include adolescence and marriage, stages that are missing from any of the discovered Lawrence papers.

When was Lawrence's "moment of revelation" that this design would

Elizabeth's maternal great-grandparents and her maternal grandmother lived in this handsome Victorian house on Ann Street in Parkersburg, West Virginia. As children, Elizabeth and her sister visited every summer. The winter after she graduated from college, Elizabeth lived here with her grandmother. (By permission of Warren Way and Elizabeth Rogers.)

be repeated, or, in Lawrence's important variant, "relived"? Elizabeth often talked intimately about herself with Ann Bridgers, and it may have been during those discussions that Elizabeth began to put words to her feelings. In the essay she considered a child's "alternate longing to be with others, and the desire to be away from them. The need to replace the confusion of association with the order of solitude is provided for instinctively by a child. To that end he builds houses in trees, and finds secret places along the banks of streams. Grown people remember the necessity, and learn to plan to be alone.

"The retreats of childhood are not merely a momentary escape from the emotional strain of adjustment to others. They are a reserve created for those future occasions when actual physical withdrawal is impossible." "Retirement," "refuge," "retreat," "escape," and "reserve"—Lawrence chose words from her lexicon that she rarely used, moving further into her own private world. "In crowded years," she continued, "one can go back to uninterrupted mornings spent among the roots of an oak tree with hollyhock ladies and four-o'clock children; to riding a pony across fields etched in rime; to long afternoons of intimacy with the life of the banks and waters of small streams, the world of crawfishes, minnows, eels, tadpoles, frogs, and the sweet-smelling water bugs that skate over the surface of brown pools." In these allusions, Lawrence drew directly upon her vivid memories of summers in Marietta, where she and her cousin Harriet made dolls out of flowers under the oak tree in the side yard of her grandparents' house, and in Garysburg, where, alone, she rode her pony cart to the banks and small streams.

Abruptly, she left those scenes for the house in Parkersburg, to observe, "Children learn very early that only places are unchanging in mood." An illustration followed:

> When Stevie [an unidentified boy in Parkersburg] was little he came into the library and found me sitting all alone in the firelight. He squeezed into my chair, and sat as still as I sat until we were called to dinner, feeling a repose rare if not wholly absent in a household of smooth surfaces and swift undercurrents. The next night, at the same time, he came to me and said, "Will you come with me and sit in the library?" And I went knowing what was to follow and not knowing how to prevent it. After a few minutes of wiggling, he slid from the chair with a very long sigh, and went back to his soldiers on the playroom rug.

The little boy had been unable to recapture the magic of the night before in the library because his mood had changed. In describing Stevie's experience, Elizabeth implicitly acknowledged two truths: the illusion of permanence and the illusion of peace. Nowhere else does she make such an honest admission about "a household of smooth surfaces and swift undercurrents," certainly one of the most recognizable aspects of many domestic environments.

In relating another enigmatic incident, Elizabeth acknowledged another revelation: the memory of disgrace. Nothing more had occurred than that while she and her grandmother were walking, they met a man who had been a visitor to their house, but whose familiarity in public—suddenly calling their names—was embarrassing. Out of something so incidental, Elizabeth drew a larger conclusion: "The incidents of first childhood are well-springs of emotion whose deep and still waters are drawn upon again and again. One of the most poignant of these is the dread of disgrace. To those of riper years the smallest embarrassment brings a flood of shame that is out of all proportion to the occasion, because the mind goes back to some half-remembered happening of early childhood."

Elizabeth concluded her essay with another incident from childhood, one that seems related to the making of a gardener. "I was very little," she remembered, "when I became aware of spring as a season that had been before and would come again. . . . "

> I went out of the gate, and crossed the sandy road to the pine barrens that stretched in front of the cottage. There were birds-foot violets in the pine barrens, and I wandered Persephone-like from flower to flower until I was entirely lost. But I did not know that I was lost, being absorbed in the spring; before I found it out a neighbor's boy met me, and returned me to my own door step, and to my great-grandmother. My great-grandmother was of a generation that moved and thought and spoke quietly. Without breaking the spell of the woods, or separating me from the violets, she explained gently—but not without emphasis—that young ladies were to play in the yard, and never go beyond the gate alone. And she sent me to the nursery for meditation. When I went into the darkened room I could see through the half-closed shutters of the blinds the flowering April outside. It seemed to me that I was the dark room. And I thought, sun and soft air and flowers are not the spring, the spring is inside. I was too little to write it down, for I had not been to school, but I sat a long time watching the sunlight slant through the shutters, trying to crystallize the moment, trying to put it into words. I had sat still for so long, Grandma thought I had been punished enough, and came to release me from solitary confinement.

If this memory dates back to Elizabeth's visit to Parkersburg when she was four or five, before she went to school, and we guess that the piece was written when she was in her late thirties, it took her more than thirty years to "crystallize the moment, trying to put it into words." "I was the dark room," she remembered feeling. "The sun and soft air and flowers are not the spring, the spring is inside." In disobeying her great-grandmother, she had discovered the flowers of spring, and when she was told that she was never again to go beyond the gate alone, she was made to go into the nursery. There, in solitude, she meditated, not upon the experience of having been disobedient but upon the experience of having discovered April. If she could not go outside the garden gate, she saw, through half-shutters, that she could bring the garden inside.

In recovering memory, Elizabeth had found her own language for the "outside-inside" mystery that the garden would always hold for her. Some thirty years later, she was at ease writing for a large public audience: "I am sure that Mrs. Boyleston's garden will never seem lovelier to me than on that cold March morning when I saw it silent and secret through the gate and over the hedge."[2]

CHAPTER NINE

Writing Poetry

To stir a memory no longer clear.

"How little I remember," Elizabeth wrote late in life about another experience in her childhood. "How vivid it all is." She and her cousin Harriet had been visiting one of Harriet's friends, Pippa, whose family spent summers at Malbone, their estate in northern Georgia. When Harriet and Elizabeth were alone together, they were close friends, but when Pippa came between them, Elizabeth was left out. "When Pippa and Harriet were bored," she remembered, "they united in teasing me. I spent most of the visit in tears, at the same time in an ecstasy of being allowed to exist, being at Malbone, moving in such grandeur."[1]

While the grownups slept, the children played croquet in the shade, according to new rules that Pippa and Harriet made up to make sure that Elizabeth would lose. They asked her if she knew where babies came from, and when she said that she did not, they told her to ask the adults that evening. "In order to curry favor," Elizabeth did ask. "A painful silence hung over the table, & after endless time [Pippa's mother] said, 'Elizabeth, we prefer not to discuss illness at meal time.' " On another occasion, Harriet stole a letter that Elizabeth had received from her mother, and began reading it aloud: "My darling sweetheart," she tittered. Suddenly, Pippa came to Elizabeth's defense, and snatching the letter away from Harriet, she handed it back to Elizabeth. "Her gray eyes became very black, & she said, 'That's the way my father always wrote to me.' "

The taunts of children, the embarrassment at the dining table, the color of Pippa's eyes—these were painful memories, which, years later, were mixed with pleasure, too. It was that weekend that she had drunk her first "grown-up tea, without milk," and had discovered that it was "the cup that cheers." And at Malbone when she had withdrawn from the others, she had the sense of "being there—standing alone on the lawn, looking at the ringing mountains around me." There had been a feeling of "ecstasy."

In writing about Malbone many years later, Elizabeth found words for the bittersweetness of experience. Her childhood memory can be read as an early dawning of poetic sensitivity, and her writing about it, as an adult, becomes an exercise in the power of language to make sense of experience. Poetry was for her the most intimate of all places.

Elizabeth had begun writing verses as a child, submitting some of them to *St. Nicholas Magazine,* where she was disappointed to receive only "honorable mention." During summers in Marietta, she and her cousin Harriet (who was three years younger) used to read their poems to each other by lamplight at the dining room table.[2] They continued to exchange poems for many years, and in 1968 when Harriet had a book of some of her poems privately printed, Elizabeth considered it as a model of what she might do herself. Sometime in the 1960s she began copying (and typing) poems that she had been writing for some thirty years, and with Ellen Flood's encouragement, she considered arranging for their publication.[3] Nothing came of this idea, however, and except for a light verse about modern poetry that was published in the Charlotte *Observer* ("Query to the New Yorker on its 50th Anniversary"), she never published her poems. At the end of her life, however, her desire to write poetry was still so strong that she confessed (in a handwritten note found in the last papers she sent to her archivist), "Why I write, I don't know, for I hate every word I write—except poetry."[4]

Lawrence was often guarded, although she expressed her opinions in a very forthright manner, as if candor could be a shield. If she seemed to say exactly what she thought, no one would have reason to ask her questions about herself. She recognized that poetry by its very nature tells the truth, but "tells it slant"—in Emily Dickinson's phrase. The very technique that gives rise to multiple interpretations—metaphor—is the means by which a poet finds clarity for her own thoughts and feelings. Readers can plumb the meaning of a poem, but only the poet really knows what she was thinking when she wrote it. Poets can not only relieve the pressure in themselves to express what's bothering them; they can transcend the pain by the pleasure of creating a work of art. Poetry ideally suited Lawrence's need for self-expression and for privacy.

No one understood this better than Ann Bridgers, who apparently read most of Elizabeth's poems, but did not encourage her to seek publication. Once Ann herself wrote a verse, "For Elizabeth," in four stanzas that begin, "For the little girl." She concluded with these lines:

> For the little girl who sat upon the step hushed
> and tranquil
> breathing the mysterious essence of the morning
> before the clothes of day were put upon her.

Elizabeth Lawrence left some one hundred poems, mostly copied by hand on lined paper and put into small loose-leaf notebooks.[5] She called the collection, "Swans and Amber," an allusion to "Amber, or the Swans" by Lucian, in which tears of amber fall from trees and swans sing melodies. She began the collection with that poem. She then arranged the rest of the poems into several categories: Regrets, From an Asylum, A Modern Herbal, In Time of War, The Ivory Gate, Exercises & Airs, and Translations. Most of them show the importance to her of literature and gardens, and she puts some of her own experiences in classical settings.

The collection begins with a Foreword:

> These verses have apart from me
> No glitter of reality
> For they would fade, if they were known,

As instantly as sea shells thrown
Above the highest waterline
In fragments colorless and fine.

The theme of the poems in the longest section, "Regrets," is loss, and the tone is lamentation. Lawrence placed first in this section a poem that insists, "No single sorrow/Is enough for tears," and locates grief in classical literature (with Deirdre, Priam, and Helen). The second poem, "Between Us Now," however, conveys the opposite impression: "Your silence falls, and shuts you off from me." She seems to speak directly to someone she has known ("When once my thought was heard before I spoke"), but something has happened to their relationship: "I call again and there is no reply." This poem is immediately followed by another on the same theme, but written in the more distant third person: "Relieved of saying all/Resolved to say no less/He let a silence fall/Upon her eagerness." The last two stanzas of the poem are:

He could recall no word
To lessen her distress;
Like music scarcely heard
His tentative caress

Dissolved into despair
Too deep for bitterness.
He found no passion there.
But much unhappiness.

Then, like an antiphonal response, the fourth poem in "Regrets" seems to speak from the point of view of the person alluded to in the third poem in the even more distanced possessive, "*her* distress."

It is the moment now
For them to be alone:
Her garment is of snow,
Is she of ice or stone?

But stone would be as ice
When breathed upon by flame,
A single breath suffice
To make the substance change.

For stronger passions are
Subdued by lesser ones:
Behold the morning star
Grown pale beside the moon.

Although Lawrence made no effort to defend or even to explain herself in the essay about Peter, she gave answer in the poems, when, for example, the pursued depends upon her suitor to break down her resistance—"as ice/when breathed upon by flame." The poems contain contradictions—"Long have I flung myself against the wall/That separates the living from the dead," she begins, and then she goes on to say that even if the wall were not there and she found him "as before,/My love would be no less, & yours no more." Who was the aggrieved in this relationship? Whose "outstretched hand" was turned back? ("It is not space that is put between us/Now you are gone to a distant land;/Denial more final than death/Turned back the outstretched hand.") She makes the ambiguity even more pronounced in these lines: "Time has not existed, since you said the word/That sent me from your presence (but of my own accord)."

In another poem, Elizabeth asserts her receptivity to love in a way she apparently did not in real life, though by the end of the poem she has retreated from being a willing lover to being an innocent child again.

If you had wanted me, I would have gone
To places you had been, but not alone,
No matter where we went I would have known
That mine was not the only voice you heard,
That yours was not the only spoken word.

That ours were not the first steps that occurred.
Through all the years, I now have been alone.
On lonely paths that now are overgrown,
Which once a child discovered for her own.

In another poem she visualizes a scene with great particularity:

If walking late,
You should see a familiar number upon a door,
And say to yourself
Here is a house where I have been before;
If you should decide to enter
—Know full well
You need not fear an encounter—
And ring the bell,
You would find me greeting you shyly,
Holding a match to the gas, and wryly
Brushing the dust from your hat.
You would find me biting my finger
—perhaps you would scold me for that—
And pushing my hair from my face, as ever;
You would not find me clever,
But pretending to attend to what you say.
You would find all the same,
Except, on the shelf by the window,
Another volume of Edna Millay.

There are other poems Elizabeth wrote as she approached her fiftieth birthday that show how much she had continued to hold on to what seems to be her memory of Peter (or some other man out of her past whom we do not know). "It might have been/Something I read in a book, or a scene/Enacted on a stage/So dim has the image become." But the poem that was perhaps her greatest achievement in coming to terms with her feelings was probably from an earlier period, when she was writing about Peter (or someone else) in the late 1930s and early 1940s. In it she closes one gate as she opens another.

> I have decided to stay in this garden
> With its aging apple tree
> Whose boughs are far enough apart
> To see the stars by night;
> By day to let the sunlight in, to green
> Untrodden grass that you have never seen.
>
> I shall not go anywhere
> That you have been.
>
> Even if I could find
> Those hidden alleys where
> You led me as they lead the blind,
> I would not go there.
> I shall never set foot in Washington Square.

One untitled poem has a mysterious history: Lawrence did not copy it in notebooks with other poems but tore it into pieces and left it in the bottom of a box of letters. It is a poem about the memory of physical desire, her only implicitly sexual poem, and because she was very private, perhaps she did not want anyone else to read it.

> The body remembers an early emotion,
> And cherishes ardor far more than the mind;
> While memory, challenged, is feeble and kind;
> And intellect sullies discarded devotion.
> The senses remember far longer than caution
> Has cared that devotion remain in the mind;
> It may be the senses, because they are blind,
> Distinguish no more than the swells of the ocean.

The Dream

The light was failing when I closed the gate,
And crossed the lawn, & stood before the door.
The door was open, & I did not hesitate.
Inside, the night had come. I called before
I went into the darkness. You were there
And heard me, & replied; without a light
I stumbled through the hall, & found the stair,
And slowly climbed the first & second flight;
I thought: my life is in this house; how can
It be removed? Then having mounted all
The steps, I turned, & called your name, & ran
Down stairs. I found the now well lighted hall,
Already unfamiliar; I heard
strange voices, and came into a new
Arrangement of the rooms.
My eyes still blurred
with unshed tears, I searched the house
for you.

Facsimile of Elizabeth's poem "The Dream." Elizabeth began writing poems as a child, and for the rest of her life she filled up small notebooks with poems. This one was written in Charlotte, where she had designed a small, one-story bungalow. There were two large old houses in her memories—her grandmother's house in Parkersburg, West Virginia, and her mother and father's house in Raleigh.

Before it was morning, I stood by my window
Cooling my temples and misting the pane;
Suddenly, fiery, throbbed in my fingers
The quickening pulses as when by the willow,
Throbbing my fingers had found yours again.
Not one of your words in my memory lingers.

A poem Elizabeth wrote about anger distances her from any particular experience, but, like the poem about desire, it shows an aspect of the poet's life that is otherwise missing in what she wrote.

The angry beast that tortured me
Lay down at your command;
I saw that you had conquered him,
But did not comprehend

That there would come an hour
When you would raise your hand,
And being in your power
He would achieve his end.

The poet depends on someone to protect her from anger, but in recognizing that person's power to save her, she also recognizes that such a person (addressed as "you") also has the power to take away protection—to let her be "tortured" by anger. This is a powerful poem, and it is uncertain who the "you" and the "He" are. Is she personifying her own anger that undermines her from within, or is the "beast" a person whose anger is directed toward her? Whichever way the poem is read, her fear of being harmed is clear. Possibly written during Lawrence's thirties, it may say something about that time in her life when she had the kind of "awakening" often experienced by women of her age.

"A Modern Herbal" includes poems that Elizabeth began as she was leaving the Raleigh garden and making a new one in Charlotte. She grieves over the necessity of leaving most of her plants behind, at the same time that she looks forward to starting over. Writing about some of the plants is a way of keeping them permanently in her memory. She follows the classical model of short verses about well-known herbs associated with magical properties.

Rosemarinus officinalis
Take rosemary from my garden,
Let it bloom elsewhere
To stir a memory no longer clear.

Ruta graveolens
Take away the garden rue
From one who needs no clearer view
And bring, if any such there be,
An herb to help me not to see.

CHAPTER TEN

Garden Design

I design gardens but cannot bear to be called a Landscape Architect.

ELIZABETH LAWRENCE had decided on a practical course when she enrolled at North Carolina State. As the only woman in her class, however, she had no one like her with whom to talk over the future. Male graduates in the program moved more quickly into professional positions. By 1938 they had found jobs operating plant nurseries, working for the North Carolina highway division, and superintending parks and institutional grounds. Only one graduate was in private practice in Raleigh.[1] Lawrence took a different path. She was going to use her own garden as a "laboratory" for learning about plants. As for going to work outside her own backyard, she said, "I design gardens but cannot bear to be called a Landscape Architect."[2]

Nationally, other women were making names for themselves in the gardening world, but, as in other professions, women who lived in the Northeast achieved status much earlier than women in the South.[3] Two schools for landscape architecture in New England had been established specifically for the education of women. In 1901 the Lowthorpe School opened in Groton, Massachusetts, on the country estate of Judith Motley Low, who had studied horticulture in England. The curriculum at the Lowthorpe School paid special homage to the influence on landscape design of Gertrude Jekyll. In 1916 the Cambridge School in Cambridge, Massachusetts, came into being because women were not admitted to the Harvard School of Landscape Architecture, and a Harvard professor, Henry Frost, had decided to tutor some of them in his office. Struggling to find an institutional sponsor, the Cambridge School became affiliated with Smith College from 1932 to 1938, while maintaining its campus in Cambridge, but by 1942 its enrollment had declined, and from the effects of World War II the school was closed.[4]

The two best known American landscape gardeners were women who had not studied in any formal program, but whose successes were models of encouragement: Beatrix Jones Farrand and Ellen Biddle Shipman. A brief look at their lives and careers gives us another way of understanding Elizabeth Lawrence's differences and distinctions.

Beatrix Jones was born in 1872 into the upper echelons of society, with connections in New York City; Newport, Rhode Island; and Bar Harbor, Maine. Everywhere she lived, she lived in a beautiful house. Her mother, Mary Cadwalader Jones, was a Philadelphia blue blood who knew interesting and important people—Henry James, Theodore Roosevelt, and Edith Wharton (who was her sister-in-law)—and did good works; improving conditions in hospitals and asylums was her special mission. Beatrix's father, "Freddy," was his mother's indulged boy, with lots of money and charm—and few accomplishments to his own name. But money and houses were only the beginning of Beatrix Jones's inheritance: she was to be the most distinguished of five generations of gardeners. She could have been idle (like her father), but as a very young woman, Jones (more like her mother) exhibited the energy, creativity, and determination that would earn her the reputation best defined by her biographer as ("almost") the "female equivalent of America's most well known landscape architect, Frederick Law Olmsted."[5]

Beatrix Jones (who did not marry until she was forty-one) got an impressive start because she discovered in her childhood that she wanted to make a beautiful world more beautiful. At Reef Point, her parents' estate in Bar Harbor, Maine, she learned from studying the natural landscape of Mount Desert Island and from the designed gardens of the summer residents, many of whom would provide her with her first commissions. Given the run of Harvard's Arnold Arboretum with the great Charles Sprague Sargent, its director, as her "teacher" (she also was invited to explore his estate in Brookline, called Holm Lea), she had access to a superb education, without ever having to succeed—or fail—in college. On long travels abroad, she studied great estates, training her eyes to follow classical lines and shapes, and continuing to make drawings in her notebooks. When she needed to improve her skills in surveying and engineering, she learned them at New York's School of Mines. Her professional associations were as well connected as her personal ones: she became one of the charter fellows of the American Society of Landscape Architects.

As if life were not already full to overflowing, in 1913 she and Max Farrand, a Yale historian, made a marriage of true minds, enriching each other's pleasures in life and work (among her academic commissions was one at Yale). Looking over a client list that includes many of America's great institutions (the White House) and families (the Rockefellers), most people would consider her greatest achievement to be Dumbarton Oaks, the Georgetown estate of Mildred and Robert Bliss, who were introduced to Farrand by Edith Wharton. Beatrix Farrand's papers at the University of California at Berkeley constitute an important collection of garden designs that will tell us more about the field of women in landscape architecture.[6]

What do we have to learn from the life and work of Beatrix Farrand that helps us understand Elizabeth Lawrence? For one thing, it probably matters more where a landscape gardener is born than it does in almost any other profession. What we think of as "the accident of birth" determines what we see when we awaken to the world. And when it comes to places where one can train the eye to find beauty and form, Parkersburg, Marietta, Garysburg, and Raleigh were no substitutes for New York City, Newport, and Bar Harbor. By the time Lawrence was helping the Wake County Garden Club to beautify some of Raleigh's city streets and helping local gardeners to choose plants for their perennial borders, Farrand had designed gardens for the very wealthy in Bar Harbor. In 1932, for example, one of Farrand's new clients was the Northeast Harbor Tennis Club. The same year, Elizabeth and her mother were on their way to a small North Carolina town for a meeting of the local garden club, which would begin with a hymn singing, followed by a reading of the minutes. After Elizabeth spoke, she distributed plants that she had brought from her garden. Then, whoever from the club had the most beautiful garden would invite Elizabeth and Bessie home, show them her garden, get their good ideas, and send them home with plants wrapped in old newspapers.

In comparing Lawrence's gardening life with Farrand's it is easy to see how they excelled in very different realms. Documenting garden designs, by women especially, is difficult at best, but because Farrand had the foresight to keep careful records, we are able to see her achievement in terms of commissions and plans. We not only appreciate Farrand as a professional but, in comparison, we see that Elizabeth Lawrence did not set out to establish herself in the business of landscape architecture. The "bread and butter" letters that were exchanged after Elizabeth Lawrence had spoken to a garden club or been consulted about a garden design are plentiful among her papers, but records of designs she may have drawn or fees she may have been paid during her years in Raleigh are largely missing. Only in later years, after she had moved to Charlotte, do we find evidence of her consultation on landscape design projects. Just as dramatic a difference between the two women could be arrived at were we to put a photograph of Lawrence's small backyard garden in Raleigh alongside one taken from the air of Farrand's vast estate at Reef Point (both made in the 1930s). Farrand's gardens seem "the equivalent of another planet" (her biographer Jane Brown's phrase for how alien the California landscape seemed to Farrand, when she lived in San Marino with her husband).[7] Since Southerners came late to American garden history, it helps us to find Lawrence's place in it by knowing what advantages Beatrix Farrand had in becoming so successful. Elizabeth Lawrence had neither the background, the training, nor, perhaps, the desire, to become a successful garden designer. Another thing we learn from putting Farrand's and Lawrence's biographies side by side (Farrand died in 1959, when she was eighty-six; Lawrence was fifty-five at the time) can be abstracted from history. Late in life, Farrand found herself disappointed on several fronts: she had failed to break into the business as a landscape designer in California; when she was a consultant at the Arnold Arboretum, the new managers did not appreciate her as much as Charles Sargent had (Sargent died in 1927); and, most hurtful of all, she was unable to raise funds to support the upkeep of her garden at Reef Point, and sold it off. Having had her expectations dashed, Brown observes, "She settled in the warmth of her own small world, largely of her memories and dreams."[8]

"Memories and dreams" is a good definition of Lawrence's sphere, and she settled early and late into the warmth of her own small world. She was not destined to become well known for having designed other people's gardens, but for having inspired other people's dreams of gardens of their own.

The American woman landscape architect with whom Lawrence had some personal acquaintance was Ellen Biddle Shipman. The record of their association, like most of Lawrence's records, is contained in a personal letter.[9] When Shipman was in her late sixties, in the fall of 1935, she came to give a lecture in Raleigh, and Lawrence, amazed that no one else seemed poised to have her as a houseguest, invited her to stay with her. Shipman accepted the invitation and said that she would be arriving on the night train from New Orleans. Lawrence was thrilled, and perhaps too naïve to be uneasy. In her files was a photograph of Shipman that she had saved when it had appeared with an article two years earlier in *House & Garden,* acclaiming Shipman as the "dean of American women landscape architects." The facts about Shipman's practice were impressive: her own office in New York City; her large, well-trained, all-woman staff; and hundreds of important clients all over the country. Shipman's success could have intimidated Lawrence, who was still trying to find a place for herself in the local gardening world. If she had also known that Shipman was "utterly sure of her own tastes," she might have hesitated before mailing her a letter of invitation to be her houseguest, but perhaps not.[10] Lawrence—intuitively—followed her senses. The photograph of Shipman, in profile, showed her as being as "beautiful as Botticelli is beautiful. That beautiful long line of jaw, wide mouth and flaring nostrils." "I said to myself," Elizabeth wrote to Ann

Bridgers, "here was a person I wanted to know." "Please," Elizabeth exclaimed, "imagine her coming to Raleigh & no one else wanting to entertain her."

Shipman had the kind of eclectic background that encourages in an artistic person a sense of freedom. Her father was Colonel James Biddle, a career soldier from an old Philadelphia family, and when he married Ellen McGowan from New Jersey, they went on an assignment to a military outpost in Texas. Their daughter was born in Philadelphia (1869) only because Mrs. Biddle had gone to her husband's home for the birth. Until she was a teenager, young Ellen reveled in the adventures of horseback riding and camping out in the wilderness of Nevada, Colorado, and the Arizona Territory and dancing at military balls in San Francisco. Her high spirits were fed by opportunities that few young girls in America could have dreamed of. By the time she was sent to finishing school in Baltimore, she must have received numerous introductions to people and places, and developed a strong sense of her own powers. Her grandmother's garden in New Jersey helped inspire her to pursue a course that would become her professional life. When Ellen was twenty-three, she married Louis Evan Shipman, an aspiring writer, from a well-to-do New York family, and they had three children. In 1927, however, they were divorced, and Shipman concentrated her energies on her New York office, entirely staffed by women, many of them graduates of the Lowthorpe School. Making use of her good connections with women in the garden club movement to find her client base, she hired women architects because she thought their work was superior to that of men in the profession. "Before women took hold of the profession, landscape architects were doing what I call cemetery work," she explained.[11]

In the 1930s, when Shipman embarked on the lecture tour that would bring her to Raleigh, North Carolina, she was known for having designed residential gardens for many of America's most prominent families, including the Astors, Du Ponts, and Fords. Her signature designs were found up and down the east coast and as far away as Washington state and Louisiana: lush herbaceous borders, after the style of the person who had most influenced her, Gertrude Jekyll; pools and pergolas defining private spaces; geometric beds; and inviting copses. Shipman began to learn the profession as an apprentice to architect Charles Platt, who was adapting features of the Italian landscape to American estates. Working with Platt gave her the kind of training that other women were receiving in horticultural and landscape studies at the Lowthorpe School in Groton, Massachusetts, and at the Cambridge School—and, perhaps more important, working with him gave her introductions to a base of clients who could afford to pay her when, in 1920, she began her own practice and moved her office to New York City. With the Depression and the war years, her career brought her South to design gardens, and to lecture. At least a few of the members of the Raleigh Garden Club probably had seen the garden that she had designed in 1929 for Dewitt and Ralph Hanes in Winston-Salem. The Haneses had been ready for Shipman to carry out her design work for their garden just when the stock market crashed. However, Dewitt Hanes, perhaps Shipman's equal in confidence and opinions, insisted to her husband that the garden must be created, even if they had to cut corners someplace else. Dewitt and Ellen had their way, and the garden was established, with its brick walls, arched gates, pigeon coop, axial paths, and geometric perennial beds.[12]

Lawrence herself may not have seen the Hanes garden, but she surely had heard about it from her friends in Winston-Salem. But what may have drawn her to Shipman was not her designs but her person—as we will discover when we return to the letter Elizabeth wrote to Ann about her houseguest. Because it reveals so much about Elizabeth, the letter is worth quoting.

> I thought the lecture [in Raleigh] pretty poor—not at all well thought out; she just said whatever came into her head, which is charming but not very helpful at a garden school where you go to learn. She told me with pride, that she never reads her lectures. "Mrs. Cary" [perhaps garden writer Katherine T. Cary], she said, "reads her lectures; of course it takes much more out of you to speak, but it is the only way." She is right,

of course, but a really good lecture has got to have been thought out in detail beforehand & turned in your mind. Then you have to think it all out all over as you say it, and then it sounds spontaneous, but makes sense, too....

She [Shipman] had flown to New Orleans to see about a garden [probably the garden of Edith and Edgar Stern] that wasn't getting along as she liked, straightened it out, and came all the way here which takes over twenty-four hours, and it was nine thirty when we got home. And she is nearly seventy. I said, when we got home, "Wouldn't you like to go right to bed?" And she said, "No, if you are not tired, I would like to sit down and talk to you." I said, "Mrs. Shipman, I think it is extraordinary (I was mimicking her—she calls everything 'extraordinary'—I don't know whether from reading Henry James or being born in Philadelphia), that you can do gardens all over the whole United States. Aren't you the only landscape architect who does?" She said, "I really do not know. I really don't know anything about what other landscape architects do. I have three children and five grandchildren so I don't have much time."

I said, "But you must be extraordinarily versatile to do gardens in such different places as New York, Los Angeles, New Orleans, Winston-Salem, the middle west."

She said, "But the principles are always the same."

To make up, I said, "That is the secret. It is because you do not try to express your personality, but your client's—so you can never become stereotyped."

Then to prove her great interest in plant material, she got out a little notebook, asked the name, height, blooming period, and characteristics of the milk-and-wine lilies, saying, "You see, this is how I pick up information wherever I go." Whereupon Bessie got out her blooming date books & began to reel off bulbs of the South. Poor Mrs. Shipman, never having heard of any of them before, & being a worse speller than I, tried to take down *lyinnus squonigui; hymenscallis occidentalis; amaryllis belladonna, childmanthus fragrans, sterbergia lenton*—looking utterly bewildered. Finally, she said, "Frankly, I am no botanist, you know. I think gardens are best when they are planted with a few things that you know will do well & have the right effect. I am not interested in horticulture."

"But how do you get the individual character of each place?"

"Because I am architecturally minded."

"And what about plant materials? Surely you can't know the plant materials for all those places." (It takes a lifetime to learn it for one.)

> This, of course, is the whole thing. She was very much annoyed and at once on the defensive. She said you don't need to know the plant material. She said, "I ask my clients what they like and I use that. A garden should be a portrait of the person for whom it is designed."
>
> I said, "Mrs. Shipman, you are not a gardener, you are a landscape architect." She was indignant at that. She said, "But I am a gardener."
>
> I said, "But no, you are not, you don't love plants for themselves. You only think of them as part of the design."

At that point, Elizabeth, characteristically, left the argument without any resolution, and ended the scene: "Bessie kissed her good night. She left her door open while she undressed, & kept talking to us." The next encounter took place the following morning when Elizabeth carried up hot milk and orange juice to her waking guest.

To have been present as a hidden observer of this scene in the upstairs guest bedroom at the Lawrences' house in Raleigh would have been as amusing as an evening at the Little Theatre—which, in fact, is probably what Elizabeth had in mind in recreating the scene for her playwright friend, Ann Bridgers. She even included some stage directions: At the end of the first scene, Elizabeth wrote to Ann, "Mrs. Shipman looks right at you when she talks and her pupils get very small and sharp and bright." Scene two ended with Mrs. Shipman "sitting up in bed with the tray in her lap, and in a blue dressing gown," and the Lawrence dogs "sitting on the rug staring at her."

But that was not the end of the little drama. The final scene occurred after Mrs. Shipman had left.

> When I told Sammy [Elizabeth's father] how beautiful Mrs. Shipman is, he could not bear not having seen her. I told Mrs. Shipman this, and she laughed, and said he would have been disappointed when he saw a wrinkled old woman. She said it the way Nana said she was a wrinkled old woman, knowing she was, and knowing it didn't matter.
>
> When I told Sammy about Mrs. Shipman, he said wistfully, "I wish you could have seen more of her while she is here." He seemed to forget that the garden school is what she came for. I said, "Oh, but I saw her a lot; last night, & taking her to the Woman's Club, & this morning before

she got up. It isn't the amount of time you see a person, it is how responsive they are in that time. Mrs. Shipman doesn't waste a second."

Sammy said, "Did you tell her you are a landscape architect?"

I said, "No, she isn't interested in what I am."

He said, "You were afraid to."

He said, "Why didn't you ask her where to study?"

I said, "I did not want her to think I asked her to my house for what I could get out of her."

Sammy said, "Isn't that what you asked her for?"

This scene as written for Ann Bridgers's entertainment is most revealing: Lawrence had been candid with Mrs. Shipman, her father (still alert and charming, in spite of the fact that his stroke had severely affected his speech) had been candid with her, and she was candid with Ann Bridgers. What it tells us is that Elizabeth had been considering further studies, and that her father had encouraged her to consult authorities who could give her the best advice about where she should go. The degree program at North Carolina State had only been intended as preparation for further training in a professional school. The Lowthorpe School and the Cambridge School were ideal in that they specifically enrolled women, and they had faculty and alumnae who were successful in the field. In the mid-1930s, the Cambridge School had eighty-two graduates reporting to the alumnae office that they were employed in partnerships, working on public projects, or teaching landscape architecture (mostly in the Northeast). Lecturers at the Lowthorpe School in the 1930s included Louise Beebe Wilder, one of Lawrence's favorite garden writers, Beatrix Farrand, and Ellen Shipman.

Lawrence may have been considering attending at least one of these schools. The name of Dr. Henry Frost and the address of the Cambridge School appear in one of Lawrence's (undated) address books, and Lawrence had her transcript from North Carolina State sent to the Lowthorpe School in September 1934. Unfortunately, no records have turned up to indicate whether she was accepted in either place, and if she had applied to the Lowthorpe School the year before Shipman's lecture in Raleigh, it is puzzling that she didn't say something about it in her report to Ann Bridgers. Because Sam Lawrence's health was poor, Elizabeth may have come to the realization that there was no money for her to return to school, or that, if money was available, she could not leave her mother alone to look after him. It is also possible that she had discovered that she could learn what she needed to know by staying at home.

Working with Miss Isabel Busbee, Lawrence undertook designs for which there are scant records, but a few examples suggest the kind of work she did: a community park in Farmville, North Carolina; landscaping for the new Little Theatre; plantings of shade trees for city streets; and small, residential gardens in Raleigh and in nearby towns.[13] Each project reflected the knowledge of plants that she had insisted upon with Ellen Shipman. When Martha Fillmore wrote to thank her for coming to help her with her garden in Tarboro, she said she was "enchanted" with her "plans for planting." Her most significant garden designs, however, would be done after 1948, when she and her mother moved to Charlotte to live next door to her sister and her sister's family. On several occasions, friends invited her back to Raleigh to check on their gardens and to suggest new things that nobody but Elizabeth Lawrence seemed to know about. It was the highlight of Lucille Aycock's week when Elizabeth came to spend the night in her house on Blount Street, where the next morning they would walk about the garden, making plans for the Aycocks' long borders. But it was in Elizabeth's own gardens, first in Raleigh and then in Charlotte, and in her writings about them, that she left the most vivid and complete record of herself as a landscape designer.

In Raleigh in the 1930s, Lawrence began a life that she continued to perfect for almost a half-century. In turning back toward home, she had found her way. Fortunately for her, living within a few blocks of the Lawrence house, there were educated people whose lives were models for what she might achieve. The pride of the neighborhood was the small "estate" on nearby Oberlin Road, which had been developed by Isabelle Bowen Henderson, a well-known portrait artist, whose house was a showplace for early American furniture and crafts (including Jugtown pottery—Henderson had grown up with Jacques Busbee, who lived a block away). In the late 1930s, Henderson perfected her gardens—front garden, resplendent with what she called an "English-style perennial border," a display garden seen from the terrace, and an herb garden in the approach to her studio. In 1942 the Henderson estate was featured in *House & Garden* magazine. There was also Miss Isabel Busbee, who already had her own practice in landscape architecture. There was Baker Wynne, a bachelor professor at North Carolina State and member of an old Raleigh family, who had a fine garden. And there were Ann and Emily Bridgers.

Miss Isabel Busbee was a member of an old Raleigh family that included lawyers and artists. In 1917, the year after the Lawrences had moved from Garysburg to Raleigh, one of the Busbee family homes was being torn down, and a newspaper reporter observed that it had contained "much of the history of Raleigh"; it was a place where great statesmen, such as Henry Clay, had been entertained. The Busbees were a family filled with interesting people. One of the men, Jacques Busbee, Miss Isabel's brother, was an artist; he had married Julia Royster (a St. Mary's graduate), who, as a member of the state federation of women's clubs, had lectured throughout the state and was studying and collecting old pottery. Jacques and Julia had lived for a time in New York, where they were leaders in an arts community, and had begun to circulate stories about the crafts in North Carolina. When they returned, they moved to Seagrove, North Carolina, where they were instrumental in reviving pottery making in the state. In the women's federated movement and in their neighborhood in Raleigh, the Lawrence and Busbee women became friends. Miss Isabel was a leader in the Raleigh Garden Club, the largest in the state, and Bessie and Elizabeth Lawrence were active members. Miss Isabel persuaded Elizabeth to take charge of various committees, to teach in club-sponsored garden schools, to present talks over the radio, and to accept invitations to give lectures. Elizabeth fell in with Miss Isabel's plans for her as an assistant in the business of landscape design.

Isabel Busbee was like many women of her generation, a professional in terms of her knowledge and experience, but one who had not graduated from a professional school. In fact, Lawrence's own studies at North Carolina State predated by a few years the formal organization of a "school" of landscape architecture. The Busbee sisters—Isabel, Sophie, and Louise ("Miss Toose")—were all single and living together in the family home near the Lawrences. Their sister, Miss Christine, was living in New York City, where she and Ann Lawrence occasionally saw one another. They were enterprising young women who supported themselves—in 1912 Isabel was secretary to the president of North Carolina State College, Sophie was a clerk in state government, and Louise operated a kindergarten in their home. Miss Isabel's real passion, however, was outside, in her garden. She had a good collection of garden books, and when Elizabeth left Raleigh and moved to Charlotte, Miss Isabel gave Elizabeth her library. Relying on her great knowledge of plants, her own beautiful garden, and her personal contacts with many Raleigh gardeners through the garden club movement, Isabel Busbee opened her own landscape practice and took on Elizabeth Lawrence as assistant. Elizabeth set up her drawing board in her studio downstairs in the Lawrence home, and went to work.

But first, there were the usual interruptions. Bessie, Sammy, and Nana loved to talk. Elizabeth found their needs irresistible, especially since she loved to talk herself. From 1929, when Nana moved to Raleigh from Parkersburg, until she died in 1933, Bessie and Elizabeth included her in the life of the family. By 1934 Sam Lawrence was an invalid, and Bessie and Elizabeth helped see to his needs. Bessie was still out and about—active at Christ Church, the Red Cross—and Sammy depended upon his beloved Elizabeth for news in Bessie's absence. Still, it was difficult to start one's career when one's father needed cheering up, one's mother needed help in the kitchen (in addition to the paid cook), and one's friends liked to drop in, often. Apparently, Elizabeth had not thought about the demands or rewards of her job.

In spite of interruptions and the informality of her business "practice," however, Lawrence took her cue from Busbee, who had come up the same way, and quickly found her professional niche in the Raleigh gardening world. Through radio talks, garden school lectures, and work with the Raleigh Garden Club, she established a reputation for knowing plants and for sharing her plant knowledge with other gardeners. She and her mother began planting their own garden in back of their house, each keeping records, making out catalogue orders together, buying plants from nurseries when they could, attending meetings of the Garden Club, and traveling together when Elizabeth gave a garden talk.

How much Lawrence had control over her own life, however, seems questionable. One example suffices. In the summer of 1934, having a lovely time at the New Jersey shore with Louisa and Warren Way, who had been head of St. Mary's, Elizabeth was considering staying longer. When Bessie began to suspect Elizabeth's intentions (in Elizabeth's words, "she smelled a rat"), she sent her a telegram—"Miss Isabel waiting for you to go to work."[14] It is not clear whose need—Mrs. Lawrence's or Miss Busbee's—summoned Elizabeth back, but whether she was at the drawing board the next morning or eating toast and jam with Bessie in the kitchen, Elizabeth was always glad to come home. It was hard to be cross with Bessie; even if she did interrupt Elizabeth's writing in the garden, she had come out to give her daughter the little curved pruning saw that Elizabeth had wanted for so long. Most important, Bessie ran the household, was good with numbers, kept up with her investments, and paid household bills. She might have been exactly the kind of office manager Elizabeth could have used in establishing fees for services. Elizabeth must have recognized, however, that it was easier to give her mother control over her life than over an independent career. Every indication we have is that Elizabeth allowed her professional standing to drift naturally into the domestic sphere, which is where we find her so often. In limiting their arguments to whether to sit out in the "sun-catch" on a winter's day, and by conceding business decisions to Bessie, Elizabeth saved her energy for what really mattered: the garden, always the garden. So what if she had to come home early from a vacation? Truth to tell, she never liked to leave the garden for very long, anyway.

Garden designers as distinguished as Farrand and Shipman, who moved easily in a world of wealthy clients, had a hard time finding work during the Great Depression, when commissions were almost at a standstill. It seems unlikely that even if Lawrence had been a more determined careerist, she would have been able to make a living in the 1930s in Raleigh as a garden designer. Dewitt Hanes certainly would have heard good things about her from any number of expert women gardeners in Winston-Salem, but Lawrence's reputation was no match for Shipman's—which may have made Lawrence especially anxious to match wits. If her account of Shipman's visit was not exaggerated for Ann Bridgers' benefit, we can say of Lawrence what Shipman's biographer said of her: she was utterly sure of her own tastes. Her education did not launch her into a successful career as a garden designer, but after studying at North Carolina State and working with Miss Busbee, she did become more certain of her knowledge and her tastes.

CHAPTER ELEVEN

A Writer's Life 1932–1942

I sat down to the typewriter, keeping firmly in mind that it bears me no grudge.

AT SOME POINT in the early 1930s, Ann and Emily Bridgers collaborated on a plan for Elizabeth to stay at home, to do what she was good at—gardening—and to earn some money. Up to that point, she had been writing only poetry. Recognizing how unlikely it was that Elizabeth could make a career out of writing poetry, they must have said to her that she should write about gardening and try to place her articles in popular magazines. From 1900 to 1940, in what Virginia Tuttle Clayton has called the "golden age of magazines," the *Atlantic Monthly, Scribner's, The Ladies' Home Journal,* and *Woman's Home Companion* included gardening articles among others on science, the humanities, politics, current events, and families, for millions of avid readers, both men and women. Other magazines such as *Country Life in America, American Home, Better Homes and Gardens, Gardeners' Chronicle of America, The House Beautiful,* and *House & Garden* gave special emphasis to gardening and published articles by both professionals and amateurs.[1]

These garden magazines, especially in the 1930s, reflected the domestic mood of the times, suggested in the titles of two of the most popular: *House & Garden* and *Better Homes and Gardens.* These magazines had regular features on monthly garden chores and practical advice about how to grow roses, chrysanthemums, camellias, and other showy flowers that would exhibit themselves well for neighbors and could be cut and made into bouquets for the dining table. The house was the center of the universe, and the housewife was expected to be a competent manager. Magazines were filled with advertisements for appliances that would make the lives of women easier and better—

electric refrigerators, washing machines, stoves, food choppers, Dutch ovens. Pillsbury flour for baking pies, cakes, and biscuits was essential to the well-being of an American family. If a woman indulged herself by owning delicate underwear, she could add years to their life by washing them in Ivory Flakes. And the house must be clean and efficient.

In the same optimistic spirit, garden columnists and garden writers wrote mostly for housewives who wanted to extend the beauty of the home out into the garden. Their prose floated in air, but was rooted in the practical. Eating in the garden—"divine"—made for a "cooperative" household. The father was said to enjoy it more than a picnic, and the children were eager to carry plates from the kitchen. Growing flowers was easy enough as long as the gardener had an attitude of "Let's get started!" During the winter, gardeners should sit back and imagine their gardens; no one suggested that they spend months poring over seed catalogues. In summer, gardeners must not forget to water. Children were to be encouraged to learn how to grow things—they were photographed happily digging holes and listening patiently as their mothers gave instructions. All in all, the message was: with a good plan, everything is possible—a tasty meal, an efficient house, a beautiful garden.[2] Ironically for Lawrence, the idealized woman in the house and garden was a *wife*.

Garden magazines published in Britain were special favorites of serious American gardeners, and Lawrence read them with avid interest. She was glad to read that on January 11 an Irish gardener in Kilkenny had picked twenty-four different kinds of blooms, and that her list, like Elizabeth's, included "violets, snowdrops, violas, winter aconite, jasminum nudiflorum and the Christmas rose." "She is a little ahead of me," Lawrence lamented. "I think I had twenty varieties on that day." In the "straightforward" prose of some of the magazines published on the other side of the Atlantic, she found "whole stories of families and social histories." "There is certainly a novel in a half-column account of the Starry Columbine," about a gardener in Edinburgh growing the plant her mother had introduced into cultivation thirty years earlier.

Emily and Ann Bridgers kept up with these current publications too,

Ann Preston Bridgers in 1928. She and George Abbott achieved overnight success as coauthors of the Broadway hit Coquette. *Ann divided her time between New York and Raleigh, where her family lived across the street from the Lawrence household. In the early 1930s she and her sister Emily helped Elizabeth become a garden writer.*

and they must have been aware of the career possibilities for a writer with Elizabeth's knowledge of gardening in the South. Although they probably did not know the market well enough to predict her success with any certainty, they knew Elizabeth. She needed to be productive—a word that Emily and Ann may have inserted into her thinking. And so Elizabeth took their advice, and it had a joyful result—she began to look forward to the hours they would spend together thinking up topics for her to write about. In June 1935 she wrote to Ann:

> Alas! I discovered immediately after your departure that it was your enthusiasm that made writing gardening articles so simple, and you had no sooner left than the magic vanished, like midnight in a fairytale, and it got to be the same chore it always was. However, I reminded myself that I

> am doing you a favor, and went bravely on; and due to your soothing influence I sat down to the typewriter, keeping firmly in mind that it bears me no grudge, and conquered the spacing system in a sitting. In time I hope to be able to strike the right key one time out of ten.

She concluded, "Writing is the only thing I don't like about writing . . . that is what I like about poetry, you can express the most with a minimum of ink."

Garden articles written in the 1930s were Lawrence's first efforts at finding her public voice and her audience. The delight of her life, then and later, was that when her words appeared in print, so many readers wrote back. Lawrence had begun—in Emily Dickinson's phrase—her "letter to the world," and no one would have less reason to complain that "it never wrote to me." Letters flowed to the "Kind Flower Lady" in North Carolina. An exchange of ideas, information, and friendships began that would sustain Lawrence for the next half-century.

Lawrence did find out just how tough it was to fit her ideas to popular taste, though house and home and the garden beautiful were exactly the subjects on which she was an expert. "It is too bad that I am so full of material and devoid of personality," she lamented, after one of her submissions had been returned. Her classical approach to gardening (a gardener, she believed, should know both the Latin and the common names of flowers, and where in literature they have been described by poets) was going to be tested; her search for her own audience would proceed slowly, step by step.

When Lawrence began writing garden articles, she did not know how much time they would require and how hard it would be to get them published. So many hours would be spent "tearing up today what I did yesterday."[3] She had already learned that she felt bound to sacrifice her working days and nights whenever family and friends needed her. In July of 1937, in two weeks of uninterrupted work, she "got a lot done in the garden, and my files in order, and magazines caught up with, and material organized, and an article written. In summer," she added, "I only get called to the phone on an average of twice a day."[4] Her garden required even more of her time: experimenting with new plants, making records about the plants she already had, and gathering information by writing daily letters to gardeners and botanists all over the country.

Elizabeth loved to write letters, and, once correspondents learned to read her microscopic handwriting, her letters brought great pleasure. When she wrote to well-known botanists and nurserymen, she kept her letters short and to the point, including enough information about her own gardening habits for the so-called experts to recognize a true colleague. With friends, she was anecdotal and humorous, naming names and places and going from one thought to the next in long, winding sentences punctuated haphazardly with parentheses, ellipses, and insertions. The greatest verbal extravagance was saved for letters to Ann Bridgers, often written in what Elizabeth called her "lyric mood," especially when she was pensive. But when she had to show her first drafts of articles to Ann (for praise) and to Emily (for editing), she focused on her subject—gardening. This tutorial under the guidance of the Bridgers sisters was necessary if Lawrence was going to become a published writer, and she did not argue with their suggestions for changes. Any time she could show off what she had learned from them, she did so, even pointing out to them that she would never send an article through the mail without having made a carbon. The carbon copies of her typed garden articles—both those that were submitted and those that were rejected—are neat examples of care and compliance. Sometimes they were typed by Emily Bridgers from Elizabeth's handwritten manuscripts.

To begin an article, Lawrence concentrated on a limited subject and organized her information very succinctly, as if following an outline.[5] Her first three acceptances (in 1932, 1933, and 1934) were from *Garden Gossip,* published by the Garden Club of Virginia and the Federated Garden Clubs of Virginia. It was a modest-looking publication, but its editors—Violet Walker, and then Elizabeth Rawlinson—were good gardeners and writers. *Garden Gossip* did not pay its contributors anything, but Lawrence had broken into print. Although there is nothing especially to admire about the writing (straightforward and factual), she showed that she knew her subject and could write about it as if she were talking to a fellow gardener. This immediacy of voice would become more distinctive as Lawrence became a more experienced writer. Visitors to her garden would always remember how generous she was in sharing information and how happy she seemed to be when she talked about her favorite plants. This personal intimacy (for Elizabeth, the garden *was* intimate) was exactly the tone she conveyed in what she wrote. She also was invited to present programs to garden clubs, and she enjoyed them, especially when people wrote to tell her how much they had learned. Word spread—Elizabeth Lawrence in Raleigh was an exceptional gardener, writer, and speaker. In her article "Summer-Flowering Bulbs," published in *Garden Gossip* in December 1933, she personalized her style in the first sentence. "Instead of agonizing over perennials that will never be at their best in our climate," she began, "we should use plant materials adapted to our hot, dry summers." The term "plant materials" immediately gave her away as a serious gardener. She couldn't help herself—she *was* a serious gardener. Lawrence observed her plants with the close scrutiny of a scientist, though she could not avoid drifting into moments of adoration. It is these two voices—scientific and lyric—that are heard early and late.

Lawrence reported on her own failures and successes. The *Amaryllis belladonna* "has bloomed for me in the poorest soil in both sun and shade. The charming *Lycoris squamigera* bloomed for two years and then disappeared. I have since learned that it was planted too deep.... One of the things that I covet, but have had no success with, is the summer hyacinth, *Galtonia candicans*. I know that it does well here, so I think I must have put it in the wrong place." Also tucked into one of her six paragraphs is an allusion to "the country women" who bring bulbs to the Raleigh market in May. And so we have promise of everything to come: plant information, lack of pretense, confidence about what she likes, reports on her own gardening, and women who advertised plants in state market bulletins.

Perhaps her willingness to share her failures as well as her knowledge was what immediately endeared her to readers. They felt as if they could ask her anything or trade with her long-distance. "Please tell me the name of the old pillar rose that is in bloom now here and in Winston-Salem," wrote Mrs. Sheets of Reidsville. Lawrence was just as likely to be rewarded for her help. "I see that you wish to try *Vallota purpurea*. I have several & will be glad to exchange for some bulbs I do not have," Mrs. Knock wrote, from Crooks, South Dakota. Dozens, then hundreds, of postcards and letters followed, asking and giving.

Writing was hard work for Elizabeth, but it was going to be fun. She could not wait to see her words in print. Her first published articles did not come easily and held no promise as a way to earn a living. In 1936, writing to her mother, who was traveling in England to recover from the long illness and recent death of her husband, Elizabeth wondered whether, after all the trouble of finally having an article accepted, a $25.00 check was worth the effort. It clearly was not going to help support the household, and not making much money lowered her sense of worth. But the writing had started, and there was no stopping it. With Emily and Ann Bridgers reading and correcting her manuscripts, Elizabeth had what she needed: encouragement. Much later in life after Elizabeth had moved to Charlotte and had published three books, she still turned to them. "Thank you for all you do for me," she wrote the best editors she ever had. "I am sure you have no idea how much." And she added, "It is impossible for anyone to write without a reader, and it is impossible for me to write without a sympathetic reader."[6] The Bridgers sisters were Lawrence's ideal, sympathetic readers, unique in that they were more interested in how she wrote than in how she gardened.

Although the short pieces in *Garden Gossip* were not remarkable in themselves, they led to the same kind of satisfaction that Lawrence received from her later books—friendships with gardeners and an exchange of information and plants. The editors were notable leaders in Virginia garden circles. Five years after Lawrence's first appearance in the magazine (advertised as "the only magazine recording the activities of gardening in the mid-south"), Rawlinson wrote to say that she would be "thrilled to have anything for *Garden Gossip* you can spare me." By then, she had met Elizabeth and her mother, who had invited her back to Raleigh to visit them after they had met at a garden lecture. In their usual fashion, Elizabeth and Bessie had showered their guest with special attention, introducing her to friends they knew she would enjoy and loading her up with plants (and a box lunch) to take home.

Lawrence aimed higher the next time out. In 1936 *House & Garden,* a nationally known magazine with a large, mostly female audience, published four of her submissions. She was hitting her stride with longer manuscripts, filled with suggestions about plants that would grow in Southern climes and encouraging gardeners to try new things. She had researched the names of plants and where they grow, and she often checked information with horticulturists at the Arnold Arboretum, the New York Botanical Garden, the University of North Carolina, and the Memorial Garden of Duke University. When she needed help identifying a specimen, she often sent it to B. W. Wells, Professor of Botany and her former teacher at North Carolina State College. She even wrote to nurserymen as far away as Oregon and California. While her primary source would always be her own garden, increasingly she also wrote about the experiences of other gardeners.

"Twenty-one Plant Facts for Gardeners in the Middle South" was a transition piece, tightly organized, but within her numbered paragraphs, her writing was personal. Furthermore, she named her place—"In Southern gardens," she began, going on to say that it was better to grow plants that tolerated the climate than to struggle with other plants that could not take hot summers. "On the other hand," she immediately cautioned, "we should not be too sure that desirable plants will not grow in the South until we have given them a fair trial."

This encouragement to try something new was to become one of Lawrence's most original contributions to garden literature. Her mailbox began to fill with letters of appreciation from gardeners who thought she was writing especially for them. "Dear Madam," W. E. H. Porter of Towner County, North Dakota, wrote after Thanksgiving in 1936, "I am glad to hear of your interest in *Lallemantia cornesceus*... I take pleasure in enclosing a few seeds collected from my own plants in the fall. You can send me 15 cents in postage stamps if you like." Porter had met a kindred spirit. "I am experimenting in a small way," he confessed, "with a view to establishing hardy perennials in North Dakota, as this state is still mostly wilderness and from a scenic view point altogether so." If baby's breath was "doubtful" for Southern flower borders, Elizabeth suggested that gardeners try "the charming wild spurge, *Euphorbia corallata.*" If French hybrid lilacs failed, perhaps they had not been given the proper care. The ginger lily is a valuable accent plant for borders in late summer and fall.

Along with specific plant information, Lawrence introduced a standard of gardening that she would return to again and again: "We can have flowers nearly every month of the year." She took it for granted that Southern gardeners made the same use of their gardens that she did of hers—the garden was a place to be enjoyed every month (every day) of the year, a place "where one may sit out of doors on mild days in winter." By the time she introduced the image of a "sun-catch" as a place to sit near warm bricks, protected from the cold, and "elevenses" as a morning time for visiting with friends on the terrace, her readers felt at home with her. Southern gardeners felt as if, finally, someone who understood the caprices of the Southern clime was writing for them. Even readers in places like South Dakota and Maine, with their long and severe winters, were encouraged to find more plants that might prove hardy and more days when a surprising change in the weather was a chance to be outside. Over time, many gardeners came to live by Elizabeth Lawrence's calendar.

By contrast, garden literature in popular magazines tended to focus on smaller pieces of the landscape—how to plant a rose garden, when to prune, how to get bigger blooms—and how to arrange flowers for the table (subjects that did not much interest Lawrence). She could think about a new idea as well as a new plant, and as her passion for the latter became documented in her daily notes and her publications, she began to realize that—like her father—she could "live" in the mind. In writing articles, she was having to think about her philosophy of gardening, but she would not be ready to express it directly until the end of this long apprenticeship.

In the fall of 1936, Lawrence took up a subject that would interest her for the rest of her life: growing bulbs. "We are beginning to learn," she announced, "that many of the bulbs from tropical and subtropical countries could be grown with success in the Southeastern United States." Thus began her lesson on three bulb families, the *Amaryllidaceae,* the *Liliaceae,* and the *Iridaceae.* In a carefully planned garden, she concluded, her recommended bulbs would bloom "almost continuously from early spring to frost." High on her list was *Zephyranthes candida,* "one of the little bulbs that travels from garden to garden." In her Raleigh garden in 1936, she remembered that it had come from south Georgia. In 1957, when she devoted an entire book to her subject—*The Little Bulbs*—she would write at greater length about the zephyr or rain lily, remembering that hers had come "from Mrs. Lay," a friend in Chapel Hill. Recently, Pamela Harper, a contemporary garden writer who knew Elizabeth Lawrence (and with whom she is often compared), included *Z. candida* in her book of *Time-Tested Plants.* Knowing that Lawrence was writing about this bulb in one of her earliest articles confirms the reputation she enjoys with gardening readers, namely, that her ideas have stood the test of time.

In 1937 Lawrence had two articles published in *House & Garden,* and one in *The American Home,* another periodical with a national audience. In the first of these three, she introduced a new subject that was to remain one of her favorites: "Rock Garden Plants for the Mid-South." She gave suggestions about how to grow alpine plants in a Southern climate where all the ideal conditions—a short growing season protected by a heavy blanket of snow and an abundance of moisture—are absent. She set out to name the plants that are easiest to grow in the Southern garden, especially the dwarf achilleas. By recommending "little used" species, she continued to enlarge gardeners' selection of plant materials.

Nineteen thirty-eight showed some modest successes, with carefully researched articles that were read by very small audiences—"Milk and Wine Lily" appeared in January and *"Torenia bailloni"* in October in the newsletter *Garden Gossip.* In her short article on the yellow-flowered annual, Lawrence said that after a "long search" she finally was able to have it in her garden. Her first attempt to grow the plant did not "survive my desultory sowing," but she kept trying until "a careful nurseryman" grew five plants for her from new seeds she had ordered.[7] In April Lawrence published an article on phlox in the first issue of a Raleigh magazine, *Southern Home and Garden;* another on rock gardens appeared in November.

These nonpaying publications hardly represented the kind of success that Emily and Ann Bridgers might have hoped for, for Elizabeth, who expressed more concern about Ann's failures (to find audiences for her new plays) than she did about her own. Meanwhile, she was working in her "experimental garden," as it was now known on garden tours, trying out hundreds of new plants, and keeping careful records. There was to be a lapse of some three years before she published again, but she was working on the manuscript that would secure her reputation for all time.

Lawrence probably would not have produced a book manuscript, nor would she have had the temerity to send it out, had she not been seasoned by years of writing garden articles. It had been a useful apprenticeship for a writer, but it had also taught her a lesson about the difficulties of publishing. Sometimes editors required her to make changes before they would accept an article. Dorothy Hansell, for example, wrote that members of the editorial board of the American Rock Garden Society, with headquarters on Sixth Avenue in New York, had found some "serious mis-statements" in her "interesting and very well-written" article on biennials, mostly having to do with climate differences, "which must be the main guide in the way we handle our plants." Apparently, Lawrence did not revise and resubmit her article. (It had already been rejected by *The American Home* and *Better Homes and Gardens.*) In March 1939, Hansell, as editor of *Gardener's Chronicle of America,* told Lawrence that her article on biennials would be accepted if one or two "minor changes" were made. Canterbury bells were the subject of debate: the editorial advisory committee argued that raising them from seed was not satisfactory unless the flowers were "protected from bees." Furthermore, "in several cases you have given the height of some plants that does not seem to coincide" with the experience their gardeners had had. Lawrence made the changes, and the article was accepted. Demands for a high degree of specification and concerns about "accuracy" were to be the bane of her existence with editors for the next forty years.

The harshest kind of letter from an editor can be illustrated by one from Robert Lemmon, the editor of *Real Gardening*. If the magazine title did not say it all, the subtitle did: *The Magazine of the Gardener, for the Gardener, by the Gardener*. Lemmon was returning her article on Southern hollies. "As you've probably guessed by this time," he wrote, "*Real Gardening* has a good many points of difference with other magazines in its field." One of these differences, he went on to explain, was *Real Gardening's* decision to use only contributors "who are definitely and professionally connected with some form of actual horticulture." In a tone of patient condescension, he concluded, "I'm sure you understand that this is no reflection on your writing, or on that of a number of other amateurs." Apparently, Lemmon was forgetting that the year before, as garden editor of *House & Garden,* he had found "perfectly good material" in Lawrence's submission to that magazine. Lawrence was not put off by Mr. Lemmon, apparently. She gave him a chance the next year to look at an article on conifers. The handwritten letter to him that she left in her files (and probably never sent) thanked him for being "so kind about telling me why you couldn't use the articles you returned" and asking if he would be interested in an article on gardening in the South. Apparently, he was not. Eight years later, however, Lemmon, by that time editor of *The Home Garden,* wrote her an unsolicited letter, asking if she could help him obtain "a few roots" of a Southern trillium he had "been hearing vague reports of." Lawrence's files do not contain her response, but it is likely she sent the "roots." A decade after he had dismissed her as an "amateur," however, he could have learned about many species of trillium in *The Little Bulbs* (and forty years later, in her article on trilliums published in *The Newsletter of the North Carolina Wildflower Preservation Society)*. Lawrence would not live to see all her lost causes found, but there were some. "Gardens in Winter for the Mid-South," rejected by the editors of *House & Garden,* was rewritten for one of her most popular books, *Gardens in Winter,* published in 1961.

In the 1930s, Lawrence had learned that there was almost no money to be made writing garden articles, but she became well known to many of the best gardeners and garden editors in America, who would continue to solicit information and articles from her. The best part of her work was that she was making so many friends. Along the way, she was also finding her subjects—not only the little bulbs and gardens in winter, but people, places, and books. If the editor of *The American Home* was not interested in Lawrence's submission because it gave so much space to first-hand information about irises, Caroline Dormon, who was growing irises at Briarwood in Louisiana, was just waiting to meet a gardener like Elizabeth. But rejection letters took their toll on Elizabeth's feelings and on her style. Step by step, she was having to move away from expressive writing toward a more scientific approach to "plant materials." More and more she would quote other authorities at great length. The editor of *The American Home,* returning her article entitled "A Night Garden," explained that they had no room in their magazine for "imaginary and hypothetical gardens." In fact, Lawrence had grown all the plants she described in the article (artemesias, herbs, petunias, and lilies), and had said only that the design of the garden was partly imaginary. The fact that the unpublished article on a night garden was one she had revised several times for Emily and Ann Bridgers suggests that they may not have correctly understood her audience. They (knowing little about gardening themselves) may well have encouraged her to be more "literary." Lawrence herself had not learned to judge her own best work.

But she had begun the difficult task of learning to be a professional writer. She had publications to her credit, and she had the respect of experts in her field. She had acquired some of the necessary skills to be successful—she knew her subject, she revised manuscripts many times, and she was tenacious in dealing with editors. She had not mastered her own emotions when it came to feeling inadequate with editors as opinionated as herself. She was still trying to find her own style, one that would accommodate her literary tastes and her scientific knowledge. She already was certain of what she knew and how to find out what she did not know, but she wanted to tell an interesting story about the world of gardening. It seemed to her so broad and deep that no single category—such as horticulture—could reveal its glories. A garden had a history—past, present, and future—and the writers she admired were not shy about writing themselves into it. To compare herself to the garden writers she admired was daunting: after all, she lacked the prodigious resources of Gertrude Jekyll, the originality of Elizabeth von Arnim, and the collaborative enterprise of the Loudons (all of whose gardens—as described in their books—she knew as well as her own). But Elizabeth Lawrence was a good gardener, and she would borrow from the best to amend her native soil. As a student, she had never had confidence in her own ability, but with Emily and Ann Bridgers to help her, she was on her way toward becoming the writer she wanted to become. And by the end of the 1930s, Elizabeth Lawrence was ready to assume a role she had been preparing for—the author of a book that could be compared with the great gardening classics.

In the meantime, the question must have occurred to her: Where was the kind of family support that Ann Bridgers relied upon? She could not live without Bessie, she knew that. Then one day her mother got a letter from Elizabeth's sister, Ann, with a very surprising proposal: "I think it's too exciting about another article of Libba's. If I felt that Libba would really get down to business, I would come home and be her business manager. That idea has just come to me, and I believe it is the solution to our financial problems. We will talk it over when I come home. If Libba would only be serious I believe we could build up a rip roaring [landscaping] business. Tell her to be sure to go see E. Thompson's friend in Durham so that I will have something to work on."

Apparently, Elizabeth rejected—or ignored—her sister's offer; Ann did not come home to be her business manager. Why? With no discovered letters between the two sisters explaining why, we can only try to understand what was going on in their lives that would have deterred such an arrangement. Ann was having a grand time living in New York City; Elizabeth was having a grand time writing her articles for Ann and Emily Bridgers. What was different about the relationship between the Lawrence sisters that prevented them from working as closely together as the Bridgers sisters? Ann often saw Ann and Emily Bridgers when they were staying in their New York City apartment. Had they suggested that she propose to work with her sister? Or was it Ann Lawrence's idea, one that Elizabeth had discussed with Ann Bridgers? We'll never know why the Lawrence sisters (and their mother) did not build up a "rip-roaring business," but we do know that Elizabeth was carving out a life for herself in Raleigh.

CHAPTER TWELVE

Writing A Southern Garden

I think it is a classic. I think it is Vergilian.

JOSEPH MITCHELL

IN 1942 Elizabeth Lawrence's first book, *A Southern Garden*, was published by the University of North Carolina Press, and despite wartime concerns, the book immediately found an appreciative audience.[1] Any attention given to a gardening book at such a time was impressive, and Lawrence's was published only months after one of the darkest days in American life, the December 7, 1941, bombing of Pearl Harbor.

Noted journalist Joseph Mitchell conveyed his good opinion to Elizabeth years later in a personal letter he wrote to her in the summer of 1955, after he and his sister Laura Braswell had visited her Charlotte garden. A few days after the visit, he bought the book in Chapel Hill, and when he had returned to New York and read it, he wrote to thank her. "I admire its subtlety and its exactitude and its humor and the strength in its sentences," he explained, and proclaimed it a "classic" and "Vergilian." "I know it is one of the books I will be re-reading all the rest of my life." Mitchell's experience of going back to *A Southern Garden* "time and time again, re-reading a selection here and a paragraph there," has been one that many readers have shared.[2]

The testament of a writer as accomplished as Joseph Mitchell made Lawrence proud, but what a hometown reviewer said about it when it came out gives a sense of the kind of reputation that Elizabeth Lawrence was already beginning to enjoy in North Carolina. In an article published in the Raleigh *News & Observer,* Charlotte Hilton Green began by speaking of the difficulties people faced during a time of war: rising costs, rationing of food and gasoline, and the need to spend whatever

Elizabeth was both a "dirt gardener" who tended her own beds and a student of gardening. She learned from many other gardeners and from books. Here she is working in her Raleigh garden in early spring, 1942. (Reprinted by permission of The News & Observer *of Raleigh, North Carolina.)*

money they had to buy defense stamps and bonds. "We need such a handbook for the gardening that will do—and is doing—so much for our morale. . . . We are going to turn more and more to our gardens for solace and comfort and peace of mind—and for physical and spiritual re-creation. And at such a time, above all times, on limited budgets of time, of money, and of strength, we want to garden right."[3]

Everyone was being urged to plant vegetables to help swell food production, and victory gardens were the pride of many Southern towns and cities. Popular regional and national magazines featured articles on how to convert a flower bed to a space for growing tomatoes, beans, beets and carrots, lettuce and onions.

It was also a time to cultivate beauty as a distraction from the ugly reality of war. Most victory gardens had at least a few borders of flowers to brighten the day. It was also a time when a quiet voice speaking as if to a friend might take one's mind away from the din of the world. So it was that Elizabeth Lawrence's book found its first readers, who learned about gardens that "planted for winter green and winter bloom have an air of spring when warm days come and redbirds flash into the open." Like "the pearly buds of the snowdrops," gardeners were "waiting for a little warmth."

At a time when confidence was called for, it is ironic that Lawrence began her book with "An Apology for Myself as a Gardener." Such a tone was contrary to the spirit of the times, when Uncle Sam looked you straight in the eye, and Rosie the Riveter flexed her muscles. And yet, Lawrence's disclaimer somehow *was* a morale booster. Every gardener secretly may have yearned to say with Elizabeth, "If plants are miffy, let them go."

Her book unfolds, season by season, beginning with winter and "the flowering of the first paper-whites and sweet violets," moving into spring and early bulbs, then to summer's perennials, the flaming of red-spider lilies in mid-September, then frost, and the garden year begins again. "Today is the fourteenth of November," Lawrence writes. "I have been sitting in the sun eating my lunch and staring at the barbaric scarlet of Tithonia Fireball against a cold blue sky."

Nothing about writing a gardening book happens quickly: it had taken Elizabeth Lawrence most of a decade to grow the plants in her own garden and to make meticulous records of how they had done for her. In promising her readers that what had grown for her would grow for them, she had to make certain that her observations were careful, her assumptions as correct as possible. When she did not know something, she said so, and when she had failures, she reported them. As Lawrence's garden had matured, so she had come into her own as a gardener and writer. Seasons of growth in the gardener as well as in the garden proceed at their own measured pace, taking their own sweet time. Elizabeth Lawrence had also had to learn the pace of a determined writer. And after she had written the manuscript, she had to find a publisher for her book, and her experience with magazine editors had often been discouraging. What always worked in her favor, however, was that she made friends—and even if others were slightly perplexed by her handwriting or bemused by her stubbornness over small details that mattered to *her,* no one came away feeling that she was an amateur at anything. She knew what she knew, and she wrote well.

The reason that Lawrence had been able to take her time through each of the stages of the book was that she loved what she was doing—gardening and writing about gardening. In many respects, the experience she had in writing her first book was as close to ideal as Elizabeth Lawrence would ever have: she was excited at last to be writing a book, her Raleigh friends and neighbors Emily and Ann Bridgers were with her through most of the steps, she had amassed a large correspondence with gardeners whose experiences in different places she could draw upon, and her own garden had come into its own, and was beautiful. Now if she could only tear herself away from the distractions of family and friends, she would luxuriate in the materials. In the history of first books, *A Southern Garden* belongs among those whose authors thoroughly enjoyed the process of putting them together.

In the summer of 1937, Lawrence wrote to Ann Bridgers that after two "peaceful" weeks she was caught up on her work in the garden, her files were in order, and she had written a new article. "I didn't realize how much material I had collected this year," she explained, "and I sat down and wrote without thinking how long it was, and before I came to, I had nearer six thousand words than the less than three thousand" that the editor had wanted.[4] Learning to write "without thinking" was a big step toward being ready to write a book-length manuscript. But it was not often that she had the time to be expansive, and a few months later, she unburdened herself to Ann Bridgers: "I have got little done on the book, and am frantic." By late August 1940, however, Elizabeth had finished an "outline" of her book, which she sent to Emily Bridgers to critique. As the manuscript neared completion, she confessed to Ann, "I have something perfectly awful to tell you—it doesn't matter whether my book ever gets published or not. I have had the fun of doing it, and I have learned what I need to know."

Beginning in 1940 Lawrence wrote to various New York publishers to ask if they would be interested in reading her manuscript when it was finished. Some of them wrote back to say no, explaining that there was not much of a market for books on Southern gardening. One suggested that she contact the University of North Carolina Press, which had also been recommended by some of her friends in Chapel Hill. When Elizabeth Lay Green (who was married to the playwright Paul Green), and William Lanier Hunt spoke to the editor of the University of North Carolina Press about her, Lawrence followed up with the briefest of letters to the director, W. T. Couch. In her first sentence she described the manuscript: "I have written a garden book for the Middle South based on my own records which I have been keeping for a number of years with a book in my mind, for there is no book for gardeners in our section, and there is a need of one." In the second sentence, she asked, "If you would be interested in reading it, may I bring it to you, and when will it be convenient?" It was signed "Sincerely, Elizabeth Lawrence," and dated "Thursday evening." (It was postmarked March 20, 1941.)[5]

Couch answered quickly, inviting her to come to see him in Chapel Hill the following week. The visit went well, they talked about books they liked and her ideas for his garden, and Lawrence left the manuscript with him. That day, he sent the manuscript to Dr. H. R. Totten in the University's Department of Botany. Two months later, Couch wrote with good news: the manuscript had been recommended for publication. He enclosed Totten's remarks. The university botanist admired her informal style, her willingness to discuss her own failures as well as her successes, and her reports from her gardening friends. These materials, Totten argued, "lighten parts that from their nature are largely encyclopedic." He did not think, however, that she had given adequate attention to native plants, adding, "I get bored with the gleanings from foreign experiences and books." That aside, Totten concluded, "There are so few garden books applicable to this section, and interest in gardening is growing." It would serve a useful purpose in Southern horticulture, and he believed it would sell. He rightly predicted what readers would especially like about it: it was "a reference book to come back to often."[6]

Elizabeth was visiting Ellen Flood when Couch's letter offering her a contract arrived. Her mother forwarded it to her in New York. Lawrence wrote Couch at once to say that she accepted Totten's suggestions. The following week, when she returned to Raleigh, there was a contract waiting for her, dated June 6, 1941. She signed it, it was witnessed by a lawyer (H. B. Hines Jr.) and a former St. Mary's classmate living in Raleigh, Sylbert Pendleton, and she mailed it off. An edition of 2,000 copies was to be published; the author was to receive twelve free copies, and she would receive 10 percent of the retail list price for each copy sold (which amounted to thirty cents per copy). By the end of the summer, Lawrence had seen sample pages and had approved the layout for the title page. America was at war, and there was hardly enough money for books of any kind. Lawrence was told that the press would not be able to do a "deluxe job."

Everything seemed to be running smoothly until soon after Thanksgiving, when Lawrence was notified that the manuscript she had submitted was much longer than expected because she had added so much new material. She drove to Chapel Hill to talk directly with Mr. Couch, who was worried about the number of changes she had made, beyond what was customarily allowed for an author. She would have to pay (about $165). The delays continued as Lawrence continued to make revisions (in February she paid another hundred dollars). The original manuscript of 240 pages was increased to 264 pages, and Lawrence had to agree to leave it at that. In March 1942 *A Southern Garden: A Handbook for the Middle South* was finally published. It sold for three dollars.[7] None of the final details meant more to Elizabeth than the dedication, which read "For Ann." Although most people who knew the family would always assume that she had dedicated the book to her sister Ann, Elizabeth had dedicated it to her friend Ann Preston Bridgers.

In the decade between Lawrence's first article (in *Garden Gossip*) and *A Southern Garden,* she had learned to convey a body of scientific information in a readable way. In perfecting the style that was to become her signature achievement in garden literature, she wrote as if readers were friends in her garden. After reading *A Southern Garden,* Opal Flick wrote her from Carthage, Indiana, "I felt as though one flower lover was talking directly to another—Me!"[8] Many letter writers over many years were to express that exact sentiment, and many tried to offer something in return. Sarah Stetson, who gardened in Williamsburg, Virginia, wrote to suggest places where Lawrence might order *Pallidus praecox.* If someone questioned what she had written, Lawrence spent hours, sometimes days, trying to learn more about the subject and writing long letters of explanation. To Mr. Marshall (who had differed with her over identifying a narcissus), she responded, "Sincerely and humbly," "Please don't think I ever make rash statements. I am overflowing with enthusiasm, but wouldn't have the confidence to pose as an authority even if I knew a great deal more than I do," adding, "If you have any suggestions for study I shall try to pursue them."[9]

A Southern Garden made its mark among a small number of readers, but its mark was indelible. Still in print, it is routinely called a "classic" in all important discussions of American garden literature.[10] With a great deal of clarity, Lawrence conveyed the kind of exact, and expansive, horticultural information that had won her a following in newsletters and magazines. Sometimes she wrote in a more lyrical style: "The special charm of a Southern Spring is its earliness, it is as long drawn out as it is sweet." Her own romance of childhood remembered was sometimes palpable: "There are days in February when the sun is warm, and children play singing games in the street, when, if you shut your eyes for a moment and listen to the whir of a lawnmower as it goes over lush winter-grass, you will be shocked upon opening them to find no leaves on the trees." While hoping to avoid the sentimental prose of late nineteenth-century garden writers (most of them women), Elizabeth Lawrence projected a strong personal voice, an approach that had been made popular by one of her favorite writers, Louise Beebe Wilder. (Wilder, who was about the same age as Lawrence's mother, had died in 1938.) She wrote about people she knew as if her readers already knew them. In spring she visited Miss Edna Maslin's garden and reported their little exchange: " 'That,' Miss Edna said, 'is the Chinese bamboo.' 'But it couldn't be a bamboo.' 'Yes, Elizabeth, it is a Chinese bamboo.' " Perhaps only a few Raleigh friends knew that Maslin and Elizabeth's mother had been friends since before Bessie married Sam Lawrence.

Lawrence often relied on memory, which, of course, is often a gardener's best friend. She was remembering Nana in Parkersburg when she wrote, "I used to know where to find [the native witch-hazel, *Hamamelis virginiana*], and I would go there in November with my grandmother to gather branches bare of leaves and fringed with sulphur-colored flowers. Now there are houses and gardens where the woods used to be." And in another passage, "If you think back to quiet gardens in little towns passed by in modern times (you will have to go off the main highways to find them) you will remember the delicate pattern of the Silver Bells against dark cedar trees."

As *A Southern Garden* began to make its way into the hands of gardeners outside North Carolina, admirers in Shreveport, Louisiana, discovered that many of their bloom dates corresponded to hers in Raleigh. Many of the Louisiana garden club members gave programs based on *A Southern Garden* so that when the author came (as she did in the fall of 1944), they greeted her like an old friend, and invited her to see as many gardens as she had time for. Inez Conger, who had a fine garden in Arcadia, kept Lawrence's book next to the Bible on her reading table. Many readers wrote to share information as well as plants; many sent her plants asking for help identifying them. Outside the South, readers were surprised to discover they could grow many of the plants that Lawrence grew in her garden. And when the climates were too different to share the same plants, they shared her interests in literature, mythology, and the naming of plants. In this way, Elizabeth Lawrence became far more than a "regional" gardener.

It was personal praise from unknown letter writers that most pleased Lawrence, but she also paid some attention to reviews. *A Southern Garden* received a good review in *Booklist,* which described it as "a straightforward, sensible, informative and pleasantly readable book by a Middle Southerner who knows from personal experience precisely what she's talking about." Reviewing the book for *The National Horticulture Magazine* (April 1942), B. Y. Morrison, founding editor, said that Lawrence's writing "put many others to shame." "Our climates being what they are," he added, "this book may be useless as a guide of the recipe book style, but for the rest of you, read it for your own undoing!" Another national garden authority, Hamilton Traub, editor of *American Plant Life,* thought it would prove to be "a model for regional gardening books all over the continent. . . . The book is original and is entirely free of pedantry and is not complicated in makeup. Therein lies its chief charm. One realizes at once that one is reading a classic in the sense that the book is ageless." Its charming presentation from personal experience "leaves the impression of a prose poem."[11] From California, Lester Rowntree, writing in *Golden Gardens,* began by noting that "Gardeners in that section of Virginia and North Carolina called the Piedmont are a folksy lot, continually swapping plants and comparing notes," creating the kind of gardening communities everybody should aspire to. But does a book on gardening in the Middle South have anything relevant to say to West Coast gardeners? Yes, Rowntree concluded, because many of the methods of achieving year-round bloom are the same. It was not Lawrence's methods that the reviewer chose to recommend to readers, however. It was Lawrence's style that recommends the book: it "reads very much like a letter from one gardener to another." Her searches for plants reflect a "gardener's spirit."[12]

CHAPTER THIRTEEN

The Church

Lift up your hearts.

THE EPISCOPAL CHURCH was an intimate part of Elizabeth Lawrence's life; she loved the familiar services, taken from the Book of Common Prayer, and she knew the creeds and prayers by heart. At home, she read her favorite family prayer, which began, "Almighty and everlasting God, in whom we live and move and have our being; We, thy needy creatures, render thee our humble praises." Perhaps what meant so much in that prayer to someone who could not sleep (insomnia, she said, was "a form of madness") was its expression of thanksgiving for having been delivered "from the dangers of the past night." She loved the Book of Common Prayer and the dramatic setting that the Church provided—a high altar, a stately chair and pulpit, and a man in priestly robes, speaking in a sonorous voice. The service was unchanging, and beautiful. For as long as she could remember, she had heard, "Lift up your hearts," and she had responded, "We lift them up unto the Lord."

In the 1960s and 1970s, when the Episcopal Church changed—the Book of Common Prayer was revised, and women were ordained to the priesthood, both of which decisions Elizabeth and her family opposed—Elizabeth suffered such feelings of regret and anger that she almost stopped going to church. But there had been an earlier time, when she herself had led a protest against an "established" church position, and that opposition is a unique chapter in her history in the Church. Perhaps it would not have surprised her Uncle Jim, the priest who had baptized her as a child at St. James Church in Marietta, Georgia.

Sam Lawrence's younger brother, James Bolan Lawrence, was for forty-two years rector of Calvary Church in Americus, Georgia, one of the best-loved churchmen in the South serving one of the South's most beautiful churches. A graduate of General Theological Seminary in New York City, he had come to Americus early in his ministry and, with a small group of communicants, had begun to build a new church, to be designed by Ralph Cram, the leading church architect in America. But his greatest ministry may have been in helping to build small country churches around Americus, where he was a friend to everyone, including farmers he helped at harvest time. Lawrence did much of the work himself in building a small church of log and stone at Pennington, which he named St. James after the church in Marietta, where he had been baptized as a boy. A bachelor, he was well known for entertaining at home, where one and all participated in his lively conversations and drank from his silver cups. Each summer he was the visiting priest at St. Mary's Church in Manhattanville, New York, where (having saved money by sitting up all night on the train from Georgia and making other Spartan choices), he indulged himself by buying a new piece of silver at Tiffany's—or ordering a copy of Plutarch's *Lives* from Brentano's.

Uncle Jim and Elizabeth had much in common—the church was as much his place of meaning and beauty as the garden was for her. They shared a great interest in reading the classics, and she sought his help in translating difficult Latin, French, and German poems. When he died in 1947, there was a mile-long procession of his friends, the rich and the poor, black and white, following his casket to his burial place at the little Pennington church. "Brother Jimmy" had made arrangements for a bus to transport his black friends to his grave and to have the casket opened for them to pay their respects.

Uncle Jim's particular influence on Elizabeth was not so much that of a priestly man who deepened her faith in God, as it was that of a good man who deepened her faith in people. A time came when she acted upon his example.

In Raleigh the Lawrences were communicants at Christ Episcopal Church in downtown Raleigh, where many of the leading families worshipped. For more than one hundred years, the large and affluent church had had a mission chapel called St. Saviour's, also near downtown Raleigh, but in the mill district. The little chapel there was as sweet as Brother Jimmy's log church at Pennington, and it had a special appeal for Elizabeth Lawrence.

St. Saviour's had a long history: In 1875 members of the distinguished Devereux and Mordecai families of Raleigh bequeathed a gift of property to Christ Episcopal Church in the factory district, intended as land for a mission and school to serve factory workers and their families. In 1894 it finally became the site for a small wooden chapel designed by the architect Adolphus Gustavus Bauer, well known for his work on the North Carolina Governor's Mansion. The mission work went forward for a half-century; then in 1924 gifts were made by other prominent Raleigh families for the purchase of another tract of land near the old chapel and for the building of a larger one, to be called the Edgar Haywood Memorial. The handsome new St. Saviour's chapel (made of stone) was built the year after Elizabeth Lawrence graduated from Barnard. She was drawn to it. She volunteered to teach a Sunday School class of young children, and spent a good deal of time trying to find songs, poems, and pictures that would enrich their lives. After a while, however, she began to despair. "I am utterly depressed by the poverty in this world," she admitted. "I had forgotten those places under the railroad, and I couldn't bear for those very little children who came to Sunday School and begged to sing 'All Things Bright and Beautiful' to have come out of them. I went home to Bessie in a funk, and she had no patience with my maudlin tale, and said people always had lived like that, and always would, and they liked it." Nevertheless, Elizabeth did not share her mother's attitude. As she tried to find time to write, work in the garden and in the house, remain active in the garden club, and give lectures, she gave weeks of her time to St. Saviour's. "You cannot stand aside and behold 'a beggar born' without doing something about it," she confided to Ann Bridgers.[1]

The annual Christmas pageant at St. Saviour's was one of Elizabeth's favorite services, and she helped the children in her Sunday School class prepare for it. Even the poorest families found some way to let their children buy small gifts for one another, and Elizabeth was especially touched one Christmas Eve in 1942 to find an old woman standing at the door waiting for her with a paper bag full of little packages. She was "Peggy's grandmother," who had brought the packages because Peggy was in the hospital, and they both wanted the children to have them. Elizabeth was touched by the ways in which children were able to find meaning in the Christmas story, and once when they were watching slides of great religious paintings, one of the children whispered, "Oh, Miss Lawrence, look at the little angels. Doesn't the one leaning on his elbow look just like Dinky?" Elizabeth agreed that he did. "If you think all joy has gone from the world," she wrote Ann Bridgers, "you should see a St. Saviour's Christmas party."

In 1945 there was talk of closing the mission church. Elizabeth responded with a vehemence that surprised people who knew her as the shy Lawrence daughter who lived at home and gardened. Offended by the "very underhanded manner" in which the priest at Christ Church was attempting to get rid of St. Saviour's and its curate, the Reverend Charles Wulf, Elizabeth took it upon herself to speak to some of the individuals who could prevent it. After church one Sunday she came away "sick and exhausted" from a morning of talking to as many of the Christ Church vestrymen as she could corner, delaying their quick departure for dinner with their families (and for some, an afternoon of golf). The women in the parish staying behind to tidy up the sanctuary must have nudged one another to ask what Elizabeth Lawrence was up to. When she did not get any reassurances, she decided to take matters into her own hands at a congregational meeting at St. Saviour's. More than a half-century later, someone who had been at the meeting remembered what had happened:

> Elizabeth was sitting with the group of vestrymen from St. Saviour's—they were working men, carpenters and plumbers—and they seemed to be feeling very out of place. Christ Church was trying to prepare them for the fact that they wanted to break the deed and sell the real estate that St. Saviour's was on. Someone from St. Saviour's was giving a report and Elizabeth stood up and interrupted him. "Speak up, speak up," she urged.

> She thought that the vestry of St. Saviour's was capitulating to Christ Church, and she was trying to tell them what rights they had. I was just a teenager, but I was listening to every word. I thought of her as a busy dove. I had never seen her attack, turned into a fighting character. I was very proud of her because she was standing up, a gentlewoman, and these men were not used to speaking, and she was trying to put words into their mouths. She was ardent, and I think a lot of people were amazed. She had shocked the aristocrats in the church, and I was thrilled that she had this spirit—and she was an aristocrat herself.[2]

But it was a losing cause. The vestry at Christ Church voted to close St. Saviour's, effective December 31, 1948. St. Saviour's was financially dependent upon Christ Church, and support for the mission had declined. During the war, people had rallied behind God and country to make whatever sacrifices it took to support the troops and look after the widows and orphans, but in the heady optimism after the war—the belief that now life was going to be a lot better—many of these people were now ready to move on. And moving they were—out to the suburbs, which is where the vestry at Christ Church thought there should be another church. The vestrymen at St. Saviour's, however, won an important victory when they were granted ownership of the church and rectory, and, without any financial support from Christ Church, they continued to operate for another decade.

But there were many angry people who felt that a rich church had abandoned its poor relation, and Elizabeth Lawrence was one of them. Family was family.

CHAPTER FOURTEEN

Ann Lawrence

My sister Ann, whose name should be Candide,
says everything always works out for the best.

ELIZABETH LAWRENCE TO ANN PRESTON BRIDGERS, UNDATED

In June of 1926, as Elizabeth Lawrence graduated from Barnard and Ann from the junior college at St. Mary's, their lives were about to diverge dramatically. Apparently alone, and with much on her mind, Elizabeth was quietly packing up to leave New York City after four years and no loosening of family ties; she would be spending the winter with Nana in Parkersburg. Ann, after "crying her eyes out" because she was having to say goodbye to her many friends at St. Mary's (and because she was expressive), had the most exciting prospect she had ever imagined: she was going to study in Europe for a year.

The University of Delaware was the first American institution to offer a junior year abroad, and in 1926, the director began the third summer of taking students from a number of different schools. Posing for a group photograph on board ship as it was departing from New York were some thirty young people, holding up banners from Miami, Cornell, M.I.T., Amherst, and Wellesley. Behind the Delaware banner, front and just to the right of center, was Ann Lawrence. If family members studying the photograph agreed, as they would have, that she was the most striking, it would be easy to see why they thought so: she *was* pretty. All the women had on close-fitting hats (the men wore suits and ties), but Ann's with the wide white band and the slight tilt to one side gave her an especially sophisticated look. Students and faculty on the trip might never have heard of St. Mary's before, but they certainly would remember Ann Lawrence, not as the girl who had been giddy with excitement (as they all likely were), but as the only student who thanked her overseas landlady before departing for home. Ann Lawrence was Nana's grandchild, after all.

The program began at the University of Nancy in Alsace, where for six weeks the students had intensive training in the language. Living with families gave each of them a chance to speak French, before they departed by train for Paris. In Paris, while continuing to live in French homes, they spent a good deal of their time in a building that housed offices for the University of Delaware, with study rooms and a library. At the Sorbonne they picked up cards that would admit them to classes, and most took the "Cours de Civilisation," designed to give foreign students an overview of French literature, history, art, philosophy, and economic and social development. Ann, like most students, wrote home about her life outside the lecture halls. She and her friends did what American students today do when they travel abroad—they walked the streets, ate the food, danced the dances, sang the songs, rode the trains to nearby cities and countries, went to tourist sites, and promised never to forget a single moment of their amazing year together. Before leaving for home at the end of August, Ann wrote her sister from a Whitehall Residential Hotel in London's Russell Square to say that she was glad that her "darling Libba" was soon going to be in New York, not only because she could meet her when she arrived, but because Libba would have "such a good time." She confided that "Porky" had waited three weeks so that he could go home on the boat with her, exclaiming, "Can you imagine any one being so foolish as to wait for me that long? well, luck to him, I hope he feels himself rewarded!" She had had a letter from "Milton," who was "quite a lad," inviting her to West Point; and one of the boys that she had met on the ship had turned up and was going with her to Paris. "I haven't broken the latter to the family," she advised her sister, "So please don't say anything about it." She mailed the letter to Ellen Flood's address in New York, with an additional warning written on the back of the envelope, "Don't send this home!"[1] It contained a confession only someone confident of being trusted and loved could have written: "You'll probably think I'm crazy to write all this but it's the first time that I have been able to express myself because you are always under the family's wing. I can hardly wait to get home, it's going to be a great life showing the family the real Ann after I've played up to what they expected me to be for so many years. I can't play forever you know."[2]

In fact, Ann did not disappoint her family, but enrolled at the University of North Carolina in Chapel Hill, where many of St. Mary's junior college graduates went for their last two years, and she earned her degree in 1929. With no abating of the thrill of having gained her independence in France, however, she was determined to keep going. After a few years of trying to find a job that suited her, she chose the right place—New York City, where, despite her disclaimer, the "new Ann" was recognizable as the "old Ann" to the many friends of her family who enjoyed her good company.

In New York, Ann moved about with great confidence, unlike Elizabeth, who was always afraid to let Ellen out of her sight. With Elizabeth's encouragement to stick it out until she found a job—and Ellen's weekly, and sometimes nightly, invitations to supper (with Ellen's father, her husband Jack, and their children—Bracelen and Mary Ellen)—Ann soon fit into the New York scene as happily as Ellen. She took a room where other single girls like her were living—in the Sutton Hotel on East Fifty-sixth Street—unpacked, and wrote home at once: "Can you believe I'm here? I can't!" She started looking for a job, and as her luck would have it, she was hired to work at Macy's. She wrote her family that it did not matter that the job was part-time or that it was wrapping gifts—she would watch for job announcements and, meanwhile, she'd be good with paper and bows. When applicants for a full-time position were interviewed, Ann Lawrence was the one hired. When half the people in one department were fired, Ann was kept. And later, when she was fired, she told Mr. Bracelen (Ellen's father, who was general counsel for AT&T), who made a few telephone calls, and she was back on the job the next day. Ann was irrepressible, and irresistible. "Dearest Libba," she wrote, "Finally after having started out to be President of

Macy's, I got sifted down to selling toys... I told Miss Tildsey that I wanted to work to be an executive and that I was willing to start at the bottom." In another letter to "Dearest Poppa," she said that despite rumors that lots of people were going to lose their jobs or be moved to different departments, she felt confident: "As long as I keep my job, I do not care what goes on, and I like being changed around." When Ann wrote home that if only she were in charge she could make Macy's a more efficient operation, Elizabeth said, "That's what I love about my sister Ann!"[3]

In an article in *The State* magazine, "Tarheels in New York," that appeared just before Christmas in 1934, Ann Lawrence was the subject of a profile about her job at Macy's, where she was one of some fifteen thousand employees. "Far from being dismayed by the noise and confusion [of Macy's Toyland] which swirled around her, Miss Lawrence, who is small and blonde and animated, was enthusiastic about her work." Ann had told the reporter that she was interested in getting into the personnel end of merchandising. The reporter noted that in spite of having graduated from St. Mary's and the University of North Carolina and having studied in France, "Miss Lawrence felt that she needed the school of actual selling in such a place as Macy's."

Ann's social calendar stayed full too, weeknights and weekends, with a round of friends and entertainment. Friends from Raleigh who came to New York looked up Ann Lawrence, as well as friends from St. Mary's, from Chapel Hill, from her trip abroad, from West Virginia, and from Georgia. Uncle Jim complained, with some amusement, that he could never find her in. She went to movies, operas, the Ballet Russe, museums, an exhibition of African Art, the zoo, and the Russian Tea Room, and ate dinners out in fine restaurants. She was "a great girl," willing to help "finish the evening off" with someone after others had dropped out and gone home to bed. She was like a member of Ellen's family, a special favorite of Ellen's father, who asked her advice about family matters. When Ellen and Jack Flood divorced, Ann knew it before Elizabeth did. When Ann and Emily Bridgers were spending time in a New York apartment, they often had Ann over for dinner. She attended the twenty-fifth anniversary of the Girl Scouts (Eleanor Roosevelt was the speaker) and wore "peach chiffon with its full flowing skirt," a flower pinned at her waist, and long white gloves and pearls, "and really looked quite well turned out." Heated discussions about FDR and the New Deal raged among her young male acquaintances, and when Ann wrote to tell her family, she was careful not to let them think she had been persuaded by her friends' critical views. She was "devastated" when she missed a chance to meet President Roosevelt, who was visiting his daughter Anna in the same building where one of Ann's friends lived, and they had been invited up.

Ann Lawrence was both worldly and naïve, spontaneous, unguarded, and without pretense. She understood people, and they understood her. And she was not a worrier—she took life as it came, and tried to make it better. She felt guilty "of shirking my duty" when things were not going well at home—her father was sick, Nana required attention, the house was cold, they had lost their help. But it was Ann that Elizabeth, back home, worried about, knowing that Ann really could not be doing as well as she said she was on fifteen dollars a week. Ann thanked her:

> Dearest Lizzie, Your sweet letter was much appreciated. I am not really discouraged, it's only that I do not think that I am doing as well as I ought to when I have so much to go on. As a matter of fact I think that you have decidedly the worst of a poor bargain because at least I am having fun and you are not. . . . I am trying to work out a plan of coming home . . . I am not neglecting it and will come as soon as I can. The older I get the more devoted I become to you. I was feeling guilty and felt that I should not withhold my financial plight from you and was afraid that in my enthusiasms I had led you to believe that I was making a living when I was not. However do not keep everything from me because I would much rather know how things are going than not.

To her father, she wrote, "Dearest Pap, you are such a dear to think so much of your good for nothing Annie and I appreciate it more than I can tell you. I am going to put away enough money to get home on as Nana said you should always have enough money set aside to get home on. You are a dear sweet daddy and I do appreciate you even if I do not always show it." When Nana was dying, Ann wrote to Elizabeth, "It makes me feel very bad to think that you and mother have all of the worry and that I am not there to share it with you. We have always been so close when anything did happen." Another time, either when Nana had come to live in Raleigh or her father was very ill, she wrote, "Mother dearest, I cannot tell you how sorry I feel for you and Liz and it just breaks my heart that I cannot be there with you. Of course that is out of the question so that is all there is to it. I am sure that the moment you think it is necessary for me to come you will let me know."

When things were going well at home and Ann thought that manners were not being attended to, she could be as bossy as Bessie and Nana. She complained to her mother that it was rude of Elizabeth not to have let Ellen know that they were coming to New York for Christmas, and she scolded Bessie for not planning to go to see the Ways in Atlantic City. The more independent of the two daughters in making her own decisions, Ann—perhaps because she did live in a larger sphere—was also more conscious of what other people thought.

When it came to Elizabeth's career, Ann took a very practical approach: "Well," she exclaimed, when Elizabeth heard good news about her submission to *House & Garden,* "your article! I do not know what to say about it. I was so pleased I nearly died, doesn't your name look wonderful in print." She had bought a copy, and sent copies to Mrs. Sammel and Mrs. Way, and took hers with her when she went to Ellen's for dinner. When one of Elizabeth's submissions was rejected, Ann lectured her, "You must not be so easily discouraged and it is good for you to have every other article refused, and as for [the editor's not] answering your letter, what do you think New York is, have you become so provincial that you do not remember the hustle and bustle of the city life? You should see the pile of correspondence in our office, it would take seven writers seven years to clear it all up." Ann's frankness was in stark contrast to the kind of gentle encouragement that Elizabeth was getting from Emily and Ann Bridgers, and it may have been the reason Elizabeth apparently rejected her offer to come home and help her run a landscaping business.

When their father died in the summer of 1936 and Ann came home for the funeral, she talked Bessie into going to Europe, just as Nana had done after her mother died. Ann returned to New York, "low in her mind." Elizabeth, on the other hand, having been with her father through more than a year of his dramatic decline, felt a sense of relief and release. Traveling with Bessie was Sylbert Pendleton, one of Elizabeth's St. Mary's classmates and, like Elizabeth, a daughter who looked after her mother. Elizabeth was free to rest—and when Mrs. Bridgers and her daughters Ann and Emily invited her to come to the mountains, she went.

For the next several years, Ann Lawrence continued to live in New York, her energy still at the full, and she warned the family to expect a letter anytime with the news that she had found a man she wanted to marry. Indeed, she had—and he was a man everyone would approve of: Warren Way, whom the Lawrences had known when they first moved to Raleigh, and Warren's father was head of St. Mary's. Way had been working in New York and visiting his parents in Atlantic City on the weekends, and Ann was a frequent houseguest there. When she took him for dinner at Ellen's apartment, Bracelen and Mary Ellen were beside themselves with pleasure. Ann was glad, she told them, because he was the man she was going to marry. Although Ann and Warren were thinking about getting married in the Episcopal Church of the Ascension in New York, they changed their plans and scheduled the wedding for the chapel at St. Mary's, much beloved by both families. After seven years in New York, Ann was ready to return to North Carolina, which, except for living on military bases while Warren was in service, would be her home for the rest of her life. On the second of January, 1939, Bessie Lawrence wrote in her garden book: "Lunch in the garden. Candytuft and the first white violet in bloom. Ann's return."[4]

Warren Wade Way Jr. was a graduate of Virginia Episcopal School and the University of the South and had been working at Chase National Bank in New York City. The marriage took place at noon on

Elizabeth's sister, Ann de Treville Lawrence. Fashionable and spunky, she went to New York at the height of the Depression, got a job at Macy's, and made many friends before returning home to marry Warren Way in 1941. (By permission of Warren Way and Elizabeth Rogers.)

December 30, 1941, in the chapel of St. Mary's School. The officiating ministers were Warren's father and Ann's Uncle Jim. Her late father's brother Donald Lawrence came up from Marietta to give her away. Among the out-of-town guests were Ellen Flood and her two children. Mary Ellen was maid of honor. Apparently, Elizabeth either did not wish to be her sister's maid of honor or was not asked to be, though there appears not to have been the slightest displeasure on Elizabeth's part about her sister's marriage. After the wedding, Bessie Lawrence entertained with a luncheon at their home. Among the guests were Warren's brother Roger and his sister Evelyn, who was now a professor of classics at the University of Mississippi in Oxford, and Betty Sammel (Bill's younger sister), from Parkersburg, West Virginia. An announcement in the Parkersburg newspaper noted that Ann Lawrence was a "member of an old Parkersburg family" that traced its ancestry to the earliest pioneer, Captain Neal. On their honeymoon at the Arthurdale Inn in Arthurdale, West Virginia (where Bessie Lawrence knew the owners), Ann wrote "Mother darling" that they had not been able to get up the hill in the car because of deep snow, and had been driven up in a sled. The trip in the snow had been a "dream." She was in "extasies" (neither Ann nor her sister was a good speller). Warren was "twice as sweet" as she had thought he was. The luncheon had been "done right."

Ann was thirty-three years old, Warren thirty-six. Each had waited longer than many of their contemporaries to marry, but when they did, it was to be a marriage of great happiness. When Way, who was a reservist, was called to active service in World War II and sent to Esler Field near Alexandria, Louisiana, Ann went with him. In long, frequent letters to her mother and sister, she described life as a new bride: setting up housekeeping in rented rooms, trying to live on a tight budget ("If you pay so darn much for rent, it just means that you have nothing left to spend on beer"), and making new friends. She cooked from her mother's "receipts" ("some very satisfactory sour milk waffles") and, like her mother, she volunteered at the local Red Cross Office (she made two hundred bandages one afternoon). Unlike her mother's reserved courtship letters to Sam Lawrence, Ann's letters were "extatic": she thought Warren Way was perfect, and he thought the same of her. When they had two children, the small circle that had been so diminished by Sam Lawrence's and Nana's deaths expanded, and when they all came to Raleigh, the large old house on Park Avenue suddenly was livelier than it had been since Elizabeth and Ann were young. All of them—Ann, Warren, Bessie, Elizabeth—were ready to be a family together.

In the first year of their marriage, Warren and Ann were so happy that their pleasure echoed in letters flying back and forth between Louisiana and North Carolina. It was as if Ann had found exactly the life she had been restlessly looking for. Warren was, for Ann, a man like her father—handsome, intelligent, and charming. He must have loved the comparison because Warren always looked up to Sam Lawrence. Ann was for Warren a woman he would always want to hurry home to, anxious to tell her about his day, anxious to hear about hers. Even in the worst of times, when in later years Ann had terminal cancer, she and Warren never gave up their end-of-the-day talk. And Ann did not insulate herself in this company of two. She always made friends—no sooner had she and Warren rented rooms near Esler Field than Ann went over to borrow her landlady's Dutch oven, so that she could cook a roast for the two families. Her spontaneity, her courage, and her "poise" (Elizabeth's word for Ann's ability to adapt to every situation) had always impressed her family and friends, but after marriage, Ann came into her own in another way. She joined the Colonial Dames, the Junior League, the Red Cross, the church guild, and for a few years took a paying office job—everything her sister rejected for herself—and still remained centered in the family.

In the summer of 1943 in Louisiana, Ann and Warren were undecided about whether she should have her baby there or he should bring her home to Raleigh. As the time came closer, Ann and Warren did not want to be separated, and it was only after Warren had made a close study of things that he decided that it would be best if he drove Ann home to Raleigh. He wanted to make sure that after the birth Ann and the baby would get the best care—and he didn't know how he would manage that by himself. As it turned out, Warren left Esler Field to go to Officer Candidate School at Duke University in Durham after the baby was born, but he was not there for the birth. And so in early June Ann was back in Raleigh, Warren had to return to his base, and Bessie and Elizabeth took over. Elizabeth suddenly was "in charge"—making sure that Ann ate well, rested, and walked—and she began to organize her own time around Ann's needs. When the baby—named Warren W. Way III and nicknamed "Chip"—was born, on August 4, Elizabeth was weak with relief—and as happy as Ann. When he was first handed to her, Elizabeth was shocked by what a newborn baby looked like, but, as she was later to remember, when a door slammed and he jumped, she suddenly held him close to her. Elizabeth was learning to be a nurturer. When they came home from the hospital, Elizabeth began at once looking after baby Warren so that Ann could get some rest. When Warren Jr. was home, Elizabeth got up early to bring Chip into her bed, where she would read to him, so that Ann and Warren could sleep late. As often happened to wartime couples, Ann's and Warren's separation was hard on them, especially on Warren, who had to get a special pass to come home to see his son. Men in the military (there were few women) missed out on many of the important family events, and Warren apparently felt that he had missed out on Chip's birth. Before he was transferred back to North Carolina (for OCS School at Duke University and his next assignment at Camp Polk in Wilmington), Elizabeth had already begun to think of Chip as her baby, too.

Two years later, Ann and Warren had a second child, a girl named Elizabeth, born in a Raleigh hospital on September 28, 1945. At first they meant to call her "Brady," which had been Bessie's name in school, but as soon as they cuddled the new baby with a head of blonde hair, they nicknamed her "Fuzz." Elizabeth wrote at once to tell Emily and Ann Bridgers (who may have been out of town at the time). "Ann is fine, but the doctors nearly scared us to death again, and we have decided not to have any more children . . . I am so relieved."[5] The "we" says a good deal about Elizabeth's sense of being a "mother."

After the births of the two children, the Lawrence household took on a new attraction for friends, who dropped by with their children and grandchildren. "We have turned into a sort of day nursery," Elizabeth reported to Ann Bridgers. "I am continually dealing out crackers and grape juice and settling squabbles and drying tears, and taking to the johnny, and getting Mr. Cayce [the dog] out of one place into another." Chip and Mr. Cayce had a special attraction for each other—always on top of one another—and Chip's father thought that the dog was the problem. Despite her brother-in-law's efforts to teach Elizabeth to walk Mr. Cayce using a training collar, she felt "self-conscious on the street, muttering, 'Steady, Boy.' " ("It seems that my method of hanging on for dear life was all wrong.") Out in the garden with a new batch of plants to get into the ground, she struggled when Mr. Cayce and Chip both wanted to lean against her. Elizabeth began early trying to teach her nephew the names of plants (later, she was to admit that he was her greatest failure). "This is *Oxalis Bowieana,*" she said, and he "leaned over close and said, 'Hi, Bowiana!' " Chip also liked playing that he was Mr. Cayce, slipping the collar around his own neck and handing the leash to his mother, who "obligingly led him out in the garden." Elizabeth was enthralled. Now as a busy aunt, she had to juggle more things —working still as a volunteer at the Red Cross information center, and writing. "Annie" helped her read galleys on a study guide for the University's library extension services, but though her sister was "a very fine proof reader," it took them several days to do it because they could only read when Chip was asleep, "or on top of us." For three days of steady rain, she had Chip and Mr. Cayce underfoot in her studio: "It took me an hour to get them settled. Then I worked another hour and they were back on top of each other again."

Having a boy and a girl was just about perfect, and Elizabeth found Fuzz "enchanting," but it took two years for her to learn "the intensity beneath. She is so cool and self-contained, with even her tempers like a small storm that is soon over. . . . She hates to be read to, and always takes the book and says, 'No, Aunt, I read to you,' and improvises long stories. She is so sophisticated that it is hard to believe that she is only two. She said, 'Chip, talk if you want to, but lower your voice, and do not shout.' " Fuzz was, the pediatrician had assured her mother, "the brightest two-year-old that he has come across in his practice."[6]

When visitors to Elizabeth's garden told her that they would never be able to have anything that required so much work because they had children, Elizabeth's response was always the same: I have children, too. These early scenes show why she felt this way.

CHAPTER FIFTEEN

The *Move* to Charlotte 1948

I hope that I have done a wise thing and that we will all live in harmony.

ELIZABETH AND BESSIE could look back on their thirty-two years in Raleigh with quiet gratitude: they had lived through two World Wars and the Great Depression, and they had suffered less than most North Carolina families. Their great loss had occurred in 1936 when, after a long illness, Sam had died. They grieved that he had not lived to see Ann marry Warren Way, whose father had been, with Sam, a member of the Sandwich Club. Now that the Second World War was over, however, and Warren was getting out of service, he and Ann wanted to make a new life together with their two children. It was a happy time. When Warren was hired to work for the Internal Revenue Service in Charlotte, and temporary housing at nearby Morris Field became available to former military families who were making the transition back into civilian life, Warren, Ann, "Chip" and "Fuzz" moved to Charlotte.

Meanwhile, Elizabeth had surprised herself by how well she adapted to changes: She had experienced the losses of Nana and her father without faltering, and she had assumed their roles in looking after Bessie, who was now seventy-two years old; she had learned to concentrate on her own work, had made a garden, and had written an excellent first book; and she had made good friends. At forty-four, she was astonishingly youthful. Ellen Flood's daughter, Mary Ellen Reese, remembered how Elizabeth had looked in her forties: "She wore her long hair in a bun, rolled up. Occasionally, she let it down—her hair was soft and long. She was extremely pretty. In life, she came across prettier than in a photograph."[1]

Elizabeth had also discovered for herself a way of life that sustained her. Perhaps she wondered if she would ever live as contentedly again. On varying days in the garden, she had "one sunny breakfast after another," and at night she wrote letters by candlelight in the "Summer House"; on hot summer afternoons she took long soaks in the tub reading Shakespeare sonnets; she lay on the Busbees' couch with her eyes closed while the Busbee sisters sat side by side with their sewing, listening to radio broadcasts of concerts by the New York Philharmonic; at night she sat on the porch steps and played her shepherd's pipe, and heard a nearby neighbor playing hers. There were never enough hours to do all the things she enjoyed doing, and time was "opening and shutting like a fan."[2] Then, with the births of Chip and Fuzz, two new compelling interests had been added to her life; she was not surprised that they meant so much to her—she had always loved childhood, and having a niece and nephew was a way of reliving her own happy memories.

And yet, at the same time, adjusting to changes always took its toll on Elizabeth's emotional energies. Louise Busbee ("Miss Toose") had died, and Elizabeth was feeling very sad. The Busbees had been an "integral part" of her life. Working at the filter center during the war with other volunteers and entertaining soldiers had been fun; now she woke up to find "peace very depressing." After the camaraderie she had experienced in keeping the home fires burning, while many other American women were celebrating a return to traditional family life (marriages were on the increase), suddenly her own struggle for existence was troubling. The worst of it was that her mother had not been well, and Elizabeth felt that she "could not face another depression, and this old house and a sick parent and no servants."[3] Her sister was faithful, but it was hard on Ann and Warren and the children to have to travel back and forth between Charlotte and Raleigh. Elizabeth did not think she could cope alone any longer, and she made the decision herself: she and Bessie needed to move to Charlotte to be near Ann and her family.

"I hope that I am not fooling myself," Elizabeth wrote Ann Bridgers, "but I think that I can do more work if we are not always either going to Charlotte or the Ways coming here. I hope I have done a wise thing and that we will all live in harmony. I am sure that the children will be happier, and that is the most important thing."

By late fall of 1948, Bessie had sold the house for $18,000, six thousand dollars more than they had paid for it, and Elizabeth, who was trying to learn something about finances from her mother, was relieved that they could get as good a price. The neighborhood was changing as many families wanted to move to a suburb. Bessie and Elizabeth had once before gone through the steps of selling an old house and emptying its contents when they had moved Nana from Parkersburg. This time they sold a barrel of family china, but they took boxes of books. For months, Elizabeth had been thinking about how she would design shelves for their new house. The most difficult decision was made for them: they could not take with them the "old and dear and sprawling garden."[4]

The move to Charlotte was begun. Bessie bought the two families adjacent building lots in Charlotte on Ridgewood Avenue, a quiet residential street of lovely but relatively small houses and backyards, near the mansions of prestigious Myers Park. Mostly a neighborhood of young families with children, Ridgewood Avenue was a perfect place for Chip and Fuzz to grow up, but it was a different kind of neighborhood from the one Elizabeth had enjoyed in Raleigh. With her desires focused on the happiness and well-being of the children, Elizabeth seems to have had no requirements for her own life—she was not, after all, a wife and mother, nor was she interested in becoming a member of Charlotte society, which was larger, richer, and more business-oriented than Raleigh's. Elizabeth was willing to take Bessie to a reception of the Colonial Dames at the Myers Park Country Club, because she could rush home to write Ann and Emily Bridgers a long letter about how much Bessie had enjoyed it, and how amusing it all was. Bessie and Ann met people by volunteering at the American Red Cross, and Ann moved easily among members of the Junior League and the arts organizations. None of these, however, was Elizabeth's cup of tea. And yet, Elizabeth

The three Elizabeths: Elizabeth Lawrence, her mother, and her niece looking into the Raleigh garden. In 1948, when Ann, her husband, Warren Way, and their children moved to Charlotte, Elizabeth believed that everyone would be happier if she and her mother, Bessie, lived close by, and so they moved to Charlotte and built a house next door to the Ways. (Courtesy of Robert de Treville Lawrence.)

was prepared to make a life as good as the one she had had in Raleigh, and she plunged in with enthusiasm. One of the great benefits of the move was that Elizabeth was able to design a house around her and Bessie's needs: "a small but roomy house all on one floor," with a living room opening onto a terrace, and a long narrow garden "with flowers around a series of little courts and shrubs beyond." Family and friends were always to remember the simplicity, the beauty, and the peace of the house and garden that Elizabeth created in Charlotte.

For their part, Warren and Ann seemed pleased that they would all be together. Living next door to her mother and sister would mean that Ann would help look after Bessie, and, as it often turned out, her older sister. Ann was quite a good cook, and her sister did not do much more in the kitchen than toss a salad and mix the drinks. Warren expected that Elizabeth would be as self-sufficient as his wife, but in that he was disappointed. But as they all anticipated living in Charlotte, the family dynamic was recognized and admired: they were the attractive sisters who lived next door to each other and looked after their mother. The neighborhood was welcoming. Down the street from where they were building, Eddie and Elizabeth Clarkson had one of the loveliest gardens in the city. There were young children to play with Chip and Fuzz. As families on Ridgewood Avenue looked out their windows to see who was about to build, they were bound to be pleased with what they saw: the tall, handsome man, the small, vivacious wife, the lively tow-headed children, and the little old lady commanding everyone's attention. (In time, according to neighbor Hannah Withers, they would all fall in love with Elizabeth's mother. "Bessie had an opinion on every subject," Hannah remembered. "She was a little Prussian empress, and we all loved her." Once at a party on the Lawrences' terrace, Hannah's daughter, Hannah Withers Craighill, overheard Bessie correcting a guest who had called her "Bessie": "The brevity of our acquaintance does not merit your use of my Christian name.")[5] What most of the families on Ridgewood Avenue did not know was that "the southern gardener" was about to become a neighbor, and that their children would be invited to tea and taught the names of flowers, which they told their mothers were Miss Lawrence's "friends."

Before Christmas, Elizabeth and Bessie had settled themselves into a rented house on Melbourne Court in Charlotte, while their house and the Ways' house were being built. At once Elizabeth saw the advantage of living all on one floor, and she and her mother got along very well without employing anyone to help them. With Ann and Warren busy getting their own family established in Charlotte, Bessie and Elizabeth had time to spend with the children. One of the things they enjoyed most was taking Chip and Fuzz to church. The Ways and Elizabeth and Bessie all joined St. Peter's Episcopal Church in downtown Charlotte. Elizabeth took great pleasure and pride in showing up with two such attractive children, and she loved to write Ellen Flood and the Bridgers family in Raleigh about their Sunday mornings. Those old friendships continued unbroken. Ellen, against everybody's wishes, thought nothing of driving through the night from her house in Connecticut to visit the Lawrences and Ways in Charlotte. As the years passed and her mother died, Ann Bridgers stayed in Raleigh more, feeling that she needed to do as much as she could to help Emily, who had become more crippled, but both of them continued to read Elizabeth's manuscripts. Elizabeth did not like going back to see her house because it had begun to look very shabby, but an overnight visit with the Bridgers family was a tonic, especially when her mother's health failed, and the times were hard.

For hard times would descend upon Elizabeth, but in 1948 as they were starting over in Charlotte, it was an exciting time for Elizabeth because she got to make important decisions. She had designed the one-story house that she and Bessie would share—it was just as she had envisioned. It had the look of a cottage, with gray shingles, and the front door opened into a small entrance hall that could be closed off from the rest of the house (perhaps an informal version of the entrance hall to the Victorian house on Ann Street), with the kitchen on one side of the front hall, and Bessie's room and bath on the other. Elizabeth's bedroom was next to her mother's, and her studio was in the back, where she could look out a bank of windows into the garden. She designed a long counter to serve as a desk, and below it were drawers that would never be enough to contain her multiple files and papers. When she had guests, she would give them her bedroom, and sleep on the daybed in the study. The best feature of the house was the living room, with a lovely fireplace and corner bookshelves, and a long, plain refectory table for dining, next to the window, on the Ways' side. In later years a stand of bamboo would afford both families a measure of privacy. Across the back of the house, French doors opened onto a terrace and rock garden.

Next door the Ways' house was red brick and accommodated a family—with bedrooms for children, and a family room. Neither of the narrow rectangular yards had been landscaped, and it was Elizabeth's expectation that she would garden both in her yard and in Ann's.

As the years passed, as shrubbery was allowed to grow up between the two houses, and Warren consistently turned down Elizabeth's offers to take the overflow of plants from her garden to his, Elizabeth accepted that gardening was her passion and not Ann's or Warren's. While Elizabeth was creating a garden to ensure her privacy, Warren's privacy depended on the success of maintaining a separate household in such close physical and emotional proximity to the one next door. No matter—Ann was a marvel at making everything work, and everyone depended on her to do so. Perhaps what had not been discussed was how she was to do it; after all, she and her sister had lived apart since they had gone off to college, and in the intervening years, their lives had taken different directions. As long as Bessie could run things next door, and Elizabeth could garden, Ann was free to live her own life, and it was freedom that the irrepressible Ann had always enjoyed.

After Elizabeth had designed the house, she turned her attention to designing a garden that perfectly served her needs, having learned in Raleigh that a garden is a place for people as well as plants. Across the front of the lot, she planted various species of sasanqua so that there would be a sequence of blooms. A pink climbing rose, Old Blush, was planted to grow up a black cherry tree near the front door. The design of the private garden behind the house was simple and symmetrical—five intersecting paths and four rectangular beds. The paths were laid with Catawba pea-gravel and wide enough for two to walk together to a pool at the center, where they could sit on a bench. She designed an allée of cherry laurels, running down a narrow bed from the house to the back of the lot, and when they grew and she kept them pruned, they looked like parasols, throwing a feeling of the warm Mediterranean over the whole garden. She laid rock steps leading down from the terrace; wide perennial beds on three gradually descending levels, each defined by a rock wall; and a back garden of pine trees and shade plants.

Against the back wall there was a bench, and against the wall a bas-relief Madonna. All in all, Elizabeth had perfectly fulfilled her own requirement that a garden have "pattern and privacy."[6]

Elizabeth believed that gardens also needed features such as statuary, a pool, a sundial, a gate—whatever reflected the sensibilities of the gardener. The garden must have an intimate relationship with the house, and life in the house should flow into the garden. She opened up the space by taking the central path to the back of the garden, where there was a "room" of pines and shade plants. She designed her garden for color (mostly light pastels) and for fragrance (evergreen daphnes, sweet box, osmanthus and Confederate jasmine). But Elizabeth was still think-

After moving from an old and sprawling garden in Raleigh, Elizabeth drew a simpler design for the barren backyard that became her new garden in Charlotte. She described it as "a small city back yard laid out in flower beds and gravel walks, with a scrap of pine woods in the background." Outstanding features included an allée of cherry laurels, intersecting paths, and rectangular beds. (By permission of Kirk McCauley.)

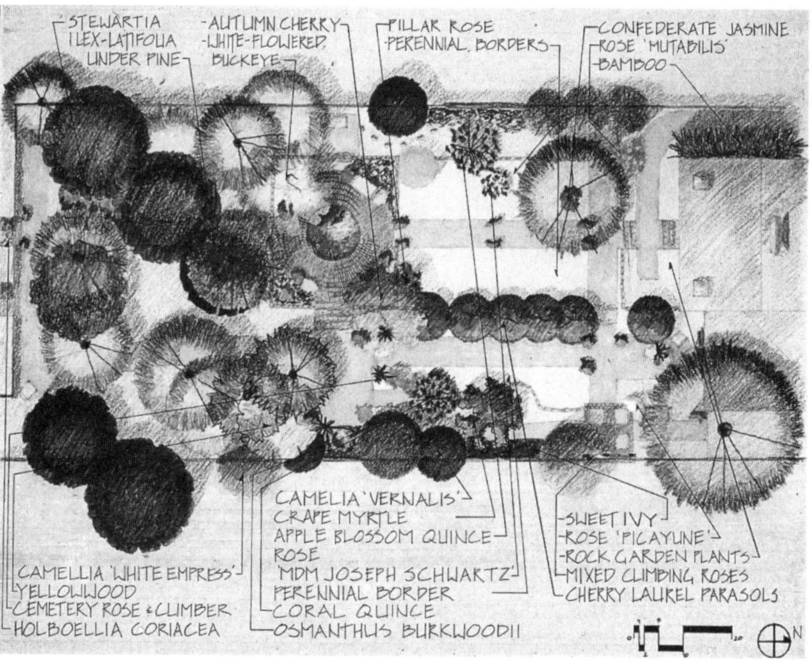

ing about plants she had left in the Raleigh garden. She enlisted Isabelle Bowen Henderson's help in trying to find out what was still blooming, and whether the new owners would allow her to remove more plants. Henderson, however, felt more comfortable sharing plants from her own garden than she did intruding upon the new owner of the house on Park Drive. She dug up hemorocallis, ferns, irises ("Starshine has the finest substance and form of any iris I know"), and a few canna ("they perform best when everything else is used up and pooped").[7] Elizabeth returned with Isabelle's plants after a visit with the Bridgers family, and she was comforted by putting them into the soil in her new garden. Having plants from the gardens of friends was always a great comfort, and in time, as the Charlotte garden became crowded with what they had shared, she could walk among her "friends."

Little by little, Elizabeth planted, and the garden grew, as hundreds, thousands of new plants—natives and exotics—were added. After she had lived seven years in Charlotte, Elizabeth observed, "I find that the new garden—although about a quarter of the old one's size—demands exactly as much time of me as the old. It demands every single moment that I have to spare, and every ounce of strength that I have left in me."[8]

Chip and Fuzz ran freely back and forth between the two houses, where "Aunt," as they called her, allowed them to play in the pool with their friends and to help in the garden. Elizabeth always had a special way with children, talking to them as she would to an adult. She observed about herself, "I have always been in sympathy with the very old and the very young."[9] The vulnerability of children was something Elizabeth Lawrence felt very acutely all her life, and her capacity to experience what children experienced made her especially sensitive to their needs. Now that they were growing up and she saw how soon they would be gone, she dropped everything when Chip and Fuzz had time for her, no matter how much work she had to do at her desk or in the garden. Ann and Warren were generous parents, who allowed Elizabeth to develop this very important role in their children's lives. Chip and

Fuzz did not think of her as another mother—she was their aunt. And they knew not to carry tales between the two houses. Although there were inevitable frictions, as there always are between sisters and neighbors (intensified, perhaps, when sisters *are* neighbors), they did not involve the children. Since Aunt did not have to discipline them, they enjoyed a sense of freedom. Each had a special day to go visit Aunt. She would set up card tables for supper in front of the fire in winter. Even as a young boy, Chip knew that he was going to be an engineer, and he shared his interest in science with his aunt, whom he regarded as a scientist herself. He reminded her of her father. She gave him a box with index cards to make notes about his own experiments. They discussed current events, and she enjoyed having him explain the *New Yorker* cartoons to her. Elizabeth remained an ardent Democrat and shared her passion for John F. Kennedy with Chip, who felt the same way she did. Fuzz also had her special rituals; she was sometimes allowed to bring a girl friend, and the two of them would lie on the couch and read. Sometimes Fuzz went up in the attic to find a scarf or costume she could dress up in. Annually she got the urge to grow something, and she would come over and Aunt would help her pot some plants; when they died, she would come back and try again. Fuzz was observant and intuitive. Elizabeth had been wearing pants for many years—as a young girl she wore knickers—and now she wore jeans to work in the garden. "Aunt, what are you going to do now that pants are fashionable?" Fuzz teased her, and Elizabeth laughed with delight. (It was exactly the sort of teasing that her father had always been known for.)

Friends talked about what a "good team" Elizabeth and Ann were in looking after Bessie, but they also appreciated their differences. Neighbors got to know Ann more easily; Elizabeth seemed much shyer. This difference was obvious at the Clarksons' annual Christmas party. Elizabeth—whose best clothes were sometimes borrowed from her sister, and who added only a trace of lipstick in honor of the holiday occasion—sat quietly and let friends come one by one to her. Friends later remembered her "whispery voice," and something more dramatic —"a hush before she spoke, a silence just before something is about to happen."[10] Ann moved easily into the room, happily greeting friends. She was outgoing and sociable—"loquacious" was the word her classmates had used to describe her in the St. Mary's yearbook. Busy as a wife, mother, and community worker, she had reason to expect that her older sister would be capable of doing more than just gardening, which Ann was beginning to think was not as hard as housework. Over time, especially after the children were off at school and Ann was working in the opera office, she had reason to wonder why the Southern gardener hadn't learned to cook. While Elizabeth was showing visitors through her garden and receiving accolades for her newspaper columns and books, the spunky girl who had known exactly how to organize Macy's was keeping house. Elizabeth, for her part, took for granted that someone would look after her—someone always had. Even Elizabeth recognized the power that her mother held over her. In 1954 she explained herself to her friend Caroline Dormon: "My mother, who is seventy-nine, and I have lived alone for so long, that I cannot bear to think how I could ever live without her—not but what we quarrel all day long—but I never come in the house without calling, 'Bessie, where are you!' and if she has gone next door to my sister's, I am much annoyed."[11]

One of the great benefits of Ann's marriage was that it enlarged the family circle. They had all known the Ways at St. Mary's, and Elizabeth especially admired Warren's sister Evelyn, who also had not married. Elizabeth visited her on several occasions when she was lecturing in Oxford. Warren's brother Roger, a doctor, and his wife Connie and their children were also great favorites. Elizabeth kept up with them with letters and gifts, and when they visited next door, she always invited them to her house. Sometimes when there were too many guests at Ann's and Warren's, the "overflow" stayed with her. Bessie and Elizabeth had always felt that they were too few, and when Ann married, one of the great joys for them was the increase of family. Elizabeth also made new friends: Hannah and Ben Withers, Elizabeth and Eddie Clarkson, and Dr. Walter Brem Mayer and his wife Helen were regulars for cocktails at both houses, and the Ways and the Lawrences were handsomely entertained at their parties. Little by little, and apparently without any explicit acknowledgment of the expansion of their roles, Warren and Ann increasingly looked after the house next door. Elizabeth was, as everyone should have known, a dependent person; she thrived as long as she had family members around. Things ran smoothly as long as Bessie was able to keep up with their expenses and pay the bills, Warren was next door to answer Elizabeth's questions, about termites, for example, and Ann helped entertain her sister's guests. The children were growing up to be very lively conversationalists at the dinner table, and Elizabeth delighted in writing to her friends to tell them what Chip and Fuzz were doing and saying. Elizabeth not only had the excitement of a new garden, she was writing another book—about bulbs and her friend Mr. Krippendorf. Then when someone at the Charlotte *Observer* asked her to write a garden column and she agreed, she had a local audience and a chance every week to pursue a new subject. The phone rang with calls from friends and strangers who wanted her advice about what to plant, and she was eager to give it. In some instances they hired her to help with a particular garden problem, and she began referring to her "clients." Year by year, Charlotte was home to Elizabeth, who for the first time was the acting head of a household.

Sometime in 1957, however, things changed dramatically for Elizabeth; her mother had a stroke. For the next eight years Bessie lay in bed, alternately agitated and silent. Ann and Elizabeth met every day to confer about her care, and a system was established with around-the-clock nurses. But as anyone knows who has looked after an older relative at home, the system breaks down when someone cannot come at the assigned hour, and a family member must take over. Elizabeth was that person, and she found herself unable to leave home for fear that something would happen in her absence. Returning from a lecture tour to Louisiana and Mississippi, she no sooner had set down her suitcase than she had to go in and sit with her mother during the night. When the stresses of caring for her at home began to intensify, the relationship between Ann and Elizabeth was burdened by more responsibilities and their shared sadness at their mother's decline. Friends who had known Bessie when she had been so lively also hated to hear that she no longer got any pleasure out of life.

Day after day, and year after year, however, life went on in both houses. Ann usually did the grocery shopping and some of the cooking. Guests were always dropping in at Elizabeth's, but it was Ann's meringues that were the hit of parties. In the spring of 1959 Frederick G. Meyer, who directed the National Arboretum in Washington, and his wife came to Charlotte to visit Elizabeth for several days. Ann helped entertain her sister's houseguests, and when they returned, Meyer wrote to thank them "for the good old Southern hospitality at its best."

Bessie had been a great example to her daughters: both Elizabeth and Ann knew how to entertain guests. It was a great distraction for Elizabeth to go on having company, and she was learning how to do it without Bessie. One of her favorite and most frequent guests was Hannah Withers, and she told readers of her column about Hannah's knowledge of old roses, and how she loved "living in the past" with her. When Claude Barr, a nurseryman from South Dakota, showed up while Elizabeth was entertaining Hannah, Elizabeth wrote Ann and Emily Bridgers one of her delightful narratives about the visit. Her letter demonstrates how well she could rise above the sorrows in her house when friends were at hand and the subject was gardening.[12]

> It was my lucky day—night, I mean. Instead of being here alone (with Bessie awake and calling, no food, and me uncombed), I had just brushed my hair, made a wonderful fire, set a little table before it, and had a casserole in the oven. It was already dark (6:30), and Hannah and I had just poured a second drink (and Bessie had just fallen asleep) when the bell rang, and I found on my doorstep a rakish figure that I thought at first was Sherlock Holmes, but on second glance saw that the cap was not a deerstalker, and the pepper-and-salt-coat was not an Inverness cape. Before I could re-adjust, he said, "Claude Barr." Well! I had thought he was safe on his cattle ranch in South Dakota.
>
> So I said (not "come to my arms, my beamish boy," as he might not be

really literate, but he looked it), "Hannah, here is Mr. Barr that I have written to for thirty years and never seen before," and "what will you have to drink? We are having bourbon." He said bourbon would be fine, and I remembered that Dr. Wherry once said when he visited the Barrs on their cattle ranch he found them living on skimmed milk, so I decided to give him a glass of sherry. Which seemed to be acceptable. While he drank this, he fixed his eye on Hannah, took a sheaf of photographs out of his pocket, and gave her a briefing on the climate and soil of the High Plains and Badlands, and embarked upon a detailed account of their flora. No mention was made of dinner, or "will you . . . " I just got another plate, gave myself a paper napkin (instead of a linen one) and began to assemble the meal. As I went back and forth, Mr. Barr was saying to Hannah, "This is *Astragalus gilviflorus* not *Orophaca caespitosa*, as Rydberg erroneously called it. And this is *Astragalus spatulatus* (no one but a fool would call it *Homalobus caespitosus*), taken in a canyon right after a flash flood." And Hannah was looking as if there was nothing in the world that she would rather hear about. I said, "Dinner is served." I had to say it twice.

Mary [the housekeeper] came in while we were at dinner, and I said, "Mr. Barr, where are you planning to spend the night?" He said vaguely, "I suppose there is some sort of motel nearby?" I said he had better stay here, and without further comment he turned to Hannah, and said, "Now Alexander, at the New York Botanic Garden, did not know that *Guterrezia sarothrae* occurs west of the Rockies . . . " so I slipped out, and Mary and I made my bed up, and I went into the studio and put everything that was on the cot under it. And then I said to Mary, we had better do the dishes while we have Mrs. Withers, so we did; and just as we finished Ben came for Hannah. I don't think Mr. Barr really knew when Hannah left and I took her place, for he was saying, "That is the only place I have ever found *Lesquerella spatulata,*" and he went on without any break in his thoughts. All I could think of was Mary's gesture as she poured my untouched drink down the drain, as she started on the dishes. Mary is a tee-totaller. . . .

After Hannah left, I said Mr. Barr must be tired after his long day: lunch, and hours in the garden at Tryon; the long drive; and more hours inspecting the Mauney's Yucca collection at Bessemer City (he would have been there still, and not here, if Mrs. Mauney had not tried to get him to look at her china—it was a rare collection he could see, but he had plants on his mind, so he told her he must come on to me), but he said, "Not at all." My eyes were glazed, and one whole side was cramped (ordinarily, I can, like Hannah, listen to the ways of *Astragalus* all night, but just before dinner I had almost thought of telling Hannah not to come), when, at last, he reluctantly laid down the last photograph, *Oxytropis Lamberti* (please remember that the accent is on the ante-penult), and said, accusingly, "You are asleep."

I had a good night, and when he came to breakfast (having asked him not to appear until Mary got her breakfast, then Bessie's, and arranged that he was to have my bathroom all the time, and Bessie's, while he shaved, as mine has no plug for an electric razor), I had pencil and paper ready, and had organized my thoughts to take advantage of this opportunity of a lifetime: Mr. Barr in Charlotte. While he ate, I questioned and took notes. Suddenly, he looked up, and said (we were in the kitchen). "Here comes Mrs. Withers." It was my sister Ann, just arriving with the week-end roast, which comes to me on Tuesday.

I think I made a mistake to take him into the garden. He looked like Rip Van Winkle dropped in Times Square. In a little bit, while I pointed out *Sternbergia fischeri* almost in bloom, and wondered how he could fail to smell the perfume of *Viburnum fragrans* with one bud already expanding, and showed him the Chinese Witch Hazel that will bloom by next week, and the lovely seed heads (remember?) of *Clematis cirrosa,* he began to shiver, and said he would like to go inside. He looked suddenly old and tired; he said, "I don't know anything." . . . .

It was nearly noon when he said he must be getting on to Lynchburg, where he is going to see a man who is writing a monograph on *Ruellias.* He said he wouldn't have lunch, but would like a sandwich to take along. Just as he was leaving I saw a glint of violet under the kitchen window, and there was a perfect iris just out. He drove off with it in his buttonhole.

Bessie's decline was arduous for Elizabeth, though having helped care for her mother's grandmother, her mother's mother, and her own father had conditioned her to know what to expect. She was older, however, and she no longer had her mother to look after the household. Now she turned to the house next door. Like his father at his age, Chip attended Virginia Episcopal School, and like her mother at her age, Fuzz went to St. Mary's in Raleigh. At a time when Ann and Warren would have had more time for themselves, Ann was constantly needed next door, and she went, faithfully. Both she and Elizabeth continued to live their own lives, and they prided themselves on the fact that they were both independent. But Elizabeth's independence was more illusory, for it meant that she did not need help as a writer and gardener, but that she did need help in looking after their mother and in running a household. Many times Bessie seemed not to know anyone, but when Hannah Craighill took her new baby in for Bessie to see, Bessie rocked her arms when she saw the child, although she did not speak. Elizabeth and Ann recognized that their mother was dying, but when the minister offered to come to the house, they declined his offer, believing that their mother would not be aware that he had come. Then one day when he asked, they agreed that he could come, and he arrived prepared to serve Holy Communion. Bessie had appeared to be unaware of his presence as he stood at her bedside, but then as he began reading from the Book of Common Prayer, she suddenly opened her eyes, sat up, and recited along with him, "On the night in which he was betrayed he took bread. . . ."[13]

When Bessie died—July 31, 1964—Elizabeth and Ann felt relief that their mother's suffering was over. But now that her mother was gone, Elizabeth could easily have panicked, her depression quickening. Instead, at least as her own health remained relatively good, she began to rally.

CHAPTER SIXTEEN

The Little Bulbs

This is a tale of two gardens: mine and Mr. Krippendorf's. Mine is a small city back yard laid out in flower beds and gravel walks, with a scrap of pine woods in the background; Mr. Krippendorf's is hundreds of acres of virgin forest.

ELIZABETH LAWRENCE, *The Little Bulbs*

NINETEEN HUNDRED FIFTY-SEVEN was an especially good year for Elizabeth Lawrence. A second book had been published, *The Little Bulbs,* on a topic that she had written about since the early 1930s. She also had recently begun writing a weekly garden column for the Charlotte *Observer*. And although she had already established her habit of naming gardeners, giving us their advice and manner of speaking, and placing them in their own settings, nowhere did she make a person come more alive than in writing about Mr. Krippendorf. Readers who opened the book to find Elizabeth Lawrence and to get information on colchicums or hardy cyclamen discovered another gardener with even *more* bulbs. "Who is Mr. Krippendorf?" they wanted to know. No one in her gardening cast of characters became more beloved of readers than Mr. Krippendorf. Although Lawrence had corresponded with him for many years and had visited his woodland estate, she still observed the formality of manners in print: Mr. Krippendorf belonged in the company of Miss Jekyll, Mrs. Loudon, and Miss Dormon, as well as lesser-known gardeners—Mr. Ainsley, Mr. Bullock, and Mr. Hayward, who also figure in the cast of *The Little Bulbs.*

In April of 1945 Lawrence had been invited to speak to the Garden Club of America, meeting in Cincinnati, and she was nervous about speaking and about meeting Mr. Krippendorf for the first time. After a long afternoon walk together, however, they agreed to call one another "Elizabeth" and "Carl." Mr. and Mrs. Krippendorf lived in a large, rustic lodge, built in 1899, picturesquely set at the top of a hill on the edge of Lob's Wood, their woodland estate. If Lawrence ever saw a marriage she might have envied, it could have been the Krippendorfs': Mary and Carl (born about the same time as her parents) were both very distinctive people—Carl was a great gardener, Mary a great reader—and they were completely at home with each other. During Elizabeth's visit, when members of a garden club appeared and called out to be made welcome, Mr. Krippendorf (which is how she introduced him to her readers) called back to say they should make themselves at home, and never took his attention away from Elizabeth and Mary. Although the Krippendorfs, too, were to have hard times—Mrs. Krippendorf went blind and could no longer read, and Mr. Krippendorf grew old and sick and could no longer wander about his beloved woods—both had the lives they wanted. In 1957, their daughter, Rosan Adams, wrote Elizabeth that, when a copy of *The Little Bulbs* arrived, she had never seen "Fantie" "so pleased about anything. He fairly beams whenever the book is mentioned, and even checked with me, to make *sure* that I had read the dedication—an unheard of thing for him."[1] "To Carl with Love" is what the dedication said. Mr. Krippendorf's granddaughter, Mary (Stambaugh), was to remember that Elizabeth Lawrence became "a fixture in our family. My grandfather had an old typewriter, and he wrote to her everyday. My grandmother didn't care. My grandfather was a charming man, and women loved him. And Elizabeth was an attractive woman. One might think her a helpless southern lady, but she was a steel magnolia. She did let men take her arm."[2]

Lawrence had been introduced to Mr. Krippendorf in 1943 when he wrote to say that he had read an article she had written on amaryllids and to tell her about the ones he grew at Lob's Wood, near Cincinnati, Ohio. The Krippendorfs had named their estate for one of the

Carl Krippendorf and his woodland estate near Cincinnati, Ohio, were the subjects of Elizabeth's book The Little Bulbs, *and he became a great favorite with her readers. (Courtesy of Mary Stambaugh and the Cincinnati Nature Preserve.)*

characters in James M. Barrie's play *Dear Brutus,* whose "endless wood of great trees" is a place of magic. This letter began a correspondence that continued over "ten Ohio springs—and ten summers and falls and winters as well."[3] Both the North Carolina and the Ohio gardener always found something of beauty or interest to tell one another. Lawrence confessed to her readers, "Sometimes I am not so sure which is more real to me: finding an early flower in my own garden, or following Mr. Krippendorf's solitary ramblings across his wooded hills." Mr. Krippendorf expressed his own vivid observations in one of hundreds of letters: "I do think the last two days were the darkest I ever saw. The ground leaves have dried out, and have not the rufous color they have when wet. When wet, they seem to emanate light."

The opening pages of *The Little Bulbs* begin in Lawrence's most sustained narrative voice. She loved fiction too much—especially the stories of Jane Austen and Willa Cather—not to have fallen under the spell of bringing characters to life. The dilemma for Lawrence was that Mr. Krippendorf *was* real, and she was too faithful to her facts to feel free to "make up" a story. Thus, she had difficulty sustaining the narrative, and in later chapters, when she turned to naming and describing bulbs, she sounded more like a scientist and less like a creative writer. For those looking for information, however, the book is an amazing discovery. Here is an *authority*. Other readers will regret the absence of the mysterious voice that spoke to them in the preface and first chapter of the book, as in the following:

> At the top of one hill there is the house, and at the bottom is a clear, wide creek. On the far side of the creek the limestone banks are hung with ferns and wild flowers. On the near side is a little green meadow, long and narrow and embroidered with blue phlox. A broad path winds from the house to the meadow, with gray bridges across the ravines. In the steep places are steps made of great, flat stones drawn up from the creek bottom. From the main path, tributaries lead to other parts of the woods. Along these you can walk up and down hill for hours and never come to an end of squills and daffodils. When the leaves are off the trees, you can see through the branches to other hills, far away. Those hills are wooded too, and I suppose they are full of bulbs. There is nothing else in sight—only Mr. Krippendorf in his leaf-colored jacket with a red bandanna about his neck.

The first chapter of the book, "First Flower," begins: "As soon as spring is in the air Mr. Krippendorf and I begin an antiphonal chorus like two frogs in neighboring ponds: What have you in bloom, I ask, and he answers from Ohio that there are hellebores in the woods, and crocuses and snowdrops and winter aconites. Then I tell him that in North Carolina the early daffodils are out but the aconites are gone and the crocuses past their best." We find out that the man with the red bandanna learned to read in McGuffey's schoolbooks, that he had planted bulbs for more than forty years, that in early March he came home from a walk with a flower in his buttonhole, that he counted seeds in a thimble, that he had tens of thousands of winter aconites, that he used to have dinner with Louise Beebe Wilder at the New York Saint Regis and talk about plants, and that he is like Lawrence's father—a charming teaser. "I was surprised to hear of the paucity of bloom in your garden," he writes to Elizabeth, "as I once read a book by an Elizabeth Lawrence who listed quantities of plants that bloomed in February or even January in her garden which she alleged was in Raleigh, North Carolina."

By the end of the first chapter, Lawrence has created a believable character. The second chapter is called "Things as Helps Themselves"—what the little maid in *The Secret Garden* calls crocuses, snowdrops, and daffodils that "spread out an' have little 'uns." It begins, "The children next door came over this afternoon to ask for space for a garden. This happens every spring and fall, or whenever they see me planting something. I always allot a piece of ground, which they lay off neatly with a border of stones. Then they go about the business of digging and planting with great energy. . . . Painfully and illegibly they print the names on plastic labels (which always get stepped on before the flower blooms). . . . *Anemone blanda* var. *atrocaerulea, Crocus tommasinianus, Chionodoxa luciliae."* But just as some readers may have settled down for another "tale" of a gardener, Lawrence abandons the narrative voice for the scientific.

Information on the little bulbs makes this book one of Lawrence's most compact guides, where page after page, readers will find entries on hundreds of plants, the familiar and the unfamiliar. Although few readers would have the space (or energy, perhaps) to grow millions, as Mr. Krippendorf did, even one of each kind could bring special pleasure to the small garden.

Although *The Little Bulbs* is a book for knowledgeable gardeners, it also offers something for the novice—an introduction to basic botanical nomenclature: *Leucojum aestivum* is a snowflake; *Galanthus,* snowdrops; one reader was delighted to know that zephyranthes were "rain lilies." Lawrence explained that once she had thought that "experts" spoke only to "experts" but that she had learned differently when she wrote to the New York Botanical Garden asking where she could find *Leucojum autumnale*—and received a gift of bulbs. Here was a voice of experience, reassuring the most uninformed novice among gardeners.

Readers of *The Little Bulbs* come to know the two gardens. Mr. Krippendorf had a series of snowdrops from before Christmas until mid-April: the Byzantine snowdrop before Christmas, *G. elwesii* in January, and *G. nivalis* (in good-sized clumps of white flowers) in February or early March. Lawrence acknowledged that a five-month season was "the work of a lifetime." Mr. Krippendorf was generous in helping other gardeners to acquire some of the plants he had, and Lawrence had acquired the spring snowflake (*Leucojum hiemale*) only after Mr. Krippendorf had dug clumps from his woods and sent them to her. Lawrence reported on her snowflakes, and seemed to anticipate her readers' questions from the kinds of questions she had asked herself. *Leucojum,* from the Greek meaning "white violet," was named because of the fragrance of the flowers, but Lawrence explained that she had learned this from a book. Only by warming the flowers in her hand did she become aware of their subtle perfume. Do not put your trust in names, she warns: in her garden the winter snowflake blooms in spring, the summer snowflake in winter, and the autumn snowflake in summer. The most "adorable" little bulbs for Lawrence were *L. Autumnale,* and *Narcissus juncifolius,* their flowers like "minute crystalline bells." Like the rain lilies, they bloom at intervals, after showers. Remember where you plant them so that you can avoid letting them get weeded out or snipped off, and when the leaves die away in early summer, it is time to set out new bulbs. If you don't get to plant them in the ideal time—in early summer—you might still get good results in the fall.

Readers who liked *The Little Bulbs* were looking for very specific, encyclopedic information, and others who already regarded Lawrence as their garden guide knew that buried someplace in all the minutiae of detail there were surprises for readers patient and curious enough to wait for them. Lawrence had absorbed instinctively a good many lessons the garden had to teach her. "One of the delightful and maddening things about gardens," she wrote in *The Little Bulbs,* "is the way strange things are always turning up, and you never remember having planted them." ("So true," many readers will want to write in the margins.) That is a pretty close description of the delight Lawrence readers share in finding something they hadn't expected in one of her books. If readers' rain lilies disappeared without blooming when they planted them in the recommended damp places, they were glad to know that those in the drier soil of the rock garden might bloom for several seasons. Lawrence is just as confident in teaching her readers how to *be* gardeners as she is in showing them how to garden. "As you go over your notes," she writes, "the flowers that have died on your hands all rise like lovely ghosts to haunt you, and fill you with an irresistible longing to try them again."

Despite Lawrence's pleasure in the book, she had again faced difficulties with publishers. Two years before it was brought out by a small New York publishing house (Criterion Books), the manuscript had been turned down by an editor at Macmillan. Although the editor thought it was charming and authoritative, other readers felt that it was "too limited to make a paying book." They recommended that she try to make Mr. Krippendorf more realistic—several readers first had thought that he was a fictitious person.[4] Ann Preston Bridgers, who had read the entire manuscript, confessed that she had been disappointed that so much of it seemed written not for the "general amateur gardener" but for specialists.[5]

Lawrence took their advice to heart, revised the manuscript, and began *The Little Bulbs* with a description of Mr. Krippendorf, but kept the body of plant information essentially intact. After long delays, the manuscript was finally published in 1957. It immediately found an enthusiastic following, and Lawrence complained that the publisher was not doing enough to promote it. She spent a good deal of time suggesting places where it could be sent for review. B. Y. Morrison, who had seen Lawrence's gardens in Raleigh and in Charlotte, reported that *The Little Bulbs* "represents the findings of many years of gardening, rather then the glib pronouncements of the breathless and ignorant!" William Lanier Hunt pronounced it "an eye opener for Southern gardeners," proving that all kinds of rare and beautiful bulbs could be grown in the region. "That charmer, Elizabeth Lawrence, has done it again," crowed Caroline Dormon from the woods of Briarwood in northwest Louisiana. From Portland, Oregon, Drew Sheppard observed that *The Little Bulbs* demonstrated that "the literary garden book" was not a thing of the past. Writing for a national audience in *The Saturday Review,* Virginia Kirkus recommended it for "the almost-professional gardener," observing that the technical nature of the information was lightened by personal experience. "Refreshing as a spring rain, entertaining as a day at the circus—that's Elizabeth Lawrence's new book," wrote the horticultural editor of *Popular Gardening.*

Sales of the book were boosted when *The Little Bulbs* was chosen by the American Garden Guild Book Club—but that too caused problems, because Lawrence got her hopes up that she finally might be able to make a little money on a book, and then, after persistent efforts, she could not find out from any source exactly how many copies had sold.[6] Ellen Flood was indignant on her behalf and went to bat for her, writing letters, showing up at Criterion Books, and enlisting the help of her husband, Mitchell Reese, who was a lawyer. (Criterion Books, a small publishing house, was in the midst of a merger, and had not given Lawrence the reports they had promised when she had signed a contract.) Eventually, Lawrence received some additional royalties from Criterion (about a thousand dollars), but she was still unable to find out what inventory, if any, was left. She continued to hear from readers who were disappointed that they could not obtain copies.

But, as was always the case with each of Lawrence's books, it was not the critical opinion of reviewers that counted the most with her—it was the flow of letters that started again. Anna Sheets, who gardened in Reidsville, North Carolina, wrote Miss Lawrence: "I know you must be swamped with fan letters along with those full of questions about the 'little bulbs,' but I had to write and tell you that I do love your book, just as I knew I would. I am just real proud that you are a North Carolinian for the whole U.S. will be talking of this book!" And Sheets, like most letter writers, offered to send her a bulb—hers was a "17 Sisters" ("different from Mrs. Hart's in Greenwood, S.C."), which "is later and is cream instead of snow.... Mine came from an old house."[7] From Hastings, in Hawke's Bay, New Zealand, Gertrude Mackay wrote to say that she had checked *The Little Bulbs* out of the library and what a "congenial" book it was (though she had never heard of Raleigh or Charlotte, North Carolina). In Woodstock, New Jersey, Ruth Healey was getting over a cold by reading it page by page and making lists of bulbs (by the time she finished, she expected to be well). Bernard Harkness, recalling that he and Elizabeth Lawrence had been members of the American Rock Garden Society since 1939, summed up her appeal when he praised "the literary excellence that we have come to recognize as Miss Lawrence's mark."[8]

Elizabeth Lawrence and her readers were not done with Mr. Krippendorf, however. When he died in 1964 and his estate was acquired by a nonprofit group and opened to the public as the Cincinnati Nature Center,[9] Lawrence was invited to write about him again. The publication, *Lob's Wood,* was something of a disappointment to her. She had hoped for a large handsome book with full-page color photographs but got, instead, a nicely done seventy-six-page small "booklet." She did, however, answer her readers who wanted to know more about Mr. Krippendorf. After opening the book with the same paragraph that she had used to open *The Little Bulbs,* she added this one:

> Wherever I go, people ask me about Mr. Krippendorf. Some want to know whether I made him up (as if I could!). Once when I was lecturing at the University of Mississippi, not long before he died, I was told that the college engineer wanted to meet me. When I was introduced I said, "What kind of garden have you?" He said he didn't have any. "Then how did you happen to come to the lecture?" "I came because I have something to ask you," he said. "How is Mr. Krippendorf?" When I told him that he was not at all well, he looked troubled. "I was afraid of that," he said. Then I asked how he happened to know about Mr. Krippendorf, and he said, "I picked up a copy of *The Little Bulbs* in the library. After reading about him, I always think of him as an old friend."[10]

Lawrence continued in this vein in *Lob's Wood,* describing the work Mr. Krippendorf did chopping down trees, making wood for the fireplace, counting birds that came to the terrace. She reported that, during one mild season, hellebores had bloomed from Thanksgiving to Christmas. What delight she must have taken in revisiting that happy scene, for in her mind's eye she could see them growing not only at Lob's Wood, but in many gardens where she had shared Mr. Krippendorf's seedlings. His granddaughter, Mary Clark Stambaugh, herself a fine gardener in Newtown, Connecticut, grew up following him around Lob's Wood. She remembered that he "gave things away by the bushel load every month of the year and he never held anything back." (Stambaugh has followed in her grandfather's tradition, so that plants from his seedlings grow in countless gardens.[11]) *Lob's Wood,* like *The Little Bulbs,* is full of Mr. Krippendorf's reports of the life of a gardener who roamed the woods in every season, making a nosegay of double colchicums, pricking out seedlings, picking ripe tomatoes in the kitchen garden, chopping wood, potting up plants, grooming the dry wall, digging bulbs, feeding the birds—and writing Elizabeth to tell her what he had done. Perhaps few books so small ever contained so much of a life well lived.

Elizabeth Lawrence concluded *Lob's Wood* by describing how in November of 1966 she had visited the Nature Center, where she met the director and visited with Mr. Krippendorf's daughter, Rosan Adams. She was pleased to see that his dry wall had been rebuilt and planted with a collection of thymes and other saxatile plants, and that juncos, blue jays, nuthatches, red-bellied and downy woodpeckers, titmice, and Carolina chickadees still came to the terrace. She thought of lines from Dante's *Paradiso,* and translated them: "Those who enter into the life of the forest become one with the leaves in the garden of the Eternal Gardener, and share the grace that has been granted them." It was the most spiritual definition she was to give of a garden.

In 1963 Elizabeth Lawrence attended a meeting of the American Daffodil Society in Stratford, Connecticut, not to see the flowers —which she said she preferred seeing in her own garden—but to see people, especially Mr. Krippendorf's granddaughter, Mary Clark (Stambaugh), and her old friend Ellen Flood, who was living in Connecticut. It was to be a memorable visit—Lawrence's talk and slides were a hit with the audience, and Mary chauffeured Elizabeth and Ellen around, while they sat in the back seat and talked and argued. Mary's mother, Rosan Adams, was also there. It was like old times.[12]

The next year Mr. and Mrs. Krippendorf died within a month of each other, not long before Elizabeth's mother died. Elizabeth had seen the deaths of all three coming (they were all about the same age), but it was unthinkable to be without them. Fortunately, she did what she had always done—she made new friends, mostly through letter writing. She had sent Katharine and E. B. White a copy of *Lob's Wood,* and Katharine wrote back to thank her and to ask her to tell her more about "the fabulous and mysterious Mr. Krippendorf." Elizabeth responded by telling her about Mr. Krippendorf's boyhood, which she had not written about in either book. He was, she explained, the son of German cobblers, who started a small factory in Cincinnati. When his father had a heart attack, young Carl stopped school when he was still in his teen years, and took over the management. By the time he was nineteen, "he knew all there was to know about making shoes." And by the time he was twenty-one, he had made enough money to buy the farm that he named Lob's Wood. He and Mary had married in 1902, and he had driven them thirty miles in a buggy to spend their honeymoon there. Later on, they moved to the woods, where he got up at daylight to work in the woods before Mary took him in a pony cart to the train station to commute to work in Cincinnati.

Then, writing to Katharine White, Lawrence added that unmistakable personal touch of hers (mixing this and that): "Krippendorf-Dittman shoes were good, but not expensive," she explained, "and when Mr. K. learned that I wore the sample size he used to pick them out for me when the salesmen came back to the factory."[13]

Lawrence was to continue to write about "Mr. K." from time to time in her garden columns—one December she wrote about a Christmas rose which came from Mr. Krippendorf, "who dug the plants from his woods and sent the clump with the soil still around it."[14] In addition to sending packages of plants, he also sent Christmas wreaths from Carl Starker's nursery in Oregon, and Dry Sac sherry. He was a generous man who always gave visitors to Lob's Wood a box of plants. Elizabeth's Christmas presents to the Krippendorfs were a pretty little wrap for Mary's shoulders, and for him—a red bandanna, of course.

But again, that was not the end of this tale of two gardeners. In 1986 (the year after Lawrence died), Duke University Press brought out a new edition of *The Little Bulbs,* with an introduction by Allen Lacy. While taking note of Lawrence's attention to the little bulbs themselves, Lacy observed that, thanks to her book, Mr. Krippendorf had become "something of a legendary figure."[15] But perhaps what would have meant the most to Lawrence was the opinion of gardener and garden writer Pamela Harper (with whom Elizabeth enjoyed one of her last correspondences, and whose visits in Charlotte had meant so much to both of them): "*The Little Bulbs* has a timeless quality. It imparts a wealth of practical information with infectious enthusiasm and a charm of style that makes learning effortless. It is one of my most treasured books."[16]

CHAPTER SEVENTEEN

Writing a Garden Column

The Garden Gate is Open; Enter A World of Beauty.

THE HEADLINE that appeared in the Charlotte *Observer* on August 11, 1957, was probably not the first thing that caught the attention of readers who had wandered past the front pages of the Sunday paper. Most may have looked at the picture above the headline, of an attractive woman, slightly smiling, standing just behind a wrought-iron gate, beckoning to readers. The caption read, "Miss Lawrence Opens Her Gate into the World of Gardening." Her friends looked with double appreciation: it was a good picture of "Libba," and wasn't her *Clematis armandii* doing well over the arch?

Lawrence's first column was an auspicious "beginning"—except, of course, that she had been writing for more than twenty years, was the author of two well-received books (*A Southern Garden* and *The Little Bulbs*), and was working on manuscripts for at least three more. Her friends knew that she was no novice, but they were delighted to see her get this kind of local attention. After all, Charlotte was second only to Atlanta in size in the South, and the *Observer* was a good metropolitan newspaper. With a circulation of more than 150,000, Lawrence would have access to her largest audience. Her *Observer* pieces were going to be clipped and mailed to gardeners in other places. And in time, some of them would be edited into a book.

It was a happy assignment for Lawrence. Writing a Sunday column for the Charlotte *Observer* gave her more immediate satisfaction than anything else she ever wrote. Although she did not work well facing book deadlines, she thrived when it came to writing a short weekly column—sometimes she even wrote a few pieces ahead when she made one

Elizabeth Lawrence beckoned to readers of her first garden column, published in the Charlotte Observer *on August 11, 1957, and continued for the next seventeen years to invite them into her garden and into the gardens she had visited and read about. (Courtesy of the Charlotte* Observer.*)*

of her infrequent trips out of town. Thinking up subjects was itself a delight, for she could draw from files of materials, hundreds of letters, a library of books, many gardening friends—and her own active mind. It was good for her to get out and see what was going on in other people's gardens, and she loved writing about them. She was interested in almost everything, and even if she wasn't (she was not interested in flower arranging, for instance), she belonged to the old school of civic duty and was happy to publicize some community garden event. Talking on the telephone was time-consuming and disruptive, but she took calls from friends and strangers alike who responded to something that she had written or asked her to write about something else. Although she found the editor's changes to her pieces as irritating as those made by book editors, she did not waste much energy fighting with him; she needed to get on with the next piece, and her mind was already casting about for what that might be. Every week brought dozens of letters from readers wanting to discuss Sunday's column, and she was glad to answer. Beginning in 1957, and for almost fourteen years, she organized her weekly schedule around writing her column. And although these were her hardest years, because of her mother's bad health, she welcomed the necessity and satisfactions of good work.

So it came as something of a shock in the summer of 1971, when, upon returning from a garden tour to England and Scotland with her good friend Hannah Withers, she was told that the newspaper would no longer carry her column. Her friends were furious, and they wrote the editor to say so. The rumor was that the editor had found her too old-fashioned; she needed to be replaced by someone who could tell people what they wanted to know in a few easy "how-tos." Perhaps the editor couldn't read her handwriting. Perhaps she was too sensitive to criticism and couldn't change with the times. The reasons that she was let go are obscure; Elizabeth Lawrence's feelings were not.[1]

Her last column appeared on Sunday, June 13, 1971. Again, the headline told the story: "Nettles (Ouch) are Good for Cloth, for Herbs, Porridge, and even Beer." "Ouch" did not quite express her pain. The word she chose for how she felt was "heartbroken."

The garden gate had not closed, however, because friends and strangers still made their way to the small gray-shingled house behind the sasanqua hedge. Friends rallied around, and the world went on just as before, though perhaps readers did not find as much "beauty" in the paper as they had been promised on that August Sunday some fourteen years earlier.

For an overview of Lawrence's garden writing for the Sunday newspaper, readers will find a good sampling in *Through the Garden Gate,* a collection of 144 columns, edited by author and gardener Bill Neal and published posthumously by the University of North Carolina Press. Neal, who gardened in Carrboro, near Chapel Hill, describes his own first visit to Lawrence's home in Charlotte on a cold December day in 1974, when he saw that a witch hazel "wreathed the door in gold." Like most first-time visitors, he was drawn back to the house on Ridgewood Avenue, and each time he found new enchantment.

Several years after Elizabeth's death, still missing their good talks, Neal began to "search out" her *Observer* columns, 720 of them, in fact. Slowly, he selected a small number, representing the range of her interests: garden books, the history of plants, the challenges of the modern landscape, flowers of the church calendar, and the gardens of friends. The "great lesson" she teaches us, Neal says, is "fearlessness": trying to see what will grow for us, according to our own desires, and letting other plants go.

She set forth her philosophy in her first article:

> This is the gate of my garden. I invite you to enter in: not only into my garden, but into the world of gardens—a world as old as the history of man, and as new as the latest contribution of science; a world of mystery, adventure and romance; a world of poetry and philosophy; a world of beauty, and a world of work.
>
> Never let yourself be deceived about the work. There is no royal road to learning (as my grandmother used to say). And there is no royal road to gardening—although men seem to think there is.
>
> "Gardening is becoming very popular now that labor-saving devices have taken the hard work out of it," your editor said to me. I gave him a withering look (but he did not wither, and when I questioned this I could see him thinking that I did not know what I was talking about.).

Lawrence responded to her editor with questions: What machine would dig a hole and plant a shrub, or get up early to pick off the dead daylilies, or work on its knees to plant petunias, or sweep the walks, and so on? Apparently, the questions were only rhetorical; she doesn't tell us the editor's answers. As if to say, "that's that," she confided to her readers, "You can see that your editor is not a gardener." She was the writer, after all: she wanted the final word: "Any garden demands as much of its maker as he has to give." Hers was the opinion of a classical gardener (before language became more gender-sensitive). *She* assured her readers that "no other undertaking will give as great a return for the amount of effort put into it."

Perhaps with this first piece the die was cast between columnist and editor, though only one of them—the editor—may have thought so. Lawrence was having fun.

The next week, Lawrence wrote about daffodils needing an early start; the following week, about lilies; and in September she wrote about planting annuals and vegetables for autumn, and about the local garden club. A year later, Japanese loquats, the Australian gum tree, the *Akebia* vine, and the jujube tree were her subjects—and she didn't overlook everybody's known favorites: petunias to replace pansies as the weather turns hot. She was as interested in people as in their plants, and she named them together: *Shortia* was in full bloom in Mrs. Stone's garden on April 8; *Shortia uniflora* came from Mr. Starker in Oregon, and *Crotalaria* seeds from Mr. Barringer in South Carolina; Mrs. Huber had the finest white wisteria. Elizabeth also wrote about herself: her cousin Harriet had sent her a lavender stick from Greece; for thirty years she and her mother had recorded the bloom dates of their gardens, first in Raleigh and then in Charlotte; she had seen blue flags in Northampton County, growing just where she had seen them when she was a child; her grandmother (in Parkersburg, West Virginia) used to buy *Colchicum* bulbs at the five-and-ten and lay them in the library to bloom; Ellen Flood had sent her a job lot of garden books bought at auction; her great-grandmother had raised plantain lilies (hostas, also called "funkias"). And there were garden notes from 1935 describing a midsummer border in her Raleigh garden, and a description of the fragrant garden of St. Peter's Episcopal Church in downtown Charlotte.

She wrote so often about some of her friends that readers began to think they knew them, too: Hannah, Caroline, Dr. Mayer, Elizabeth and Eddie Clarkson, Mr. Houdyshel, Ida Bennett, Mittie Wellford;

B. Y. Morrison (who by the age of five, she told readers, was already interested in gardens). When her editor complained that she seemed to be writing for Hannah and Dr. Mayer, she said that she was, and for many others, too. She called them by first names or titles or whatever came to mind that day, without foolish consistency. It had taken her more than a year of exchanging letters with Mrs. White to call her "Katharine," but she wasn't going to call her that in her column. She tried to remember not to call William Lanier Hunt "Billy," but she usually forgot. Even her readers who were already familiar with Carl Krippendorf's woodland estate knew she was right to call him "Mr. Krippendorf." Still, it must have been somewhat frustrating to the editor at the *Observer,* trying to make Miss Lawrence conform to its style sheet, and on a few occasions, he made suggestions. She meekly agreed, and perhaps she wished also that her typing was better, the length of her pieces predictable, the deadlines more manageable. But she had so little time to worry about such matters. In December, when the thermometer dropped to ten degrees, she had to call around to find out what had escaped the cold: Elizabeth Clarkson's purple aster, brought from her mother's garden in Texas; Mrs. Dowd's Camellia buds, which she had twisted off to avoid putting extra strain on the plant. There were so *many* things to write about.

"Through the Garden Gate" was also an invitation to read, and Lawrence wrote often about her favorite garden literature: Mrs. Loudon's beautifully illustrated garden books for ladies; Vita Sackville-West's long poem, "The Garden"; passages from Thoreau and Colette; books by Louise Beebe Wilder and E. A. Bowles. And everyone should know Liberty Hyde Bailey's monumental reference books on botanical nomenclature (Lawrence used *Hortus Second*). Lawrence devoted one column to a short history of the famous Fruitland nurseries in Augusta, Georgia, started in the mid-nineteenth century by the Belgian immigrant family of Berckmans.

Lawrence challenged her readers not only to cultivate their own backyards but to pay attention to the larger world around them. When Rachel Carson's *Silent Spring*—about the indiscriminate use of pesticides, especially DDT—was published in 1962 and the chemical industry mounted an aggressive attack to discredit her, Lawrence insisted that Carson had the facts right. In a column written in late September, about a month after the book was published (it had appeared serially in the summer, in *The New Yorker*), Lawrence took what for her was an unusual position: she entered a public debate about a very controversial subject. Readers today may have to be told that Carson's book was damned by her critics, but at the time the issue was in the news. Those who wanted to keep people in the dark about what was being done to the environment knew what was at stake, and reacted accordingly. *Silent Spring* (and its critics, ironically) launched the grassroots environmental movement that has made watchdogs of millions of individuals and organizations. In one of her longest columns, Lawrence quoted one critic after another, accusing them of distorting what Carson had said: Carson had not said that chemical pesticides must never be used, but that ordinary citizens needed to be informed about the potential for harm. Like millions of Americans, Lawrence was aroused by Carson's arguments, and she relied on her own penchant for debate to take on "Miss Carson's detractors." Read today, Lawrence's column simply states what many environmentalists (a term Carson made a household word) call "the cautionary principle." This may all seem like tame stuff now, but in the fall of 1962, when the debate about *Silent Spring* was explosive, for Lawrence to weigh in with her weekly garden column showed that she could be brought out of the garden, if only to protect it.[2]

Writing for newspaper readers allowed Lawrence to demonstrate her broad interests, not those of a plant snob but of someone concerned about everything: Mr. Grier's gourds, Jack Mitchell's bees, gardening with children, castor beans and cucumber vines, lawn care, Christmas decorations, highway wildflowers, city beautification, state parks, botanical art, houseplants, and pests. Almost any one of Lawrence's columns was an education in itself. Take bees, for example. From Virgil, we learn to shelter our hives from the wind, to provide them with nearby water, some shade, and fragrant flowers. When a swarm rises, the bees are in search of sweet water and a leafy shelter. We should clash cymbals and scatter bruised balm and the leaves of honey-wort on the place where we want them to go, and they will light on the scented spot. As true today, Lawrence assures us, as it was in Virgil's time. (There are further instructions about rinsing our mouths with fresh water before getting honey from the hive—bees "find strong scents offensive.") But Virgil isn't the only one who knows his bees. Jack Mitchell knows an Indian beekeeper on the Lumber River, who calls Mitchell a honey-thief because he doesn't open the hive with bare hands. Lawrence then cites Belgian writer Maurice Maeterlinck, author of *The Life of the Bee,* who said, "The first time that we open a hive there comes over us an emotion akin to that we might feel at profaning some unknown tomb." Virgil? Jack Mitchell? the Indian beekeeper? Maeterlinck? Who the heck *are* these people, Lawrence's editor must have asked. But Lawrence was writing for the readers who recognized them, or wanted to know them.

As months and years passed, Lawrence became more certain of what she knew and of what readers were willing to learn. Perhaps the nearest thing to Lawrence's columns were those of Vita Sackville-West of Sissinghurst, Kent, England, writing for the London *Observer.* Sackville-West wrote in one of her "snippets," as she called her pieces, "Few of the English—a most sentimental race—can resist the appeal of the buttercup and those gold-besprent meadows of childhood, and the Kingcups growing along the banks of a stream."[3] Lawrence's readers would not have had to ask, "Who is Vita Sackville-West?" Lawrence had already educated them.

On June 20, 1971, when *Observer* readers opened their newspapers to read about what was blooming in Charlotte, they searched and could not find Elizabeth Lawrence's garden column, and they felt bereft. The next week, someone who was writing about gardens called her from the newspaper and wanted some help, and she gave it.

CHAPTER EIGHTEEN

Gardens in Winter

On chance-mild days when an incandescent light falls on thin twigs, throwing their fine shadows across gravel walks, my garden seems more beautiful than ever.

ELIZABETH LAWRENCE, *Gardens in Winter*

Gardens in Winter begins, "I never did care for fair-weather gardeners. Standing behind glass doors, they look out at the cold ground and leafless branches, and exclaim, 'How beautiful this must be in spring!' " This simply written paragraph, garden writer Bobby J. Ward observes, is the "real essence" of Lawrence's book.[1]

Elizabeth Lawrence loved her garden in winter more than at any other season. What could be better than finding three little hoopskirt daffodils ready to open, and having lunch in the sun-catch? There was never a time when she did not find delight in her garden, but there also was no season equal to winter in its capacity for surprise.

Because Lawrence wanted something blooming every month of the year, she looked for plants that would tolerate the coldest months—November, December, January, and February. She believed that the garden year really begins when bulbs break through the ground, and the buds of winter-sweet begin to swell, and the Christmas roses bloom. Usually by the first week in November in her Charlotte garden, a killing frost came on a clear night at the end of a brilliant day, to wipe out all color. But after the dead stalks had been cleared away, underneath she found the first Algerian iris and the violet-colored cups of *Crocus medius*. They were a sight too wondrous to have ever been in doubt.

In addition to plants, Lawrence's literary favorites show up often in this book she wrote about gardens in winter. Again, she quoted from books by old friends—Elizabeth von Arnim, Gertrude Jekyll, and Sir Herbert Maxwell. But poetry dominates. Before she was fifteen lines into her manuscript, she quoted a line from Coventry Patmore, a nineteenth-century English poet: "Sweeter yet than dream or song of Summer or Spring or Winter's sometime smiles." Next she turned to William Cowper's "A Winter Bouquet" ("While earth wears a mantle of snow") and Matthew Arnold's "Thyrsis" ("The winter-eve is warm"). Wordsworth, Austen, and Thoreau also make appearances. Then, with a description of her Boston Aunt Letty sitting out in a Southern winter sun, and with passages from her mother's December garden notes, Lawrence again left her personal signature in garden literature.

To write about the winter garden was one of Lawrence's most persistent dreams, and she began consciously to realize it in garden articles she wrote in the 1930s. In 1955 she directly expressed her wish to readers of the *Bulletin of the American Rock Garden Society* that some gardeners would write about winter bloom.[2] Two years later, however, she decided to take on the assignment herself, and she wrote to tell Caroline Dormon about a new manuscript she was working on, to be called *Gardens in Winter*. Accompanying her letter was a copy of the recently published *The Little Bulbs*. Since Lawrence had been so disappointed in the drawings in that book, she was writing specifically to ask Dormon to illustrate her next book. Dormon was not only a talented plantswoman, but an artist as well. Lawrence had greatly admired her drawings and paintings, in Dormon's book *Flowers Native to the Deep South*. Dormon began at once deciding on which plants to include in Lawrence's *Gardens in Winter;* many of them she would have to grow herself in order to know them intimately. The back-and-forth of progress reports about how plants and the manuscript were coming along constitutes a large, unwieldy, and altogether delightful correspondence.[3]

In the summer of 1959 Lawrence had "gone so far as to gather together the main points about winter in various parts of the country." One of her main observations remained as she had expressed it in an article called "Broad-Leaved Evergreens for the Mid-South," published in 1937 in *House & Garden:* more plants could be grown successfully in winter than most gardeners realized. Now she was in the midst of rereading letters that had helped her to record the names of some 350 plants.[4] As usual, she turned to her correspondents for information about their successes and failures, chief among them Caroline Dormon. In Dormon's letters, written over two decades, were plenty of "facts," but in rereading them, Lawrence told Caroline that she had experienced "a delightful sensation of having been with you for days." Now she was writing to check temperatures at Briarwood; she wanted to "get everything right."[5]

Gardens in Winter, like *The Little Bulbs,* was to be another tale of two gardens—this time, her own and Caroline Dormon's one hundred acres of pinewoods in northwest Louisiana.

In the writing of *Gardens in Winter,* Lawrence made a small but effective change in her style. She had been told by various readers that *The Little Bulbs* seemed to have been written not for the general reader but for specialists (an opinion that Lawrence herself later agreed with). Readers had responded well to her tale of Mr. Krippendorf, and, in fact, they had asked to know more about him. In *Gardens in Winter,* Lawrence sketched more scenes that required no special knowledge. Here is just one example of a lively vignette:

> In summer birds keep to themselves; in winter they come closer to people and houses. A cardinal who used to live in our garden summered with his family in the shrubbery, but in winter he always slept in the bamboo outside the living room window. His wife would follow him, but he drove her away. Cardinals are devoted fathers at the nesting season, but afterward they like to go back to their bachelor ways. This one would arrive at the window every afternoon at tea time, and flutter and twitter, and peer inside. When it grew dark he would settle on the cane of bamboo nearest the house, and when we sat down to dinner he would be fast asleep. We could see him by the candle light, handsomely red on his green perch. Sometimes in midwinter when I was up before daylight, I would find him

there, still asleep. One morning he came to the window, and found us sitting by the fire having elevenses. After that he made a habit of coming to the bamboo every morning at eleven.

We are told in the next paragraph that during a mild December Elizabeth and Bessie had elevenses in the garden, at the same time, in the same spot; and had been joined by a mockingbird. At Caroline Dormon's, wrens nested in a basket, and a phoebe slept on a twig of the Lady Banksia under the end of the porch roof. Caroline fed them cornbread. The Lawrences fed their birds suet left over from making Christmas puddings.

Lawrence continues in this narrative voice in a section she called "A walk in the woods." Beginning with an epigraph from Tennyson's "Merlin and the Gleam"—"a wintry glimmer/On icy fallow/and faded forest"—she told this story: "On a cold, wet day in winter I walked into a bare, open wood that had once been cut over. Now, all that was left was a second growth of stunted oaks that looked as if life had been drained out of them with the falling of their leaves. Rain had washed the soil away, leaving only the dark bones of the earth to support the spiritless trees on a hillside as colorless as anything in nature can ever be." Soon, she discovered an "enchanted forest," where everything was encrusted with color and design—filigree of silver upon the boles of trees, emerald and malachite on the forest floor, mosses like polished stones, rocks of oxblood and cinnamon. "Nothing moved, no animal, no bird. The air was still." By journey's end, she had turned back to a stony ridge, reminded of Thoreau's "It is a lichen day."

Lawrence's efforts to find a publisher for *Gardens in Winter* began with months of waiting to hear from Criterion Books, which had published *The Little Bulbs* in 1957. While she worked at her desk, weeds in the garden were so thick that she dreamed about them. Since answers about the sale of *The Little Bulbs* had not been forthcoming, Ellen Flood and other friends had urged her to look elsewhere for her next book, and she had agreed. Flood herself went to the Criterion office and retrieved the manuscript. Caroline Dormon had discovered an editor at Harper & Row who was interested in gardening manuscripts, and when Lawrence wrote to him about hers, she was offered a contract. Dormon was less able to deal with editors than Lawrence, and she had demanded that her own manuscript, *Flowers Native to the Deep South,* be returned. With a change of editors at Harper and the usual delays in sending letters and revisions back and forth, Lawrence became discouraged. Her fatigue is reflected in the corrections, insertions, and smudges in her revised manuscript, which sometimes make it look as if she had done battle. She complained to Caroline, "Nothing is so hard on me as arguing." The two writers were mostly bothered by the hurry-up-and-wait mentality they felt was being imposed upon them. Deadlines and changes made them both nervous: Elizabeth said that she simply could not "think" under such conditions.

Although Lawrence often found editors trying (even those she liked), the main problem facing her now had nothing to do with them. It was life at home that was interfering with her work. Her mother had had a stroke, and Elizabeth was looking after her at home, with shifts of helpers. As she wrote to Caroline Dormon, "I got a lot done early this summer, about a third of the book, and I am hoping to be able to finish it by spring, but I cannot promise anything, when my time is not my own." She was having a "wretched time." In May 1960 she "nearly went to pieces" trying to keep nurses with her mother. She "wrote all day every day for ten hours, and then nursed until eleven." In addition to the book, she felt that she must do a plant design for a new clinic recently built by her mother's doctor and close gardening friend, Dr. Walter B. Mayer. Add to that, she and Ellen Flood (and Ellen's son-in-law, who was a lawyer) were trying to resolve the question of royalties and inventory for *The Little Bulbs.*

The most enjoyable side of working on the new manuscript was that Lawrence discussed it with Caroline, who spent about two years growing and studying many of the plants and working on the drawings. Lawrence paid her about ten dollars a drawing, and when they were finished, Lawrence was delighted. She was happiest that Caroline's drawings would have a national audience and that *Gardens in Winter* might help sell Dormon's own book. "What pleases me most," she told Caroline, "is that people say that the drawings and the writing go together. Nothing could flatter me more."[6] When she sent Caroline an autographed copy of *Gardens in Winter,* she said again, "What I like best about the book is that it has [the drawings] and you, too.[7]

Although *Gardens in Winter* was admired by reviewers and letter writers, only a few of them commented on Lawrence's knowledge of garden literature. One of the critics who did was Carol Woodward, writing in the Sunday *New York Times* about the year's best gardening books. In singling out *Gardens in Winter,* Woodward noted that Lawrence, like most of the writers she was recommending, referenced writers of the past, "a sign of cultural maturity" and a sign that gardening now occupied an important place in American life. Woodward also noted, "Her own writing gives ample evidence that the lights and shadows, silhouettes and traceries, varied greens and occasional flowers give a garden special beauties during the cold months."[8] Among Lawrence's suggestions for winter reading were names enough to keep even the most demanding readers happy. Along with her familiar favorites (Elizabeth von Arnim, Gertrude Jekyll, Mrs. Loudon), there were others —E. A. Bowles, Henry Bright, Alice Morse Earle, Sir Herbert Maxwell, Beverley Nichols, William Robinson, Vita Sackville-West, Graham Stuart Thomas, and Louise Beebe Wilder. Lawrence found lessons for success, as well as consolation for her failures: What other gardener would not mind that *Viburnum fragans* had never bloomed for her, when it was "patient in neglect" for Vita Sackville-West?

As in all her books, Lawrence quoted extensively from letters in *Gardens in Winter.* (A few of Lawrence's old friends sadly observed that reading about gardeners who had died in recent years was like reading an obituary.) When Ben Morrison took her to task for quoting a gardener he did not admire, she defended herself in a letter to Caroline: "I *saw* good things in Mrs. D's garden. She must have known something."[9] Lawrence also was so scrupulous about not appropriating words or ideas from other sources that she perhaps was too slavish. (She wanted to give credit to Morrison for using his phrase "preserving a reservoir of stock material" but he assured her it was hers to use as her own.) She never failed to thank those who helped her, and to help others. Her frequent mentions of Carl Starker at Jennings Lodge, near Portland, Oregon—in *Gardens in Winter* and in her newspaper column—resulted in a big jump in mail orders for his Christmas wreaths. She had learned about them when Mr. Krippendorf had first sent her one long ago.

The immediate effect of the publication of *Gardens in Winter* was more fan mail. "Everybody is now writing about fascinating winter flowers I never heard of," she wrote to Caroline in early February 1961. When a dear friend, Ben Morrison, called from Pass Christian, Mississippi, she wrote to him at once, "I think you must be the kindest person in the world. I could not believe my ears."[10] Noted horticulturists found much to praise, and Lawrence was even happier when they admired Dormon's drawings, as John Wister did, writing in the journal of the New York Botanical Gardens that they "could give distinction to any garden book." Although she loved the letters and answered them all, with each book she had become more attentive to her audience, and more challenged to live up to her growing reputation. Moreover, the expenses of around-the-clock nurses for her mother were great, and Lawrence felt, as most people feel in similar circumstances, that Bessie's money would give out before Bessie did. Elizabeth wanted to sell more books.

In the early 1960s, Elizabeth might well have imagined that her best chance to gain a national following was through Katharine White, with whom she had been corresponding since 1958 and who appreciated the help that Lawrence was giving her in finding good materials for her *New Yorker* garden column. White's praise of Lawrence's earlier books had caught the attention of her editors at University of North Carolina Press, but Lawrence may have expected too much. When White recommended *Gardens in Winter* in her March 11, 1961, column, Lawrence was disappointed in the brevity of her remarks, though she did not tell White. She wrote Caroline to say that because of bad health White had been unable to write anything more than "comments" ("hardly a review") about the book. Lawrence must have been feeling discouraged in general, because, in fact, most writers would have been pleased to be praised even briefly by Katharine White. Among the books on winter gardens, White had found Lawrence's "the best. . . . Miss Lawrence is a classicist, and can cite Virgil and the English poets as freely as she does Gertrude Jekyll and Jane Loudon." White was herself a reader of the classics, and she probably brought to her column more knowledge of literary matters than any other of Lawrence's reviewers. Hers was high praise, but Lawrence was feeling low. Characteristically, however, she considered Katharine White's needs, begging Caroline to write to thank Katharine for her comments about the drawings—"delicate and precise as the author's prose."[11]

Sales were disappointing. "So far I haven't made a cent on *Gardens in Winter,*" Lawrence lamented to Caroline, "as I was charged for the mess the editors made, and the expensive changes in the galleys." Lawrence continued to promote her book through a friendship network. She sent those in a position to review it a copy of her book, mindful of her grandmother's saying, "Molasses catches more flies than vinegar." She went through her address book and correspondence, making a note of every possible person, including those mentioned in her book, who might help promote it, and passed the names along to her publisher. She and Caroline conferred as to whether or not a certain person might do a "nasty" review.[12]

Sixteen years after *Gardens in Winter* had gone out of print, Lawrence was able to arrange another edition through friends of Caroline Dormon's. Sara and Frank Gladney, who had gardened in Baton Rouge, Louisiana, and had set up the John James Audubon Foundation to further their gardening interests, had helped Dormon get her books published at a small Baton Rouge publishing business, Claitor's. Sara Gladney had enlisted the support of her garden club friends to help underwrite the costs, and some arrangement along that line was worked out for Claitor's to bring out a new edition of *Gardens in Winter*. Again,

Lawrence worked hard to promote her book (and Dormon's books, too) by preparing a list of possible reviewers, bookshops, and friends to be contacted. The personal connection always mattered the most to Elizabeth Lawrence, and even though the many letters between her, Frank and Sara Gladney, Caroline Dormon, and Bob Claitor took a great deal of everyone's time, many of the people on her lists did order the book. Suddenly, Christmas 1977 looked happier for Lawrence, if only because she mailed out (at her expense) copies of *Gardens in Winter* as presents—and received such happy letters. The handsome red jacket with Dormon's black and white drawing of the Lenten rose (which came from Mr. Krippendorf, who grew them from his own seed) gave her much pleasure. And she took particular pride in the dedication to Caroline Dormon and Sara and Frank Gladney, with the wisdom of Virgil: *hiemes orate serenas,* "Pray for fair (or sunny) winters."

CHAPTER NINETEEN

Elizabeth and Her Friends

No one can garden alone.

ELIZABETH LAWRENCE, *The Little Bulbs*

FROM HER EARLIEST experience, when her mother read her the Parable of the Sower and gave her a packet of radish seeds, to the last summer of her life, when she asked garden designer Edith Eddleman for help finding seeds of *Verbascum olympicum,* Elizabeth depended upon the "friendly society" of gardeners. When Carl Starker from Jennings Lodge, near Portland, Oregon, visited Elizabeth in Charlotte, she offered to cut anything in her garden that he needed for his lecture. Standing on the terrace and looking out into her garden, she said, "Everything you see is yours." And Starker replied, "I see a lot that *used* to be mine."[1] Visitors often left with treasures from Elizabeth's garden, while the plants that she sent wrapped in newspapers took root and flourished from Maine to California.

Readers of Lawrence's books and garden columns came to know her gardening friends as if they were characters in a long-running radio drama. Lawrence herself often said that she knew many gardens as well as she did her own. Some from the past, she explained to readers of *The Little Bulbs,* "still bloom in my mind." "Gardening, reading about gardening, and writing about gardening are all one," she explained. "No one can garden alone."[2]

Ruth Dormon, Felicity Wild Gardens, Shreveport, Louisiana

Soon after *A Southern Garden* was published in 1942, Ruth Dormon wrote Elizabeth that she thought that it was "one of the most delightful garden books I have ever read," and she wanted "to discuss every page, for every page has some special interest." Dormon (whose sister-in-law was Caroline Dormon) explained that she had propagated Louisiana plants for a number of years and found it "a most fascinating hobby."[3] In fact, she was operating her own nursery near Shreveport, called Felicity Wild Gardens. In the letters that followed for the next five years, Lawrence and Dormon exchanged plant information, and Elizabeth interrupted whatever she was doing to answer Ruth's letters. "Yesterday morning, in the midst of leaf-raking," she confessed, "it suddenly came over me that I had not written to thank you for the plants—and when I laid the rake down, and went in to look for the mail, there was a letter from you."[4] This little scene was repeated over and over—they had become loving friends.

Dormon had a little white trumpet daffodil in her garden that "could be traced to your North Carolina source, as they came from the garden of colonists from South Carolina who came to Louisiana about one hundred years ago and all the name they have for them is 'silver trumpet.'" She asked, "Is there any chance for us to get a few bulbs of your silver bell for comparison?" Dormon was also willing to teach Lawrence what she thought Elizabeth did not know. "Your Chapter on Louisiana Iris is good and accurate," she wrote, "but it does not go far enough." She concluded, "If there is any Louisiana native plant you would like, or if you want information on any, please write me."[5]

Soon afterwards, Lawrence sent Dormon bulbs of silver bell. The next spring, she bought more from a woman at the Raleigh City Market and sent those, too. Dormon wrote to thank her, "To say I was delighted to get the 'Silver Bells' is putting it too mildly."[6] Lawrence ordered from Dormon *Nemastylis, Eustylis, Kosteletzkya, Silene,* and several other plants; when Dormon billed her for $9.55, and also sent a sarsaparilla and shooting star, Lawrence added another dollar to her return payment. The two women continued to exchange plants, each always thanking the other for the trouble she had taken on her behalf. Lawrence's carefully dug plants, wrapped and mailed, arrived in Louisiana "as green and lush as if they had not made that long journey" (April 6, 1943). In return, Dormon kept trying to educate her about Louisiana iris. "Perhaps we are like a fond mother whose brood is as alike as peas in a pod," she wrote, "yet she sees the individuality of each and thinks them very unlike and all Charming." She had "variety" in her irises but not "quantity" and was propagating what she had and hybridizing for new ones. "We are some distance from the swamps, a day's drive, and collecting is hard work as well as dangerous. Last spring I went on a collecting trip, waded in water knee deep. And as I jumped from one 'Cotton Mouth' I almost landed upon another with his 'cotton mouth' open."[7]

Dormon offered a wealth of knowledge about the Louisiana swamps and the plant kingdom. "*Pteris multifida* is said to be an escape down around New Orleans.[8] It comes up everywhere from spores [and] is very hardy. This may be the fern you saw in Shreveport that Adelaide Dickson told me she told you she thought it is called 'Fish tail.' If you would like to try them I shall be delighted to send some to you."[9] She also had twenty-five irises registered with the American Iris Society and hoped to get a few more. She added, "It really is not a simple task to get all this done, especially as the Natives are so little known in the American Iris Society."[10] Dormon not only knew plants, she thought about their effect in her garden. She recommended that Lawrence plant the *Kosteletzkya,* native to the Coastal Plain, with *Commelina,* the dayflower, "if you want a pink and blue effect" or with *Raimannia* (*Oenothera,* the evening primrose) "if you want pink and yellow." Dormon helped Lawrence correct mistakes. "I think your sentence 'I water all summer' is the key to your failure with the Hymenocallis—they do better to dry out."[11]

Dormon and Lawrence both read the state market bulletins and enjoyed the mystery of what the advertised plants could be. "That is what the Farm Bulletin is for," Dormon reported, "to excite your interest with their 'homemade' names." When she read one woman's advertisement for "Wisendonna" bulbs, though she "vowed I would not let my curiosity get the best of me," she gave in and ordered them. Sure enough, when the bulbs bloomed, "they were just as I thought—that small magenta escaped gladiola."[12] Lawrence was equally "suspicious" that what she ordered might disappoint, but she, too, feared that something good would be lost if she didn't order it. They alerted each other to any article that might be of interest. "I was so glad you mentioned Mrs. Henry's article," Dormon wrote Lawrence in April 1943, "as I would have missed it. What with American Amaryllis Society, American Plant Taxonomy Society, American Iris Society, Mary Swords Debaillon's Louisiana Iris Society, and a few 'must' magazines I have to leave out something."[13]

In October of 1944 Lawrence was invited to speak to the Shreveport Garden Club. Realizing that she would get to meet Ruth Dormon, she gladly accepted. But something happened to spoil the visit. In a long letter to Ann Preston Bridgers, Elizabeth described the events: After having exchanged many letters and plants with Ruth Dormon, Lawrence had accepted the invitation to speak to garden clubs in Shreveport in order to meet her. "I knew she knew I was coming," Elizabeth explained to Ann, "and when I did not hear from her, I realized something was wrong, & restrained my impulse to write to say, 'When am I to see you?' " Mrs. Dormon had written to say that she would invite her sister-in-law, Caroline Dormon, to meet her, also. "I read [the letter] carefully, many times," Lawrence explained. "It didn't say, 'I want you to come to see me,' but I was sure it implied that." And so Lawrence had asked her garden club hostess to please arrange for a time for her to meet Ruth Dormon.

The day Lawrence left for Louisiana, she received a telegram from the garden club hostess saying that Dormon's husband was desperately ill and that Dormon would be able to see her only at a luncheon to which they both were invited. After Lawrence arrived, she learned that Mr. Dormon had been desperately ill for years. Why was she being discouraged from seeing Dormon's garden?

Elizabeth was also surprised to see that Ruth Dormon was not the "vigorous, spirited" letter writer she had grown to love, but a "little, worn, country woman, so darling that I could hardly keep from putting my arms around her, instead of holding out my hand." Lawrence pulled out her plant list to ask if Dormon knew a certain man, who had plants she had been searching for, when from across the room a member of the garden club came forward, shrieking, "He ought to be exposed! He's a

Negro." "But what is there to expose?" Lawrence asked Dormon. "I can't see why a Negro can't sell plants—can you?" "No," Mrs. Dormon had said, and smiled. " 'No, I can't.' And that was all I saw of her," Lawrence told Ann Bridgers.

Before the meeting was over, Elizabeth succeeded in finding out what her garden club hostess knew about Ruth Dormon. "Mrs. Dormon has had reverses," she was told. "They are desperately poor—and her place has run down. She was afraid you would expect her to have a show garden. I told her I knew from your letters that you were not the kind of person who could care about that—but she is very sensitive."

"As I talked to her friends, who worship her, I easily saw how Mrs. Dormon got to be sensitive. 'No use for you to go out to Ruth's place,' one of them said. 'There's nothing to interest you there—just a wilderness. Of course, it's pretty in the spring, with all her native iris blooming.'. . . I asked one of her friends if Mrs. Dormon had my book. 'Oh, I don't think so!' she said, then added, 'But she may have it. You never can tell what the poor will spend money on. Ruth managed to find five dollars for one bulb of that white *Lycoris radiata* that she wanted so much.' "

Elizabeth concluded her letter to Ann Bridgers, "So here I am, taking a train tomorrow after three days in Shreveport looking at gardens of the rich, landscaped by a contractor who calls himself a landscape architect, and creates an effect much like an expensive cemetery. And I left my work and took this long and toilsome trip, mainly to see Mrs. Dormon."[14]

It is not clear from the records exactly what went wrong. Just before Elizabeth's trip to Shreveport, a local newspaper columnist had reported that the great event of the week for her had been going to see the flowering of *Lycoris radiata alba* in Ruth Dormon's garden on the Mooringsport Road. A letter Dormon wrote to Lawrence when she was back in Raleigh offers further evidence that she was used to having visitors. She explained that, after she had Lawrence's letter saying that she wanted to come out to Dormon's place for "a walk in the woods," she had called the garden club woman in charge of Lawrence's schedule to confirm a time. When Dormon discovered that she had made "*all* those plans to take you to all *those Gardens*," she admitted, "I could see that she did not want to change." Yes, Mr. Dormon was sick, but he had been an invalid for years and was "very understanding" about her need to see people. Her daughter had volunteered to bring Elizabeth. "If you had wanted a 'walk in the woods' my place was the place to come. My walks are trails. I have eight acres with only a two-bedroom house. I love the outdoors too well to be burdened with a big house. With all due respect it amuses me how some of my friends adore those big 'landscaped places' and if we could have sneaked off to Caroline's!!!!! she has one hundred and thirty-five acres mostly in woodland!! What a walk we could have had."[15]

What seems to have happened is that some of the club members who had invited Lawrence as a speaker had decided to keep her for themselves, and Dormon had been excluded. Whatever "due respect" Lawrence and Dormon paid to the gardeners with big houses and landscaped gardens, privately, they disdained them. But the memory of what happened was hurtful to them both.

The two women continued exchanging plants and information after Elizabeth's trip to Shreveport, though now their letters were sent "with love." So it was with "heartfelt sorrow" in March of 1947 that Lawrence received a letter from Caroline with the news that Ruth had died. She knew that she would feel her death "more and more" every time she thought again, "I must write to ask Mrs. Dormon about that." Recently she had reread her letters. "I loved her dearly, just seeing her that one time," she concluded. "I shall miss her as long as I live."[16]

Caroline Dormon, Briarwood, Saline, Louisiana

Elizabeth Lawrence and Caroline Dormon had been corresponding for more than a decade before Elizabeth was able to accept Caroline's invitation to see her native Louisiana pines and flowers " 'as is' with no landscaping" at Briarwood, her 135-acre homestead in northwestern Louisiana. Finally, she visited in mid-October in 1958, "after the witch-hazel and before the Indian pipes," and the pine forests of Briarwood were alive with the songs of whitethroats. Dormon always waked with

Caroline Dormon was as well-known in Louisiana gardening circles as Elizabeth Lawrence was in North Carolina. In the 1950s Elizabeth visited Caroline in her pinewoods at Briarwood, where they spent hours outdoors looking at plants, and in the evening had dinner by the fire in a rustic cabin. (Courtesy of Eugene P. Watson Memorial Library, Northwestern State University of Louisiana, and the Caroline Dormon Nature Preserve.)

the sun, and the morning of Elizabeth's visit she had hurried outside her small log house in the woods to stand on the porch—still in her nightgown—and listen. She had special reason to be up with the birds: at last, Elizabeth Lawrence was coming to Briarwood. In late afternoon Caroline's friend and fellow-gardener, Inez Conger, arrived with Elizabeth. Inez had taken time to show Elizabeth her own beautiful garden in nearby Arcadia before driving her to Caroline's, but when she arrived, she knew not to linger. For forty years Caroline had been studying, growing, and drawing wildflowers. Caroline Dormon and Elizabeth Lawrence had much to talk about. Elizabeth's brief and only visit to Briarwood lived up to the promise of what it would be like when Caroline wrote her very first letter to Elizabeth on October 26, 1944: "We will have lunch under the pines and beeches—and—if the weather is like this—never set foot inside the house."[17]

When that long-awaited time came, Caroline and Elizabeth had only "two nights & a day" together, but they were magical. Elizabeth remembered: "We got there at sunset, & Caroline & Dusty [Dormon's dog] were waiting on the porch. I jumped out of the car & ran up to her and we fell into each other's arms. The supper table was set before the fire with odds & ends of china, and autumn leaves flat on the bare table. The main dish was a baked chicken. The next day we ate tea & toast & chicken, & at each meal pushed the dirty dishes aside, & got out clean ones. Just like the mad hatter's tea party."[18]

In few letters is Elizabeth Lawrence more expressive of affection than in her letters to Caroline Dormon, and yet, no close friend was more different from her. Elizabeth's two nights in a log cabin under a canopy of Louisiana pines may have been the only two nights in her adult life when she did not have a cocktail (Caroline was a teetotaler). And these were nights in which Elizabeth's energy had been drained—and rejuvenated—by a long day of trying to keep up with Caroline's frantic gestures to "Come! Look at this!" as they stooped down and stood up, when every leaf and flower seemed waiting to be loved. Elizabeth made no mention of not being able to sleep at Briarwood. And when she was back home on a residential street in a suburban neighborhood of a large city,

Elizabeth stood at her studio window and looked out long and deep into her garden and remembered Caroline.

Dormon, older than Lawrence by sixteen years, was one of the most original women anyone might ever hope to meet. The traditions of church, family, and society that had tamed whatever rebellious spirit lay in the heart of Elizabeth Lawrence had not conquered Caroline Dormon's wild urges to be free. Lawrence's small backyard garden was a place for her to create beauty. Dormon's natural woods were a place for her to discover beauty. "I can slip away to my world of birds and trees and rise serene above them," she wrote. "A swift realization comes that I possess something fine and lovely which no power on earth can take from me."[19]

Caroline Dormon had been living at Briarwood, the family estate, since 1917, when she and her sister Virginia had moved there, returning to the place where they had spent many summers. The sixth of eight children (and said to be her father's favorite), Caroline was born July 19, 1888, at Briarwood. Going there to live with her sister was like "going to heaven." By 1930, after years as a teacher and conservationist, Caroline had had enough of a public life and retreated. She said, "All I ask of life is to be able to stay in the woods, fooling with plants and birds."[20]

Dormon's successful efforts to propagate, hybridize, and illustrate native plants, especially Louisiana iris, brought her to the attention of noted botanists all over the country. Like Lawrence, she corresponded with many of them. And like Elizabeth and Bessie, Caroline and her sister Virginia traveled together when "Carrie," as Virginia called her, spoke to garden clubs—and along the way, they collected plants. Virginia was the "indoor Dormon," Caroline the outdoor one, "whooping and prancing about like some bamboo-stemmed marsh bird, swinging her arms high over her head" to greet visitors like Elizabeth, whom she so wanted to see. She was tall, thin, long-armed, angular, by the end of her life a self-described "old scarecrow."[21]

Although exchanging plant information was the primary focus of hundreds of letters, Lawrence and Dormon often wrote about their difficulties in finding publishers, and, when they did find a publisher, their difficulties with editors, who wanted to change their styles to "journalese." When either finished a book, they shared—in Caroline's phrase—"such a glow." Lawrence and Dormon were fierce admirers of one another's work. Lawrence thought that Dormon's botanical illustrations in *Flowers Native to the Deep South,* published in 1958, were among the most beautiful that she had ever seen. In 1965 when Dormon published *Natives Preferred,* she dedicated it to Elizabeth Lawrence. And in 1961, Lawrence dedicated *Gardens in Winter* to Caroline Dormon, who had drawn the illustrations.

On many occasions, Caroline grieved over the distance between them, always wondering when they would see each other again. "Why DON'T you and I live near enough to run in and compare notes?" Caroline asked. "Letters take so long."[22] Still, Caroline was not one to complain of ever being lonely, and in fact, she often complained of having too much company. "Oh," she lamented after Virginia had died in 1954, "for my sister and my little cabin on the other side of the pond" where she "could really hide, and it was heaven."[23] She was fiercely independent, often unwilling to accept help, even when she needed it. After Inez Conger's husband had died, Caroline saw Inez less. She wrote Elizabeth, "Inez went home with her soldier son, and stayed nearly three months! Never a line, till just before her return. Said 'without Ed, it's just a big old empty house, and I feel no desire to return.' Well, I got mad! I wrote, 'Yes, an empty house is just a house, but don't you want to see what's blooming in your wonderful garden? And what do you think is happening to your birds' Ha! Plenty of us live in an 'empty house.' "[24]

Dormon's letters bristled with exclamations, and Lawrence thought the letters even better than her books. "For heaven's sake," she exclaimed, "tell me the correct name of 'lemon verbena'—my poor scrambled mind can't recall it."[25] Another time, she wrote, "I draw, paint, and write a little—but am so triflin'. I have read that Audubon often painted 17 hours a day! I don't believe a word of it! It is true he had an iron constitution, but he was also nervous and highstrung. After I do such work for two hours, I have to rush out and look at flowers—or pull weeds!"[26] Even on a Sunday when it was 107 on her shady back porch, "plants *cooking*," she wrote, "Hurrah for Crepe myrtles—lovely, in every shade! My white seedling exquisite."[27]

Elizabeth was more expressive in her affection toward Caroline than she was with most people. Elizabeth signed most of her letters "Aff—" for "affectionately." Soon she was using her family's expression "with a heartful of love," and Caroline responded "With love" and "I love you." Elizabeth wrote, "Hardly a day goes by but I think of something I want to say to you, and one never goes by without my thinking how I love you, and how few such gardeners there are in the world for me to love."[28] But it was not only that Caroline knew so much about plants that drew Elizabeth to her. Caroline was an irrepressible, exuberant child. Punctuation marks, capitals, underlinings, and graphics (!!!!! and ?????) gave emphasis to her feelings, and in case Elizabeth did not hear her, she said it: " 'Nobody knows the trouble I see.' (Nobody but *you*!). I'm writing a book with this title! Top Secret—don't tell!"[29]

Elizabeth was also confiding. In the fall of 1957, before they had met, she reported that she was getting nothing done in the garden. "My mother has followed me twice and fallen down. On some days she gets some sort of hallucination that a large body of water (I think it is the Ohio River) is out there, and that I may fall in. Anyhow, there is some great peril, and she thinks she must come to save me." In the same letter, however, Elizabeth had the presence of mind to answer Caroline's questions—a semi-trailing shrub was *Abeliophyllum distichum,* the little three-leaved things, hellebore seedlings.[30]

In 1959, the year after Lawrence had been to Briarwood, Dormon visited her in Charlotte when she came to lecture in North Carolina and was Elizabeth's houseguest for "two half-nights & a day." "When she came to me," Lawrence said, "I put her on the train at 2 in the morning. It was April & very cold & dark. No stars. As we stood alone on the platform Caroline said, 'Wings—don't you hear them?' I didn't, but I am sure she did."[31] It was a time when Bessie required around-the-clock nursing care, and often Elizabeth, to save money, took the late shift. For Caroline's visit, she had made special arrangements to have extra help—a nurse during the night and her sister Ann "looking out for Bessie during the day." "That was the only holiday I have had for over a year," she wrote Caroline. "It did me a lot of good, being free and being with you."[32]

When Caroline Dormon died in 1971, her papers were given to the library at Northwestern State University in Natchitoches, less than an hour's drive from Briarwood. As Carol Wells began setting up the Dormon archives, she wrote to Elizabeth Lawrence to ask if the library could have her letters to Dormon. That request began an exchange of letters between Wells and Lawrence that resulted in Lawrence giving her papers to Northwestern as well. In rereading Caroline's letters before sending them to Wells, Lawrence regained a sense of her dear friend. Dormon had often asked Lawrence to come and live with her in the woods of Briarwood, an invitation that Lawrence knew was fanciful and required no answer. Caroline Dormon's need to pour out her heart to Elizabeth—about plants, editors, the deaths of friends, and her own frailties—brought out an emotional maturity in Elizabeth that perhaps is not revealed in other relationships. In a way, Elizabeth Lawrence was like a mother to Caroline Dormon—constantly reassuring and loving, but a mother who did not restrict her freedom. In that role, Elizabeth expressed her own originality.

William Lanier Hunt of Chapel Hill, North Carolina

For much of the twentieth century, Elizabeth Lawrence and William Lanier Hunt were arguably the most knowledgeable gardeners in the Southeast. Elizabeth and "Billy" (most friends called him "Bill," and he was amused that Elizabeth called him by the name he was called in college) were also good friends, who visited in each other's gardens, exchanged plants and information, wrote to each other, read each other's garden columns, and knew many of the same people. A record of their answers to questions posed in letters or asked at meetings would make

William Lanier Hunt and Elizabeth Lawrence were gardening friends for more than a half-century, visiting back and forth between his garden in Chapel Hill and hers in Raleigh and later in Charlotte, North Carolina. They often lectured together—and swapped plants. (Photograph by Francis Lavergne Johnson. North Carolina Collection, University of North Carolina Library at Chapel Hill.)

a unique plant history of private gardens in the region, beginning in the late 1930s. Directors of public gardens, nurseries, and botanical laboratories asked both of them for help in identifying and testing plants, and came to see their gardens. Include their friend Caroline Dormon with them, and there is a triumvirate of distinctive Southern gardeners.

Hunt was born in 1906 (making him two years younger than Lawrence) in Pomona, a small town near Greensboro, North Carolina. From childhood, he had a life made for a gardener. He grew up next door to Lindley Nurseries, then the South's oldest and largest nursery, owned by his uncle. Lindley Nurseries, founded in 1822, had four hundred acres and fourteen greenhouses, tended by a staff that included European gardeners. When Hunt went off to preparatory school at Woodberry Forest in Virginia, and later to the University of North Carolina in Chapel Hill, he took with him truckloads of plants, many of which he had nurtured in his uncle's greenhouses. His plant collection and reputation grew so quickly that by the time he had graduated from the university (in 1931, with a degree in Botany), he could be forgiven for thinking that he knew as much as his teachers.

As soon as Hunt heard about Elizabeth Lawrence's garden in Raleigh, he began coming to see her and "Miss Bessie," sometimes arriving by train. In July of 1937, he came "with an armful of March pinks and with a photographer," for he wanted a picture of a plant that Elizabeth had been calling *Amaryllis belladonna,* although she was unsure of the name. She had telegraphed him that it was in bloom, and he had come over and identified it as *Lycoris squamigera var. purpurea.* Lawrence remembered, "He had never seen it before and had a fit. Anyone would: six iridescent pale lilac lilies in a circle on top of a tapering applegreen stem."[33] After that visit, there were many others, both in Raleigh and, after 1948, in Charlotte.

In the late 1930s and early 1940s, Hunt and Lawrence were part of the Southern garden club movement, lecturing and conducting workshops. He traveled more extensively, and his garden column published in the Durham *Herald* was also carried by other newspapers, including the Shreveport *Times.* Louisiana gardeners writing to Lawrence often mentioned Bill Hunt's visit to speak at a garden club and to take the local garden club tour. He struck everyone as a charming Southern gentleman, handsomely attired (a bow tie his signature style), and as his hair turned white, he grew even more dashing. He loved everything Southern and everything English, and was especially proud that he was one of the first American Fellows of the Royal Horticultural Society. In 1948 he introduced Elizabeth Lawrence as a new member of the Society.[34]

Although Hunt's garden column was popular, he was not the determined writer that Lawrence was, and although he often said that he wanted to get started on a book, friends understood that he would never take the time from his many interests to write it. In 1982, when a selection of his newspaper columns was finally to be published in *Southern Gardens, Southern Gardening,* Hunt asked Lawrence to write the introduction. She agreed, in spite of the fact that she was in poor health and had not been able to finish her own manuscripts.

In her introduction, Lawrence began by recounting the story that her sister Ann had heard when she was a student at the University in the late 1920s: "There is a boy here that you would like; he brought his garden with him when he came to Chapel Hill." Lawrence then began to name what they had in common—plants (the oxblood lily) and friends (Violet Walker, Lester Rowntree, Camilla Bradley)—and described how they had acquired them. Her greatest admiration, however, was for Hunt's crowning achievement—his gift of more than one hundred acres of woods and fields on the edge of the University campus, a place he had first seen as a student when he walked with other villagers to admire the rhododendron blooming on Laurel Hill, above Morgan Creek. Little by little, Hunt had purchased parcels of land, until in 1960, he began to transfer ownership to the University. ("You," he wrote Elizabeth when the gift was announced, "have known about it for many years.")[35] Today the Hunt Arboretum of the North Carolina Botanical Garden is Hunt's most enduring legacy.

The friendship between Lawrence and Hunt was genuine and lasting, based on a shared passion for gardening, and generous to a fault. Although sometimes Lawrence's friends thought that Hunt took too much credit for helping to advance Lawrence (in fact, he had recommended that the University of North Carolina Press reprint *A Southern Garden* and led Duke University Press to publish *Gardening for Love*), he always said that she and Caroline Dormon were the great "spirits" of the gardening world and that he revered them both.[36] His introduction to the 1967 reprint of *A Southern Garden* shows how well he understood Elizabeth: "Through the pages of *A Southern Garden* walk many of the best gardeners and most interesting characters in the South. Elizabeth quotes from her letters from plant lovers everywhere and takes us back to many of the world's garden lovers in literature. It is not difficult to see what she thinks of her gardening friends. She sits at the feet of some, shares the joy of plant swapping with others, and makes wry little observations about a few."[37]

When writer Beverly Seaton, in a biographical essay about Elizabeth Lawrence for *American Women Writers,* said that Lawrence was a foremost authority on Southern gardening, Lawrence protested: "I thank you for your extremely flattering 'entry,' but really, upon hearing that I am a foremost authority on Southern gardening (or anything) William Lanier Hunt would have apoplexy. His column in the Durham paper is syndicated and widely read, and he is far better known as a lecturer than I. And also committed to Southern botanical gardens. . . . Couldn't you say *one* authority, if anything, though I am not an authority, only a gardener."[38] Seaton acceded to Lawrence's request, describing her as "one of America's foremost authorities."

Lawrence made her reputation in the garden, and Hunt in garden circles. His contributions were prodigious and timely. In the 1960s he helped develop the North Carolina Botanical Garden, and organized and served as first president of the Botanical Garden Foundation. He proposed organizing the Southern Garden History Society, modeled after the Garden History Society of England, and when it was formally recognized in 1982, he was named honorary president. When he died, in the fall of 1996, at age ninety, he had outlived Elizabeth Lawrence and Caroline Dormon by many years.[39]

Linda Mitchell Lamm, Wilson, North Carolina

A younger friend and a leader in North Carolina gardening circles was Linda Mitchell Lamm, who had grown up on a large farm in Robeson County in the eastern part of the state.[40] Her sister, Laura Braswell, was a friend of Elizabeth's in Charlotte, and her brother, Joseph Mitchell, was a writer at *The New Yorker.* Linda married a cotton merchant-broker, William Lamm, and they lived in Wilson. There she gardened with great energy and originality, and she devoted a great deal of time to the activities of garden clubs and plant societies. Her leadership in the North Carolina Wild Flower Preservation Society, the North Carolina Botanical Garden, and the Herb Society of America helped keep those organizations going over many years. Two of the people she often turned to for advice and information were William Lanier Hunt and Elizabeth Lawrence. Lamm shared Hunt's interest in the North Carolina Botanical Garden and the old Coker Arboretum. With Lawrence, she discussed garden literature and garden design.

Lawrence and Lamm first met in the mid-1950s on "a bright October day," Lamm recalled, when Laura Braswell invited them to tea. Lawrence came bearing gifts, as she always did: a basket of five seedlings labeled *Helleborus orientalis,* hoping that Lamm would share her passion for the Lenten roses. She did, and the plants thrived in her woods. That introduction began a friendship that lasted until Lawrence's death in 1985, and included more than one hundred letters, plus phone calls, gifts, meetings attended together, and gardens they visited.

Lamm's garden on Raleigh Road in Wilson was always welcoming. She herself loved to sit and look at it from a bay window down a long allée; friends often joined her in this room to enjoy the view and to have tea among her many books and paintings. Her collection of native plants included some she had grown up with as a child on the farm—Joe-pye weed, yellow jessamine, and a pawpaw tree. She especially liked to show off her favorite, *Baptisia alba.* Her climbing fern came from Elizabeth Lawrence's garden in Charlotte, though Lawrence warned her that she would be sorry she had asked for it—it was "rampant." Lamm also had hardy begonia, sweet autumn clematis, ginger lily, and two of Lawrence's favorites—*Clematis armandii* and hellebores. She also had grown plants from seeds that Rosemary Verey had given her of the bear's foot or stinking hellebore *(Helleborus foetidus)* that came from Verey's garden at Barnsley House in Gloucestershire, England. Lamm went on to learn a great deal about hellebores, to grow them in her garden, to share seedlings with friends, and to write about them in plant newsletters.

Early in the 1960s Lamm sought Lawrence's advice for the design of a terrace and woodland garden. These discussions began with a series of visits and were followed by letters that outlined ways to enhance the view from the window; Lawrence proposed a new herb bed in the distance. It was a welcome opportunity for Lawrence, who wrote often to suggest plants for Lamm's garden, such as Korean daisies, Japanese Aster, yucca, lilies, and peonies. She also gave Lamm cuttings from her own garden—feverfew and sweet rocket.

Lawrence had seen in Lamm's backyard landscape an opportunity to emulate something she had learned from Gertrude Jekyll. The large pine trees, and smaller oaks, maples, and tulip poplars in Lamm's backyard had made her think of Jekyll's Munstead Wood in County Surrey, England, and she had begun rereading about woodland gardens. She wrote Lamm to say, "The parallel is uncanny: the sitting-room windows [at Munstead Wood] 'look straight up a wide grass way, the vista being ended by a fine old Scotch Fir,' just like your pine. I was afraid to say too much to you, for that is so confusing, but I felt that all of the woods need thinning, especially the part toward the house, and that is something that you should think about as you sit in it or walk through it." Lawrence added that Jekyll cautioned against making quick decisions, and she added her own preference: "You can't decide in a minute. You must brood."[41]

The chance to work with Linda Lamm had awakened in Lawrence a desire to shape a garden, and in looking into Lamm's woods she was also reminded of her own. The distinctive allée of cherry laurels leading from her own terrace to the back garden of pine trees (underplanted with hellebores) had created a distinctive view through the French doors of her living room. Lamm agreed that such a view could be enhanced in her own garden. Lawrence also made sketches for Lamm's terrace, suggesting that Lamm use open urns—and, remembering that "proportion is all," that "she try out her own design preferences by setting something up in each corner (even a bucket)" to see how it looked. Lamm took all of Lawrence's suggestions.

Lamm's residential garden was one of Elizabeth's most cherished assignments, but Lamm also recommended that Elizabeth design a public garden at the Country Doctor Museum in Bailey, North Carolina. Lamm was a founder of the garden, and she and another friend of Elizabeth's, Dr. Herbert Hechenbleikner (a horticulturist at the University of North Carolina in Charlotte), were active in the North Carolina Wild Flower Preservation Society, which sponsored the garden. The speaker at the dedication in the summer of 1971 was the playwright Paul Green, whose wife, Elizabeth, had been one of Lawrence's friends at St. Mary's. The museum consists of a composite restoration of two doctors' offices built in the late 1800s. Lawrence based her garden design on a medieval herb garden in Padua, Italy, and her plant list included some sixty herbs, including bay, lavender, lemon balm, basil, borage, boxwood, chamomile, comfrey, St.-John's-wort, and sassafras.

Elizabeth and Eddie Clarkson, Wing Haven Garden, Charlotte, North Carolina

There was another Elizabeth whose garden in Charlotte, North Carolina, was as well known as Elizabeth Lawrence's, and the two Elizabeths were good friends who lived within a block of each other. Elizabeth Barnhill was a Texas native who married Eddie Clarkson of Charlotte, and in 1927, after their honeymoon, they moved into a new house on Ridgewood Avenue. It was a two-story white frame house on a flat piece of land with almost no neighbors in sight. There were a few small pine seedlings, a spindly willow oak, and a field of caked mud. When Elizabeth Clarkson looked more closely at the house, however, she saw the architectural beauty she had planned for—a fanlight with tracery over the front door, a newel post and stair like those in her home in Texas, a raised brick terrace off the living room, and large windows. And there was a surprise: a baby grand Steinway piano, Eddie's wedding gift to his new bride. Together, over the next six decades, the Clarksons would fill the house and terrace with a constant flow of guests. Good food, music, and conversation would set the stage for memorable Christmases, birthdays, late afternoon cocktails, Sunday night suppers,

Elizabeth and Eddie Clarkson were near neighbors of Elizabeth's in Charlotte, where they used their lovely formal gardens as a sanctuary for friends and nature. Elizabeth often wrote about them in her garden column. (Courtesy of The Wing Haven Foundation.)

and concerts—when the piano would be moved to the terrace and the party moved to the garden. In time, the Clarksons, with modest enough means, acquired adjacent properties, and Elizabeth developed gardens connected by paths that led visitors deeper into quiet places of peace and beauty. And to all of this, the Clarksons added a sanctuary for birds, planting hundreds of trees, shrubs, and flowers for their feed—sumac, greenbrier, chokeberry, locust, elderberry, mahonia, eleagnus, larkspur, and columbine. But the most remarkable feature of the Clarksons' concern for the birds was that they not only tried to provide for their health and happiness in the gardens, but also left windows open and invited birds into the house. Stories of a bluebird named Tommy that bathed in a finger bowl on the dining room table (with seated guests), of a wren that built her nest in a bookcase, and of injured birds nursed back to health not only were told and retold by friends and overnight guests (who sometimes had to give up the guest room if a bird had already claimed it), but even attracted national attention. A president of the National Audubon Society reported on having seen outside his door a breakfast dish of worms left for the Carolina wrens. Childless themselves, the Clarksons were also interested in everyone else's children, including hundreds of schoolchildren who followed Elizabeth about the house and garden as she told them about birds and plants.[42]

Elizabeth and Eddie Clarkson were a devoted couple, and when Eddie put a flower in the buttonhole of his white jacket and his wife came down the stairs in a long dress with matching slippers, they seemed the essence of romance. They were formal, gracious people, and whether they were dining alone in the garden or welcoming large parties of guests, they entertained in the grand style—silverware and linen napkins, crystal candelabra and white candles, porcelain bowls, and a gracious servant, or two. Lest the scene seem too elegant, however, we should not overlook the nest of rabbits in a Chinese bowl, the backs of chairs covered with protective plastic, a wren having its mealworms in the kitchen. An aura of romance combined with an attitude of practicality was perhaps the most singular characteristic of the Clarksons, who gave each other bricks and worms for presents.

It would seem inevitable that when the Lawrences and Ways moved in down the street some twenty years after the Clarksons built their house, they would become friends with the Clarksons, and they did. The two Elizabeths had the most to talk about, both being superb gardeners. Anyone visiting one Elizabeth was usually taken to see the garden of the other Elizabeth. Elizabeth Clarkson often called Elizabeth Lawrence to ask her a question about plants. Elizabeth Lawrence knew Elizabeth Clarkson's garden as well as she did her own, and indeed, her own was filled with plants that Clarkson had given her. Lawrence often wrote about the Clarkson garden in her newspaper column, and she devoted an article to what she called the "Garden of Enchantment."

Nothing makes a garden, or a gardener, pale, however, like too much idealizing. The fact is that both Elizabeths were strong women. Readers will miss the meaning of the story of their friendship unless they know the resolute determination that has long been regarded as a distinguishing feature of the "Southern lady."

Cama Merritt, a niece (and goddaughter) of Elizabeth Clarkson, remembered, "Aunt Lib knew that certain things were right, and she did what she thought needed to be done to make them right. When city trucks came through the neighborhood, for example, spraying for mosquitoes, she saw what it was doing to the birds, and she stopped them. She didn't yield. You can't be anything except tough as nails if you are going to be a good gardener. Was she competitive? Yes, I never have used that word to describe her, but she was competitive. Aunt Lib was in a class by herself, and intended to be there."[43]

The two Elizabeths respected one another's differences. As their friend Hannah Withers observed, Elizabeth Clarkson wanted her borders neat; Elizabeth Lawrence wanted flowers to spill over her paths. Elizabeth Clarkson had a show garden, where form was essential. Elizabeth Lawrence said about her own garden that it was a laboratory for plants. The Elizabeths were different in another way: at the Clarksons' Christmas parties, friends remembered, Elizabeth Lawrence sat quietly in one place, and just by being there, she seemed to attract people to her. When someone came over to talk, though she spoke softly, she was intensely interested and interesting. She liked people one at a time. Elizabeth Clarkson walked forward to greet friends, a welcoming hostess who knew how to bring people together, who "presided" with Mr. Clarkson over a room crowded with happy guests. Elizabeth Clarkson was an elegant dresser; even for the garden, she did not change into "work" clothes. Elizabeth Lawrence did not care much about clothes and seldom dressed up—at the Clarksons' Christmas party she wore a touch of lipstick. In the garden she wore socks and good sturdy shoes, serviceable dresses, and, often, jeans. Together, Elizabeth Lawrence and Eddie and Elizabeth Clarkson made Ridgewood Avenue in Charlotte, North Carolina, one of the most famous addresses in Southern garden history. What is most remarkable about this fact is that, relative to the great gardens of America, the Lawrence and Clarkson gardens were extremely modest in size, though fully expressing the intentions and obsessions of the gardeners who made them.

John Jamison of Beaucatcher Mountain, Asheville

John Jamison was a businessman living in Charlotte when he began reading Elizabeth Lawrence's column in the newspaper. A gardener himself, he much admired what Lawrence had to say.[44] Her absence from the Sunday *Observer* after her column had been discontinued in 1971 was felt keenly by her loyal readers, and any chance to hear her talk about plants was a special gift for those who came to see her. Such was the case in early 1976 when Dannye Romine (Powell), a writer for the *Observer*, invited Jamison to join her for one of her visits with Elizabeth. Dannye herself was a special favorite of Elizabeth's, not so much because she wrote for the newspaper that Lawrence had written for (Lawrence's experience of having been "fired" was still a wound)—but because she was a native of Georgia and a poet. So Dannye and John went to Elizabeth's for drinks and a tour of the garden; before John left, Elizabeth gave him an autographed copy of *A Southern Garden*.

After that first occasion, Lawrence invited Jamison back for other visits—telling him to come at five o'clock in the afternoon, when, as she pointed out, "the sun would be over the yard arm." Each visit followed the same pattern—drinks in the library and a walk in the garden. Since Jamison had just begun his first serious garden, he felt that he "desperately needed to see a *real* garden." Elizabeth was not at all well, but she was still writing every day and tending her garden, or supervising it. On a good day, she would agree to give one "last" lecture in the garden (she loved showing schoolchildren around and telling them about her favorite book, *The Secret Garden*), but on bad days, which were becoming too frequent, she had to stay in bed. Once when she had suggested that Jamison order wildflowers from Rosa Hicks in Banner Elk, she invited him to have a look at her notes for the market bulletin book. He did order plants from Hicks, but when he looked at the manuscript, he recalled, "My heart sank. She seemed so fragile, and these notes seemed to me so rough and fragmented." But nothing about her garden knowledge was missing from their conversations, and she still had strength to pot up a small seedling of tall meadow-rue *(Thalictrum polygamum)* for his garden.

Although Jamison was afraid that he took too much of her precious time and energy, she insisted that she enjoyed his visits. And while sharing information, plants, and the names of favorite gardening books, she also taught him what he calls "lessons": "Are you cruel enough to be a gardener?" she asked him, explaining that her garden was too small to keep every species she had wanted to grow and observe, and she had to be willing to dig up and discard old plants in order to make room for new ones. She also said that to really appreciate a garden, one had to see it every day. But perhaps most important as their friendship grew, was that she helped him with his life. When he came to tell her of his decision to leave his marriage, he said that part of his grief was walking away from the garden that had been a refuge during a stormy time. Jamison remembered, "She reminded me that she had walked away from a wonderful garden in Raleigh to move to Charlotte. She said, 'I made a *better* garden, and someday *you* will make a better garden.' "

Jamison married again, and today in the shady, naturalistic garden he made with his wife, Curry, "on a narrow, boney ridge of Beaucatcher Mountain" in Asheville, North Carolina, he feels Elizabeth's presence still. "Sometimes, walking in my garden, I listen for Elizabeth's little voice, saying, 'See, didn't I tell you?' " Lawrence was, Jamison confessed, "the heroic figure in my life."

CHAPTER TWENTY

A Friendship in Letters 1958–1977

And I find myself quoting 'Elizabeth.' Do I dare call you that?

KATHARINE WHITE TO ELIZABETH LAWRENCE, *Two Gardeners*

ELIZABETH LAWRENCE's friendship with Katharine White dates from the spring of 1958, when Lawrence mailed a letter to White saying how much she had enjoyed her article in the March *New Yorker*. She got right to the point: "I am very grateful to Joseph Mitchell's sister, Mrs. Linda Lamm, for calling my attention to your story about the catalogues."[1] It was characteristic of Lawrence to make family connections. She also was not above dropping the name of Joseph Mitchell, a *New Yorker* writer and North Carolina native, although she waited until the end of her letter to say that she knew Katharine was Mrs. E. B. White.

White sent off at once for Lawrence's *A Southern Garden* and, finding it out of print, borrowed a copy from Mitchell. White put stock in his good opinion: she considered his recommendation of her review to his sister "a great honor." Some writers thought White the best editor at the best magazine, and she was quick to nurture talent. Although she had had letters from many enthusiastic readers in response to her long article, nobody would hold her attention like this Elizabeth Lawrence down in Charlotte, North Carolina. She was not put off by the fact that Lawrence was a careless speller and a careless typist—though she might have been, had a Lawrence manuscript appeared as a submission to *The New Yorker*. It was clear from the content of the letter that Elizabeth Lawrence *knew* garden catalogues; moreover, she was eager to recommend several that White had not known about. By the end of her letter to Lawrence, White had told her that her suggestions would "spur" her on, "if anything could." But she wanted Lawrence to know that she was "an editor, not a writer," that it was unlikely she would be able to write another piece, and that as a gardener, she was "a rank amateur" (and she was allergic to primroses). She sent off for the catalogues, and saved the letter for what would become her Lawrence files.

Those who knew the brilliant Katharine White would have recognized her in this self-effacing letter because of the characteristic generosity she expressed to another writer. It was probably good that she and Lawrence were not meeting in person for the first time; Lawrence was uneasy in the city even when she visited her friend Ellen Flood, and White knew North Carolina only as a state she and her husband drove through on their way to Florida for the winter. (When one of her favorite *New Yorker* writers, Peter Taylor, moved to Greensboro to teach at the Woman's College there, she was pleased to be able to tell Lawrence.) Although Lawrence was a garden writer little known outside the South, and White was a well-known editor in literary circles in New York, they felt on a comfortable footing with each other. White recognized immediately that Lawrence knew more about gardening than she did, and she must have been encouraged by the fact that Lawrence seemed to take for granted that White would write more garden articles to follow the first one. White herself had not planned what she would do next, or, if she had, she wasn't saying so. But with Lawrence's help, perhaps she might "get enough good ideas" for another review. Lawrence also felt rewarded: she had received a letter from an editor at *The New Yorker,* who was married to the famous writer E. B. "Andy" White.

After the success of her first review of plant catalogues, White published a second and, six months later, a third. Even though she continued to express doubts to Lawrence that she could write another, in fact, she kept on going, reviewing not only catalogues but also gardening books and flower shows. The *New Yorker* heading for her articles—"Onward and Upward in the Garden"—seemed exactly right. Many readers became interested in garden literature because of these pieces in *The New Yorker;* in all, she wrote fourteen, the last appearing March 28, 1970.

During the same years, Lawrence was writing a weekly gardening column for the Charlotte *Observer,* ranging over some of the same territory that White was covering—nurseries, garden shows—with her own display of intelligence and wit. Both Lawrence and White were women of strong opinions, and it was fun for each of them to find someone who felt as strongly as each did, even if the subject was flower arrangements. Their letters to one another were a proving ground for their opinions, and perhaps fueled their determination to write about gardening as if it were as legitimate a subject for debate as politics, which they also alluded to in their letters to one another. (Both were JFK Democrats and stunned by Kennedy's death in 1963.)

Lawrence was a lifelong reader of *The New Yorker,* and if she could have fulfilled any fantasy, it might have been to be a writer of poems published in *The New Yorker*. She had first heard about the new magazine, founded in 1925, when she was a student at Barnard College, although she had not known anything about the woman who would be at the right hand of Harold Ross in making it the best magazine in America. But when White's "Romp in the Catalogues" appeared, Lawrence took note. And no matter if her files were a mess and her mornings disrupted and her own column delayed, she sat down to write a letter, seeking the kind of person-to-person contact that expressed her deep need to know other writers, especially those writing about gardens, and to be of help. Her letter to White was immediately answered, and the two women began a correspondence that lasted until White died in 1977.

The New Yorker had always had a prominent place in the Lawrence household, although Elizabeth often had to scramble to retrieve it from under the bed or her stacks of papers in order to write friends about articles they must not miss in the latest issue. She and her mother read it aloud together, she and her nephew Chip looked at the cartoons, and she wondered if all her sister Ann really wanted was her very own copy of *The New Yorker,* which passed back and forth between the two houses in Charlotte. Ann's daughter, "Fuzz," Elizabeth's namesake, remembers being told to run next door and get "the new *New Yorker.*"[2]

When the correspondence began, the time was right: White and Lawrence each needed someone to keep up her spirit. White had accepted her husband's need to live year-round on their saltwater farm in North Brooklin, Maine, and it was no secret that she was finding it hard to leave the city: she had to give up her desk at *The New Yorker,* meetings at the Algonquin, and parties in their Turtle Bay apartment. Not that she didn't love Maine, where they had been going for almost thirty years, where their son Joel and his wife Allene and their children lived, and where her son and daughter, Roger and Nancy, loved to bring their families for visits. The farm was as interesting a place for them as it was for readers of E. B. White's essays and stories. North Brooklin was small, but it was not without interest: natives and summer visitors were good conversationalists, and in nearby towns, shopkeepers familiar with the needs of New Yorkers sold specialty foods and the *Times.* The public library in North Brooklin was just the home for Katharine's collection of children's books, which she had reviewed for the magazine. Still, in her office in the front room of the farmhouse, across from her husband's, Katharine waited anxiously for the morning mail. There would be bags of *New Yorker* manuscripts to edit and letters from some of the *New Yorker* writers she had encouraged.

But there were problems that made the homecoming less than idyllic. Katharine's health was beginning to fail (she had admitted to Lawrence that she had little "strength" for gardening), foreshadowing a series of daunting illnesses and surgeries that would plague her for the rest of her life. She needed a good tonic for what ailed her that couldn't be x-rayed, diagnosed, or medicated: the dread of growing old and useless.

In 1958 Elizabeth Lawrence was also at a difficult place in her life. Her mother had become an invalid, living at home, which meant that Lawrence was having trouble finding time to write. Her best-known book, *A Southern Garden,* published in 1942, was out of print. *The Little Bulbs,* published in 1957, was a small book that deserved a larger audience. She could not find publishers for the manuscripts she was working on—about rock gardens, gardens in winter, and the market bulletins. Many of her friends were old and dying. During the twenty years she corresponded with Katharine White, she lost her mother and several of her dearest friends.

And yet, Lawrence was ambitious still. Her Charlotte garden, begun in 1950 after the Lawrences had moved from Raleigh, was filled with unusual plants and admiring visitors, and her mailbox was filled with letters from gardeners from Maine to California. And best of all, in 1957 she had begun writing a column for the Charlotte *Observer,* "Through the Garden Gate." Nothing gave her more pleasure than writing that weekly column. And one way she found things to write about was by keeping up with what was going on in other people's gardens. When Katharine White reported on her garden in Maine, it was exactly the kind of thing Lawrence's readers might enjoy. Elizabeth appreciated her efforts because she knew how many months during the winter Katharine's garden was under wraps, and how often Katharine's health would keep her inside the house. There was one aspect of the correspondence with Katharine White that particularly helped Elizabeth: White began to praise Elizabeth's books in her *New Yorker* columns. When Elizabeth's friends called to tell her, excitedly, that they had read White's good opinion in *The New Yorker,* Lawrence was set up, both with her friends and with her editors.

The back-and-forth of questions and answers, information, and candid opinions, as well as moments of pathos and humor, created a surprisingly lively correspondence. White hoped to be helpful to Lawrence by reporting on bloom dates in Maine. In her second letter, written in early July from her desk back at *The New Yorker* (the Whites still went to the city on occasion), she reported that in early March she had had snowdrops, and scylla and grape hyacinths in mid-June, but that they had left home just as the peonies, lupines, bearded iris, and the first roses were about to bloom. Lawrence assured her that this was valuable information and that she would always be grateful about any such reports, especially about anything that bloomed in November, December, and January. White's chrysanthemums were still in bloom the first week of November, her dark red Charles Mallerin rose bloomed Thanksgiving week, and by picking buds of Eclipse, Golden Wings, and White Wings, she had roses indoors until the last of the month. "Then came our hard freezes," she reported, December being the coldest since 1917, and they had had a blanket of snow for four weeks. Her gardening had moved indoors, and she knew that Lawrence wasn't interested in houseplants. "I am afraid that I shall not have a single outdoor winter flower to report," White regretted, and reiterated how limited she felt: "I am a sham as a gardener—no time to be scientific."

The Maine climate and the Whites' travels to Florida for the coldest months did limit what she could report, but she was also being honest about herself when she said that she wasn't scientific, at least not about the garden. The garden journal that she told Lawrence she had started on January l was, we discover, abandoned the next year, and it is easy to see why: Katharine White could not even write about plants without going back and revising her own sentences for clarity. Indeed, she was an editor. Readers would certainly not agree that she was a "sham" as a gardener, allowing for the fact that many are armchair gardeners rather than "dirt gardeners" themselves. Lawrence, on the other hand, had studied horticulture and was scientific in keeping daily, detailed records for her own gardens, both in Raleigh and later in Charlotte, but she had not described to White her thousands of index cards in file cabinets and dozens of small notebooks with minutely scribbled notes about plant names, characteristics, origins, and bloom dates. Lawrence had told White in her very first letter, written in 1958, that she had been gardening for nearly fifty years, a statement which perhaps had put White on the defensive. She did assure her that she was interested in houseplants, "not for myself—but I collect notes on everything that grows! I feel I should cover everything, as I do a column for the Charlotte *Observer.*" And she was "charmed" to hear of the roses at Thanksgiving—"just what I wanted," she said. "Here everyone at church wore a pink camellia—Debutante."

Though there were often long silences between letters and a continuing formality of manners, over the course of the first year they became more than sources of information for each other: they became friends. "I owe you more thanks than I can ever say for all your help," White wrote in May of 1959. "And I find myself quoting 'Elizabeth.' Do I dare call you that? Anyway, I'll sign myself, Katharine." "Dear Katharine," Elizabeth wrote back, attending to business: assuring her that she didn't know either why her daffodils had been short-stemmed ("Far from being an expert, I am the most casual gardener."); saying that White was welcome to anything she had ever said that would be of any use to her, without any concern about having "lifted" it unconsciously; and saying that she should not assume that she had "offended" Cecil Houdyshel because she had not heard from him since writing about his nursery in her column—he didn't write letters. (Lawrence had recommended Houdyshel's catalogues from LaVerne, California, in her first letter to White). Then she added a postscript: "I thought you did call me Elizabeth. I always call you Katharine in spirit." Mrs. White and Miss Lawrence already had written about nurserymen as if they knew them personally; now they felt freer to be themselves with each other. For almost twenty years, in spite of long lapses, and the duties and distractions of family life, Elizabeth and Katharine continued to exchange information, to laugh, and to encourage one another.

One of the liveliest aspects of the correspondence is what had inspired Katharine to write her first review in *The New Yorker*: The personalities of the catalogue writers themselves were every bit as "individualistic as any Faulkner or Hemingway." "The Burpee people," she explained, "have always been slightly mad on the subject of marigold"; "the sage" of White Flower Farm (in Litchfield, Connecticut), who signed himself "Amos Pettingill," was "peppery"; Will Tillotson had a "style of his own"—he was a "quoter." Probably it was exactly this recognition of the idiosyncratic personalities of the authors of garden catalogues that had prompted Lawrence's first letter, for in it she had introduced Cecil Houdyshel as a man in his nineties who aimed to live to be a hundred (his grandparents did), who offered a litter of cocker puppies for sale along with his plants, and who began his brochures, "Dear Flora Friends." And she had recommended *Park's Flower Book* (Greenwood, South Carolina)—though the new ones on slick paper couldn't compare with the old ones—for the photographs of the Parks: Mr. Park looked like his ancestor John Knox; his mother was "the Balance Wheel."

As soon as Katharine had used up most of her material and interest in catalogues, she turned her attention to gardening books, and Elizabeth was again forthcoming with suggestions about what to read, and where to order the books: everything by Gertrude Jekyll and the Loudons, von Arnim's *Elizabeth and Her German Garden,* and Louise Beebe Wilder. And Katharine introduced Elizabeth to books by Ernesta Drinker Ballard and Buckner Hollingsworth. Lawrence urged White to read books by her dear friend in Louisiana, Caroline Dormon; White put Lawrence in touch with her friend Grace Root, who gardened in northern New York. They exchanged books in the mail. White gave Lawrence a copy of Mrs. Loudon's *Ladies' Annuals;* Lawrence sent her own books and added Dormon's. And Lawrence sent boxes of plants—hellebore, ivy, fleur-de-lis, nandina—and "I wish you lived next door," she said. "I would fill your garden up."

In fact, Elizabeth and Katharine could not have been neighbors (the Whites would not have wanted to live anywhere except the North; Lawrence and her mother nowhere except the South). Nor does it seem likely that Katharine would have had time for Elizabeth (her time was "Andy's") or that Elizabeth would have presumed to ask for it. Although Katharine wrote several times that she hoped that she and Andy could stop by to see Elizabeth in Charlotte en route to Florida, something always came up to prevent the visit.

When Lawrence and White finally did meet—in 1967, in New York City—they had been writing to one another for almost a decade. Elizabeth was visiting her old friend Ellen Flood, and Katharine met them for lunch. Perhaps Andy had been invited, but he would not have wanted to come and probably was pressing Katharine to hurry so that they could get back to the farm. Whenever she visited the city, Elizabeth was timid and dependent on Ellen, a native New Yorker, who might have talked more than Elizabeth—she knew the city as well as the Whites. The meeting did not go well, for whatever reasons, including the fact that one-time meetings of this kind sometimes do not.

After the lunch neither wrote for the next seven months. Finally, Katharine broke the silence. In a letter written November 16, 1967, she first thanked Elizabeth for the help she had given her on her article about flower arrangements (they had enjoyed laughing over garden club rules and exhibits), and then she apologized if she had in fact never written to tell her how much she had enjoyed the luncheon—"I have written so many letters to you in my mind since last spring." The summer had been "miserable"—bad weather, poor health, no help. Katharine then was as personal as she had ever been: "Meeting you in person at last—you who have been my guide and mentor and my envy and admiration because of your knowledge and your wonderful books and your writing—was a nervous moment for me so if I acted jumpy, I hope you can forgive me. The wonderful thing for me was that I loved you at once as a person and wanted to stay on and talk for hours. Forgive me if I have written all this before."

Soon afterwards, Elizabeth wrote to Katharine, beginning by saying that she had enjoyed her article on flower arrangers, but she had been interrupted in her intention to write to her:

> Each day I set out to do what I have to do, and one thing that I want to do. Today is yours. First to tell you how I loved being with you, and to explain why I did not write before to tell you so. I was in great distress when I was in New York (and so much so that I did not stay as long as I had planned but came on home right after I saw you) about Ann Bridgers, who was dying of cancer in a hospital in Raleigh. You may remember that she was one of the authors of 'Coquette.' Ann and her sister Emily are the friends who have most encouraged me in writing, in fact, who started me out in writing about gardens when I had never done anything but poetry. Now Emily is dying of cancer. As they are much older than I, I knew I would be likely to out-live them, but I don't yet see how I can do it.

Whatever happened at the luncheon, Katharine and Elizabeth explained it to one another, and there was no lessening of feeling in their correspondence, which continued for another ten years. They never referred again to having met in New York. In the ways that mattered to them, their letters were more important.

Elizabeth and Katharine kept up each other's spirit. Katharine's praise of Elizabeth's gardening books helped her find readers, and Elizabeth thought it had helped persuade her publisher (the University of North Carolina) to bring out a new edition of *A Southern Garden,* in 1967. Although Katharine did not have the time or the strength to help Elizabeth find someone to publish the book she had been writing about the market bulletins, she told her that she must finish it, that it would be "a real contribution to the history of the culture of the South." Lawrence thanked her, "I was amazed at your point of view, and it gives me a new outlook." Both were stretching a point: Katharine had not actually seen the manuscript; for some thirty years, Elizabeth had been reading Southern market bulletins for what she learned about the lives of country people as much as for what she learned about plants. But they were true to their friendship—they cared for each other's work, and for each other. After twenty years, they were openly affectionate: in a letter written about a month before Katharine died, Elizabeth had signed her letter, "With love to you both." Katharine's last letter was signed, "Much love." The formidable Mrs. White and the shy Miss Lawrence were friends. Letters had been a means for both of them to express their uncertainties—and their certainties.

There is a last chapter to the Lawrence-White friendship. In 1977, the last year of her life, White arranged to give many of her books and papers to the archives at Bryn Mawr College, where she had been a student. She wanted to include Lawrence's letters and books also. Lawrence was proud that White thought of her in making her gifts to Bryn Mawr, and she immediately asked if she could send White's letters to her archives at Northwestern State University in Louisiana. Each agreed, and the letters were deposited.

In 2002, some twenty-five years after their last letters were written, the letters were published as *Two Gardeners: Katharine S. White and Elizabeth Lawrence—A Friendship in Letters,* edited by Emily Herring Wilson. Verlyn Klinkenborg, writing in the *New York Times Book Review*, hailed it as "one of the finest gardening books published in years, largely because it reveals as much about the character of these two remarkable women as it does about the plants they loved."[3]

CHAPTER TWENTY-ONE

The Weltys of Jackson, Mississippi

How lovely & rewarding a day like that can be.

EUDORA WELTY TO ELIZABETH LAWRENCE, APRIL 1982

ELIZABETH LAWRENCE and Eudora Welty claimed one another as friends over many years. They first met in Raleigh in the 1930s, and their last visit in Lawrence's garden in Charlotte, the spring of 1982, was especially memorable for them both. The two writers had been interested in one another's work from the beginning of their publishing careers, but Lawrence's literary affinity was with poetry, and she felt qualified to comment on Welty's stories only when the experiences seemed to match up with her own. As single daughters who looked after their widowed mothers, they were also in a position to sympathize with each other's chosen life, with its exhausting responsibilities and its deep sorrows as they watched their mothers decline.

Perhaps the closest understanding, however, existed not so much between Elizabeth and Eudora as between Lawrence and Welty's mother, Chestina Welty, a kindred spirit in the garden. Their friendship had begun in 1942 when Mrs. Welty wrote Lawrence an admiring letter after she read *A Southern Garden*. Several years later, when Mrs. Welty invited Elizabeth to stay with them when she was traveling to lecture to garden clubs, Elizabeth came, and she felt at home. It was exciting to talk with Eudora about her stories, but Elizabeth admitted that she did not always understand them. Going into Mrs. Welty's garden to admire her roses immediately set Elizabeth at ease.

The Weltys of Jackson, Mississippi

In 1904, soon after they were married, Chestina Andrews Welty, a native of Clay County, West Virginia, and Christian Welty, a native of southern Ohio, moved to Jackson, Mississippi. After the births of their three children—Eudora in 1909, Edward in 1912, and Walter in 1915—Chestina Welty became active in various women's club projects. In the 1920s she was one of the founding members of a garden club that sponsored flower shows at the state fair and helped to landscape streets and highways. As city beautification projects became more desirable, several local garden clubs decided to work together, and in 1931 they formed a central organization. Mrs. Welty herself wrote the early history of the Jackson Council of Garden Clubs. In it, she named many of the same kinds of projects that were sponsored by the Wake County Garden Club in Raleigh, North Carolina, in the 1930s and 1940s, when Elizabeth and her mother were members: juried competitions, garden libraries, streets and highways, lectures and garden schools, and (during World War II when many club activities waned) vegetable gardens.[1]

Elizabeth Lawrence's early education through garden club activities was parallel to Chestina Welty's—they learned from them, and they outgrew them. Each of them came to value an exchange of plants and information, and each soon grew tired of judging flower shows. They shared an intense desire to learn a body of botanical knowledge. In 1942 when Lawrence received Mrs. Welty's letter in praise of *A Southern Garden,* Lawrence could tell from what she had to say about plants that Mrs. Welty was "a real gardener." Chestina Welty gardened, she read about gardens, and she studied gardens. Plants—their Latin and their common names, their seasons of bloom, and the conditions under which they thrived—were intensely interesting to her. She wanted to *know* all about plants, and she was an avid and continuous learner. She and Elizabeth approached the garden in the same way: as teachers in a classroom, passionate and opinionated about their subject. Each had a discerning eye, and neither admired blossoms or gardens for their size, or gardeners for their prizes. "It was a perfectly simple matter of fact; the garden was to be a learning experience," Eudora Welty remembered, many years after her mother's death in 1966. "She had a schoolteacher's love of accuracy. She would look up everything so there would be no mistakes made and no foolishness."[2] This quest to learn was precisely what Lawrence recognized as the passion of the "real gardener."

Chestina Welty and Elizabeth Lawrence began on an equal footing with their first letters. "My dear Miss Lawrence," Mrs. Welty wrote in the summer of 1942, "I have just finished reading your book, *A Southern Garden,* and have enjoyed every page of it—though I felt selfish all the time for reading it before Eudora did when it is her book." She quickly added, "But she is reading it now."[3] Lawrence had received many fan letters, but this one was special: not only had she met Eudora and known that they were both writers and about the same age, but she could have recognized in Mrs. Welty's a voice so like her own mother's.

By 1942 the Weltys' brick Tudor house on Pinehurst Street (built in 1925) had settled comfortably into the residential landscape of Jackson's first suburb, and Mrs. Welty had a garden of her own. In front of the house, boxwood and other foundation plantings conformed to the style of the times, and there were young trees planted for the future. A water oak, which Mrs. Welty had insisted must not be cut down, did come to dominate the front yard; cedars to the side flourished long after the shade garden had gone to weeds. Flowering shrubs, crepe myrtles, dogwoods, and camellias added seasonal color to the side yard, but the more private garden behind the house was Mrs. Welty's special pride: the upper garden included perennial borders, which she had designed herself, in detailed journals, for a succession of blooms. She admired camellias and worked in her iris border, but what she especially loved was her roses in the lower garden.

Rose trellises, a wisteria arbor, two benches facing one another—Chestina Welty had laid out her garden with an eye for beauty and order. After the sudden death of her husband, Christian Welty, in 1931, she tended her beds with great care, daily for as long as she could, studying the effects she had hoped for when she had ordered seeds and plants from nursery catalogues and made drawings for where they were to go. Although she belonged to a garden club and agreed to have her garden on the annual tour (and won a ribbon for it), she had little patience with club rules—the dos and don'ts of gardening were for those who did not have minds of their own. Even though her garden shared something of the same look and plantings of other Jackson gardens of the 1920s and 1930s, Mrs. Welty knew what personal knowledge of each plant had gone into its making. When she read Elizabeth Lawrence's book, she recognized a voice much like her own, and her letter made that clear: "It is such a pleasure to read something that is applicable to our own gardens. Nearly all the writers of the North and East discuss our needs with the admonition that time of planting or blooming should be a month earlier or some such nonsense that doesn't work at all. We all have to contend with and allow for what you aptly call the 'caprices of our climate.' But your book is what you call it—a handbook—and already I have returned to it several times to verify something."

Then Mrs. Welty turned to her own garden. "I was particularly interested in dates of bloom of various things in your garden. While I have never kept a record of these, I have always started out in January with the best intentions but failed to carry them out. But it seems to me your dates and ours are very nearly the same. Take day-lilies for instance—and I am very enthusiastic about them. My amaryllis Gem and J.A. Crawford have just finished blooming. Hyperion is in full bloom now and Mrs. W. H. Wyman just beginning. That seems to agree pretty well with your schedule."

Few gardeners ever wrote to Elizabeth Lawrence without asking for help in identifying some plant, and Mrs. Welty was no exception. She did not know the name of her "most prolific" day lily. "Miss Newman of Belhaven College [across the street from Mrs. Welty's house] brought it from Virginia years ago and her friends call it 'Miss Newman.' I am wondering if it could be 'Florham,' which I do not know. It is almost the same shade and form—though mine is a little larger—as Mrs. W. H. Wyman and is just now past its peak of bloom. I counted thirty bloom stalks on a four year clump the other day."

Such a question, so like hundreds that were asked of Lawrence, and that she answered, must have sent Elizabeth out into her own garden (where Florham was two weeks past its bloom in Raleigh, North Carolina) and into her study, where she could consult her files. "Florham," she had written in *A Southern Garden,* "an old variety that is a great bloomer and increases rapidly, is the best day-lily to plant in quantity. It is like Amaryllis with its frilled petals and delightful fragrance, but it is not so good in form and substance, nor so large in size."[4] But whether she was able to identify Mrs. Welty's day lily is not known, and "Miss Newman" has not been identified. Perhaps Miss Lawrence asked Mrs. Welty to send her one so that she could study it for herself in her Raleigh garden.

Another flower that interested Chestina was the white Desmodium. "When I bought mine it was mixed—white and magenta colored—but I have almost eliminated the purplish ones and the white is lovely. And I am surely going to try your blue spirea. I thought at first you meant blue salvia—for some reason I've always wanted to call a blue salvia, a *spirea.* I think because I couldn't stand the *red* salvia, but now that I know there really is a blue spirea I am going to have some."

Whether Lawrence sent seeds from her blue spiraea *(Caryopteris incana)* is uncertain—there is none growing today in what remains of Mrs. Welty's garden—but if Lawrence followed her usual pattern of answering letters, she would have spent as many hours as it took trying to help Mrs. Welty with her garden, including packing up cuttings and carrying them to the post office for delivery to 1119 Pinehurst Street, Jackson, Mississippi.

Mrs. Welty was finally ready to put down her pen: "But my letter would be too long if I mentioned half the things that you mentioned which were of special interest to me. Let me just repeat that the book has given me great pleasure and I am sure will continue to help me."

A chance to meet Mrs. Welty came in the fall of 1944, when Lawrence, enjoying the popularity of *A Southern Garden,* was invited to talk to garden clubs in Shreveport, Louisiana, and Oxford, Mississippi. On that trip she visited the Weltys, apparently for the first time, arriving at two in the morning on the train from Vicksburg, and leaving that same evening. The next morning on the train to Atlanta, Elizabeth wrote Ann Preston Bridgers about the experience. "I wanted to sit right down to discuss art & literature," she explained, "but they seemed to take it for granted that we would go to bed. *They* did, and I took a bath & read Chekhov's letters—so that left only the day & evening to talk to Eudora, and most of that was spent with Mrs. Welty, who is a real gardener, and with the president of the garden club, and a next door neighbor, looking at camellias not yet in bloom & wondering what they would be like when they did bloom."[5] Several days later when she had arrived back home, she wrote to Eudora:

> I was so dazed after all of the people and gardens, and being with you always makes me feel so dazed at best, and I came away with the feeling that every time you started to tell me something I floated away like those long-stemmed water-lily leaves in streams that float away (I mean the leaves float away, not the streams—I feel a comma would fix those things up, but never know where to put one) when you reach for them, and then float back when you turn away. And every time I floated back you had turned away. But it is only the conscious mind that does that, the subconscious (fortunately) stays put like the root, and takes in all that goes on, and stores it up and changes it to carbohydrates or something, and keeps it in available form where you can get at it whenever you like.

She concluded, "So all the way home I dug the carbohydrates out."[6]

On a later occasion when Lawrence was back again in Mississippi for talks with garden clubs, she apparently called the Welty house hoping to see Eudora, but when she found that she was away, she accepted Mrs. Welty's invitation to come to see her. It made such an impression on Eudora that she remembered it years later (in 1987), after Chestina Welty and Elizabeth Lawrence had both died. In a Christmas note to Welty's editor at *The New Yorker,* William Maxwell, and his wife "Emmy," accompanying a gift of Lawrence's *Gardening for Love,* Welty wrote that Lawrence "once paid a surprise visit and I was by (my) bad luck away, but she stayed in my room and visited my mother and read all my books, the visit she always said was the best one.[7]

Perhaps it was a very short visit like the earlier one, when she was returning home by train and stopped off in Jackson. Eudora must have been grateful that Lawrence spent time with her mother, knowing how fond Mrs. Welty was of Elizabeth and how they shared the same gardening interests. In Elizabeth's letters to Eudora, she seldom failed to send "much love to your mother." And Eudora would respond, "Mother sends her best to you and we wish you would come back."[8]

Sometime in the late 1930s, Elizabeth had met Eudora Welty in Raleigh, where Welty was visiting her good friend Frank Lyell, also a Jackson native, who was teaching in the Department of English at North Carolina State College. They could have been introduced by Ann and Emily Bridgers at their home, a popular gathering place for people in the arts, or by another member of the English Department, Lodwick Hartley, a friend and colleague of Lyell's. To meet a young writer from Mississippi whose short stories were being talked about in New York was the very thing to enliven an evening in Raleigh. When Eudora Welty came to town, and parties were given, Elizabeth fell into the group, and finding herself among like-minded people, she immediately made friends. Welty came to see her garden, met Elizabeth's mother, and heard Elizabeth play her shepherd's bamboo pipe. Even after Lyell left Raleigh (in 1942, to join the faculty at the University of Texas), Elizabeth continued to keep in touch with him, usually through Eudora. ("Bessie sends her love to Frank," Elizabeth wrote, "and says to tell him she is ever grateful for the peach drink he taught her to make.")[9] In addition to Frank and Lodwick, two others who made up the lively company were Anna Riddick, an interior designer (whose client houses included the Governor's Mansion), and Baker Wynne, who had a fine garden. Riddick and Hartley shared a love of the eighteenth century —Riddick designed eighteenth-century interiors, and Hartley was an eighteenth-century scholar. What they also had in common was that they were Southerners, born and bred.

They all took to Eudora Welty immediately, and read each of her stories and books as they came out. A grand occasion for a party was when the Raleigh group got together to think up names for her next book.

Hartley was always trying to find a way to get Welty to come to Raleigh, but she declined his suggestion that she teach at State College, though she was willing to come speak to his reading group, since she was going to be giving a lecture at Duke University at the same time. "The prospect of coming back to Raleigh and seeing you and Anna and all warms the heart and I look forward mightily," she exclaimed. "Shall I bring along the copy of 'Spangled Unicorn' [satirical poems by Noel Coward], which I remember we all read with such rapture, or do I dare!"[10]

Elizabeth Lawrence's friendship with Eudora Welty had its own special character, loyal and loving and perfectly harmonious in their visits in both North Carolina and Mississippi. The two Southern women—intelligent, opinionated, dutiful to family, and attached to memory—were cut from the same cloth, though the patterns were different. The cloth was the geography of place. For Lawrence the pattern was a garden, for Welty a story. Sense of place is obvious to readers of both Lawrence's garden books and Welty's stories. In Lawrence's garden books readers were introduced to Gertrude Jekyll of Munstead Woods, Vita Sackville-West of Sissinghurst, Carl Krippendorf of Lob's Wood, Caroline Dormon of Briarwood, Eddie and Elizabeth Clarkson of Wing Haven, Rosa Hicks of Rocky Knob. The title of her first book locates her: *A Southern Garden: A Handbook for the Middle South*. In Welty's fictions, Sister lives at the P.O. in China Grove, a salesman travels in the desolate Mississippi hill country, Livvie sweeps her dirt yard clean on the Old Natchez Trace, strangers meet on Bourbon Street, a motherless child rides the Yellow Dog to a delta wedding, and on and on. A Lawrence landscape and a Welty landscape were recognizable to their readers—and to one another.

Many of the particulars of Welty's and Lawrence's lives were close and comforting. Lawrence noted, "Eudora is only two years younger than I [Welty, born in 1909, was five years younger than Lawrence], and she lives in the same atmosphere. Georgia and West Virginia are to me what Mississippi and West Virginia are to her."[11] Both were first children of doting parents (and grandparents)—held, read to, talked to, photographed, loved, and overprotected. Welty said that Chestina Welty tended to be a pessimist; Bessie Lawrence wasn't far behind, though she would have insisted that she was only a realist. Christian Welty and Sam Lawrence were optimists and had a good sense of humor, which was a great gift to their daughters, who learned to laugh at a very early age.

In their youth as well as later, Elizabeth Lawrence and Eudora Welty traveled similar paths. Both went to women's colleges; Elizabeth began at St. Mary's School for girls in Raleigh, and went on to Barnard College; for two years Eudora attended "the W," Mississippi State College for Women. Both wrote verses (and submitted them to *St. Nicholas Magazine*), majored in English, loved Latin, and read Jane Austen and W. B. Yeats, among many other favorite writers. Both were said by some to be "shy" and "reclusive"; in fact, they were neither. Smart, literary women who do not marry, live at home, and keep to themselves are often said to be shy recluses. About Jane Austen, whose laughter is heard all through her novels, Welty observed, "perennial objectors" wondered how a spinster who lived at home and traveled little "could have had any way of knowing very much about life."[12] In fact, like Austen, Lawrence and Welty were both very private women, who were the best company in the world. Friends could hardly bring themselves to say goodnight, even after Lawrence had added the last log to the fire (she was an excellent fire builder) and Welty had sweetened their drinks (she mixed good ones). Audiences who gathered to hear them "talk" were also enchanted, leaning forward so as not to miss a soft-spoken word. They had candid opinions and did not hesitate to express them. They did not suffer fools gladly, though they managed to ignore them in the interest of good manners. They liked bourbon and their mother's recipes, and though they did not want to spend a lot of time in the kitchen, they could do what had to be done to make their guests feel perfectly at home: Eudora did not want any help in her kitchen; Elizabeth did.

They suffered similar losses. Eudora's father died when he was only

Eudora Welty and her mother, Chestina, in their garden in Jackson, Mississippi, in the mid-1950s. Mrs. Welty and Elizabeth shared similar gardening interests, and Elizabeth visited her and Eudora on several occasions. (Courtesy of Mary Alice Welty White and Elizabeth Welty Thompson. Photograph by Rollie McKenna.)

fifty-one; Elizabeth's father died when he was sixty-one. After the death of their fathers, they both felt that they were needed by their mothers at home. As their mothers grew old and infirm, Eudora and Elizabeth managed the family finances (Welty had begun to make money; Lawrence made some, but she and her mother were living mostly on a small inheritance) and were responsible for the around-the-clock care at home, sometimes taking the night shift themselves. Each understood the other's pain in watching her mother decline. When their mothers died, in their own beds, after long illnesses—Bessie Lawrence in 1964, Chestina Welty in 1966—Elizabeth and Eudora had lived at home too long to contemplate doing anything else.

But there were also differences between them, not only in what they wrote but in who they were. As a gardener and garden writer, Lawrence designed a life for herself that was expressive but not disclosing. She was perhaps the more private of the two, the more guarded, the less likely to expose herself to questions. A writer of fiction inevitably opens herself up to questions. Welty refused to talk about herself and said that anybody who wanted to know about her could read her stories. Although Welty continued to live in the house her parents had built on Pinehurst Street in Jackson, Mississippi, she traveled quite a bit, as long as she was able. She was, she said, "locally underfoot," and other writers came to see her in Jackson—Elizabeth Bowen, Katherine Anne Porter, Robert Penn Warren. She became the most celebrated citizen in the city; even the governor came over to the Old State Capitol to honor her, on Eudora Welty Day.

Elizabeth Lawrence had her own magnetism, and her own close circle of friends, who adored her, but she was not the public person that Welty was. She was far less well known, wrote fewer books, had fewer readers, gave fewer lectures. The garden was a more private space than the literary world, and Lawrence chose to make her life there. Lawrence seems not to have struggled against the authority of her own controlling mother, but rather to have accepted it and to have taken advantage of what her mother could provide: financial security, household management, and companionship. There is no evidence that she felt the guilt Welty writes that she sometimes felt when she sought to loosen the ties that bound her to her mother. "In the act and the course of writing stories," however, Welty discovered that her passion for independence and her guilt were "two of the springs, one bright, one dark, that feed the stream."[13]

When Welty visited Lawrence in Charlotte in mid-April, 1963, Lawrence showed her the new garden that she had made after the move from Raleigh. "Some people always make you see how shabby your things look, and others make them even more beautiful than you thought," Elizabeth reflected later. "I thought the garden had never been more delightful than when I walked around it with Eudora. It was still early and the shadows were cool, and there was dew on the white tulips and snowflakes, and more of the banksia was out than I had thought. Eudora stood still in the path, and said, 'I am thinking how to tell my mother.' "[14]

The names and places of flowers often appeared in both Elizabeth's and Eudora's letters. "It's camellia and blue hyacinth time in Jackson," Eudora wrote in mid-February. "In New Orleans the sweetpeas are blooming—in the swamps, red leaves on maples and on the willow trees those green-gold threads."[15]

Lawrence always felt indebted to Welty for having put her on the mailing list to receive the *Mississippi Market Bulletin* (published in Jackson). Several years later she wrote to tell Eudora how much she and Bessie were enjoying reading the bulletins. "We came very near asking you to interview a bull dog for us, but thought maybe you were like us and had used up your gas, and he lives on Route II."[16] Welty had started Lawrence out on a passion for corresponding with farm ladies, as she called them, who advertised their seeds, bulbs, and cuttings to make "pin money." Lawrence and Welty corresponded with a few of the same gardeners and often peppered their letters with references to something they had read about in the Mississippi publication. Both loved the country sayings: "I'm sorry not to have written before this," Welty began one of her letters, "but, as old ladies that sell flowers through the mail say, must plead company."[17] Welty had put her agent Diarmuid Russell's name on the mailing list for the market bulletin, and he also became an avid reader. He wrote Lawrence to be alert to ads for beer seed, and she got interested and tried to find out what readers of the Mississippi bulletin knew about beer seed. Soon Welty, Russell, and Lawrence were exchanging information. "One answer I got," Welty wrote Lawrence, "was from a Rev. somebody on the Coast (Miss.) written on an envelope with a photograph of a church on it and a little ad of gospel services rendered underneath—he wrote with a red ribbon in his typewriter and said when he heard anything about those beer seeds he certainly would let me know, and that they were carrying on there on the Coast, 'although unmarried,' and would love to hear more about myself and my home. (I hadn't told them a thing—natcherly!)."[18] Welty encouraged Lawrence "to have up a correspondence" with Russell. Nobody could be more persistent than Lawrence when it came to finding out the answer to a question, and it was she who finally found some beer seeds. She sent them to Jackson, and Welty sent some on to Russell. "I can see now why people advertise for it [beer seeds] again and again," Welty joked with Lawrence, "because you just drink it up, and next time you're thirsty you have to run another ad."[19] Russell was less jocular: he thought the seed Lawrence had sent (which she had described as "sticky and granular and of a pale amber color") did not look promising. If she wanted to send him a whiskey plant, however, he said he wouldn't trouble her further.[20] But, Welty wrote to Lawrence, "don't PLANT the beer seeds—that will be the end of them. They won't grow up and have beer on tap at little notches in their stalks, enchanting as it seems, and almost real as it seems, now that we have 'got a hold of' the seed." She enclosed a letter from a market bulletin correspondent who said that beer was made by dropping the seeds in water. "I haven't made my beer yet," Welty advised. "Let us communicate when that brew is drunk."[21]

It wasn't unusual for orders through the market bulletins to confuse gardeners in other places. "God knows what the bulbs are," Welty lamented, "but the lady says she can spare me any number, so no doubt they are not the real sterling silver bells." And the hope that a plant would like another garden was sometimes as uncertain as its name. "The enormous rain lily with wine-dark throat sounds beautiful," Welty wrote. "I hope you can keep it."[22] "The wonder lily is up," Elizabeth wrote in the fall of 1942. "Also our silver bells came up early, so they must be some of the polyanthus group."[23] The next year Welty wrote, "I hope our Wonder, Russian, Blue Phantom, etc. lilies all bloom wondrously, Russianly, bluely & phantomesque for us in the summer. Your day lily is in bud, and we are watching."[24]

The bulletins, especially ones from Mississippi, gave Lawrence and Welty materials for their articles and stories. Neither one wanted to miss a single issue, and each would call something to the other's attention.

When Welty was living in New York City in the summer of 1944 and writing book reviews for the *Times,* she complained to Lawrence: "It was nice to hear from you—the letter got here all right though *who* forwarded it I do not know, since nobody was home—probably the postman—and why doesn't he ever forward my Farm Bulletin? I live without it and hate it."[25]

For four decades Lawrence collected plant information from the correspondents whose acquaintance she had made through the market bulletins, and she intended to write a book based on this correspondence, but she collected so much that at the end she found herself overwhelmed. "Their advertisements show the customs of the country people, their humor, and their way of speaking," Lawrence wrote. "Like Eudora's novels, the market bulletins are a social history of the Deep South."[26] Lawrence often used letters from these correspondents in her garden column in the Charlotte *Observer,* and she told her readers that Welty also found the market bulletins a good source for materials. In Welty's last story in her Morgana chronicle, "The Wanderers," Virgie Rainey, who aimed to get married on her bulb money, fanned her dying mother with the *Mississippi Market Bulletin.* As she was losing consciousness, the mother went over in her head her list of flowers that she had advertised for sale, dozens of them: four colors of cannas for 15 cents, true box, moonvine seed by the teaspoonful, five colors of verbena, apostle lilies, four o'clock, sweet geranium cuttings, sword fern, fortune grass, golden bell, pink fairy lilies.[27]

Lawrence and Welty had a good time exploring Southern culture together. When they tried to remember the words to "The Church in the Wildwood," Lawrence cleared up the mystery by ordering a record of gospel hymns from Mr. W. E. Kimery, who lived near the Tennessee line. (Apparently, Lawrence had found him in the *Mississippi Market Bulletin.*) Lawrence said that it was "the real thing," and Welty agreed. "I love the way they all (especially his sister) 'come in,'" she wrote. "I only wish they had had enough room to give all the verses. You get the very air in the room and the smell of the country flowers. I expect zinnias and gladiolas and salvia, in a tub—and the warm day. The enthusiasm is fine—it's all so expressive & Sunday-like."[28]

When Welty published a new story or novel, Lawrence was eager to read it. In 1941 when Welty's story "The Winds" appeared in *Harper's Bazaar*, Lawrence wrote immediately to say how much she liked it. Apparently they did not discuss the fact that Welty had based it upon a childhood experience of having been frightened during a tornado, but Lawrence intuitively understood the power of memory. Welty wrote back, "Nothing more pleasing to the writer could be said about a story than it seemed written for its reader, and I am really pleased that you said it was written for you." Then she went on to invite whatever thoughts Lawrence might have about its meaning. She explained, "No one is timider than I am in the face of being read, but just on account of that don't think I don't want to hear any analysis if you have it in your head. Use of analysis, I don't know about either—I believe there is no aid or help in this world for stories, maybe, at least for the particular story it's made about. For stories to come, there's hope there. But use is not so much to us, is it—why not for its own sake."[29]

Frank Lyell lent Elizabeth his copy of *Harper's Bazaar* so that she could read another of Welty's new stories, "First Love," and she was excited to discover that she had a family connection to one of Welty's characters. In one of her few historic fictions, Welty describes the perceptions of a young deaf boy as night after night he watches Aaron Burr and his friend Harman Blennerhassett talking in a Natchez tavern. Elizabeth wrote her to explain that she had played on Blennerhassett Island as a child when she was visiting her mother's family in Parkersburg, West Virginia.[30]

When *Delta Wedding* was published in 1946, Lawrence wrote Welty a long letter to tell her how much she liked it, especially the descriptions of a plantation house called Marmion, which she thought was "the best" of all Welty's fictional houses. (Welty's biographer Suzanne Marrs explains that Marmion was based on a real house, Waverley, which Welty vividly remembered having seen.[31]) Lawrence thought the novel was "like a poem," and while admiring the symbols, she admitted, "some of them were beyond me, (but none the less beautiful for that, maybe more so)."[32]

Many years later, when *The Optimist's Daughter* was published (in 1972), Elizabeth wrote to say that she had read it, "and then turned to the beginning and read it again. And it is as if I had been with you. I always feel that you are writing for me," but she added, "I suppose everyone does." Then, as if to let Welty know that she read (and personally knew) other good writers, she said, "Only Joseph Mitchell writes as well as you." She confessed, "Laurel haunts me, like those dreams you think really happened. I feel as if I knew her—or know her. She is more real to me than anyone you ever wrote about. All are real, but real as if they were in poems—Poe or Blake; or pictures—Damien. But Laurel is like a friend I can't bear to hurt."[33]

Welty was good about encouraging Lawrence's own writing—she often gave copies of Lawrence's books as gifts to friends—and when Lawrence wrote that she was having trouble finding a publisher, Welty recommended that she contact her own literary agent, Diarmuid Russell. But nothing came of Lawrence's efforts to enlist Russell in her cause. While admiring *A Southern Garden,* which Welty had sent him, he did not think that it would have a wide audience. What most discouraged Lawrence, however, was that Welty had told her that she never had anything changed in her manuscripts, whereas Lawrence felt herself constantly undermined by editorial changes. As she brooded over their differences, Lawrence wrote to Ann Bridgers, "I worked in the garden, and thought about Eudora. It came to me that Mr. Russell must edit her, and then wrestle with the editor."[34] In 1963, when this exchange took place, however, the gap between Welty's success and Lawrence's had widened considerably. Lawrence's *Gardens in Winter* (1961) was the last major book published in her lifetime, and for the next twenty years, she struggled unsuccessfully to finish her market bulletin manuscript. Welty, by comparison, was to have another twenty years of even greater successes as a lecturer, writer, and well-known American literary personality. In 1972 she won the Pulitzer Prize for *The Optimist's Daughter,* a novel that many critics believe was her way of coming to terms with her mother's death. And in 1984, she had impressive success with a series of autobiographical lectures delivered at Harvard and published as *One Writer's Beginnings.*

But even though there were great differences between these two writers, they still shared a remarkable devotion and love for each other. Two visits, in particular, are indicative of this.

Welty had come in the spring of 1963 to speak at Davidson College near Charlotte, and she spent a morning on Ridgewood Avenue. "We had breakfast by the door, and walked in the garden, and had sherry by the fire, and forgot about time until Eudora said, 'Mercy!' and I went to get a clock and put it in front of her."[35] (When the time came, Elizabeth put her on the Durham bus at noon to go to Duke University, where she was scheduled to speak. Two ladies in their fifties saying goodbye in a bus station was the kind of moment Welty herself might have captured in a novel, perhaps when Elizabeth handed a picnic basket to the driver to put overhead, and Eudora was helped up the steps.)

After a later visit by Eudora in April 1982, she wrote a letter to Elizabeth that epitomizes her pleasure in their friendship.[36]

> How lovely & how rewarding a day like that can be. Diarmuid would have called it "a day picked out." You made it happen, and as far as I was concerned it was perfect—the shortness of time wasn't of any consequence at all, it was so fixed with pleasure, and the joy of walking in your garden again and seeing how you'd kept its continuing identity and its peace [marginal note—& as is] & in the beauty of the time of year—I was so glad to see you! and to see you where you belong most, just as always, and garden & house & yourself all looking in charge of one another in the same lively and complete accord—well, it's not easy to express, but so easy to bask in and thank heaven for.
>
> The only thing was, you'd done too much for me. Starting with thinking it up and figuring the time table and making the map, and of course calling upon that dear Roger. Our sherry in the light of the garden, the tulips and the cherry tree—and the home-made cheese straws & the pepper jelly, & the cheese and the prunes in Marsala—we were living exclusively on treats, and conversation was the best one.
>
> I wouldn't take anything for a word of it. As my mother would say, 'I wouldn't take a pretty for that.' I am so glad that you are providing for

the Market Bulletin work you've given so much time & care and imagination & understanding to. I'm delighted to think anything of mine could fit in with it all in any shape or form, and thank you for seeing those kindred elements.

. . . . The lunch you made & packed for me should've been eaten in the spring woods (perhaps Fontainebleau) beside a flowing stream. But I was the one flowing, up in that jet stream. I ate the delicious ham sandwiches—& the delicious bread—and the egg! The box you fixed for it like a little square house with a round window so its lovely brown face could be inside.

And the delicious tarts! And all thought of, salt, pepper, a fork & spoon and a proper knife for the golden [ham?], and even a little wet washcloth, same as a finger bowl—It was my lunch and my supper, too. Thank you for all that day!

I got home safely last night. Take care—I'm glad we're in touch.
Love from Eudora.

CHAPTER TWENTY-TWO

Gardening for Love *and* A Rock Garden in the South

Gardeners are generous because nature is generous to them.

More than twenty years after Elizabeth Lawrence wrote about her own city garden in her first book, *A Southern Garden,* she was at work on what she expected would be her last book, about Southern farm women and their gardens. For decades she had been responding to their advertisements of plants, placed in agricultural market bulletins, mainly those published in Mississippi, Louisiana, North Carolina, South Carolina, Alabama, and Georgia. Her respect for these women was obvious, without "a single word of deprecation or hint of superiority," as Elisabeth Woodburn was to observe when she first read Lawrence's manuscript. In her opening chapter, Lawrence wrote, "These old ladies—and an occasional gentleman—who sell flowers through the mail are amateurs in the true sense of the word: they garden for love. And their love is a saving love. . . . Gardeners are generous because nature is generous to them."[1]

Nowhere is Lawrence's democratic vista more expansive than it is in this book, which she called *Gardening for Love.* She began with a passage from a letter written by a gardener in London (one Peter Collinson) to a gardener in Williamsburg, Virginia (one John Custis). The year was 1735.

> I think there is no Greater pleasure than to be Communicative and oblige others. It is laying an obligation and I seldome fail of Returns for Wee Brothers of the Spade find it very necessary to share amongst us the seeds

> that come annual from Abroad. It not only preserves a Friendly Society but secures our Collections, for if one does not raise a seed perhaps another does & if one Looses a plant another can Supply him.

Lawrence explained that many of the same plants that traveled between London and Williamsburg still appeared in twentieth-century market bulletin lists, and went "from garden to garden: fringe tree, cucumber tree, sweet gum, and sassafras" and many others. In the simple phrase "garden to garden" she named precisely her subject matter, not only for this book but for all her books. As a garden writer, by bringing many other writers and gardeners into the conversation, she enriched the tradition of people and cultures talking across time and place.

Elizabeth Lawrence apparently spent more time on what she called her "market bulletin book" than on anything else she wrote, which may explain why she never finished it. Around 1943, when Eudora Welty told her about the wealth of information about people and plants to be found in Southern agricultural bulletins, and put her on the mailing list to receive the bulletin from Mississippi, she embarked on an adventure that was as time-consuming as it was rewarding. She subscribed to every bulletin she could find (including several privately owned ones), and when the bulletins came (usually monthly or bimonthly, and mostly free of charge), she began reading everything in them, including ads for farm animals. But what interested her most were the farm women who advertised their plants for sale in order to make "pin money" and to spread the gospel according to "old-timey" ways. She wrote to them, and they wrote back. While continuing to collect plants (often exchanged for some of her own) and information in this way, she also began to expand her ideas for a book. She started creating a manuscript that was so long and diverse that it became unwieldy. At various points in its gestation, it included a long section on Mr. Krippendorf (which was later taken out and published as *Lob's Wood*), another on herbs (which she was unable to place as a separate book and which ultimately became part of *Gardening for Love*), and chapters based on correspondence with the West Coast (which she sent to *Pacific Horticulture,* where they were published).[2]

Friends who knew Lawrence in the last decade of her life were aware that she was engaged in a desperate race to finish the manuscript. As much as friends loved being invited to come to see her, they knew that their visits took her away from finishing "the book." From Maine Katharine White wrote to say that it would be a social history of the South. Lawrence's Charlotte friend, Dannye Romine (Powell), a columnist for the Charlotte *Observer,* saw what a "fret" Elizabeth Lawrence got herself into, trying to write what amounted to an encyclopedia of horticulture. But Lawrence was in the grip of the feeling writers often have when a manuscript has been under way for a long time: the fear that it will never get done. And she realized that her correspondents were also aging, and that all that they knew would disappear with them. Lawrence wanted to include in one last book all the information about plants that she had acquired over a lifetime of learning—from her own gardens, from other gardeners, and from garden books—then to mix into the brew the wisdom of the Southern American provinces. And to know both the country names for Miss Bessie's plants, sent through the mail as "hummingbird plant," "turkey-gobbler beads," and "wedding bells," and their Latin names, *Spiraea* x *bumalda, Symphoricarpos orbiculatus,* and *Forsythia viridissima,* was part of that learning.

In 1961, after *Gardens in Winter* had been published, Lawrence sent her editor at Harper's the manuscript of *Gardening for Love,* and for several years she continued to believe that he would recommend publication, but finally he returned the manuscript. The rejection was too much for Lawrence, and by the late 1960s she was asking for help wherever she might find it, mailing letters off when she heard about editors who might work with her on the manuscript. Nothing came of her inquiries, and so she began to circulate the manuscript among her friends. One of the gardeners who met Lawrence late in life was a North Carolinian, Burke Davis, an important writer of historical fiction. When Lawrence sent him part of her manuscript, he became interested in her correspondents as well and ordered plants himself from one of her favorites, Rosa Hicks. He encouraged Lawrence to "flesh-out" her characters, and when she did, he applauded her efforts: "Yes m'am. Rosa is now in residence in your narrative; if other opportunities arise later, you might use tiny touches, but she's now a personality, and will radiate throughout the plant material. I believe you've helped the reader."[3] By 1984, however, Lawrence accepted the fact that she was unable to finish the manuscript, and when an editor turned up, Elizabeth Lawrence handed over her manuscript to her.

William Lanier Hunt had told Joanne Ferguson, editor at Duke University Press, about Lawrence's market bulletin book. Ferguson, already a reader of Lawrence's other books, was immediately interested and wrote her to ask if she could come to see her. Lawrence agreed, and in the summer of 1984, Ferguson went to her home in Charlotte. They had a touching visit, each wishing that it had occurred sooner. As Ferguson left, Lawrence gave her a box of papers, neither of them, apparently, quite certain of what was in it.[4] When Ferguson examined some of the papers, she discovered the market bulletin manuscript, and recognizing that it was still unfinished, she asked noted garden writer Allen Lacy to take a look at Lawrence's materials and see whether there was a book in them. Lacy accepted the assignment because he admired Lawrence as a garden writer and regretted never having met her. He knew what he was getting himself into when Ferguson sent him the materials: pages of unfinished manuscripts and many letters. But Lacy saw immediately that there was "magic in that box." He went to work trying to make order, retaining as much of Lawrence's original intentions and materials as he could. In 1987 *Gardening for Love: The Market Bulletins* was published posthumously by Duke University Press, and it immediately acquired a following.[5]

Reviewers were generous in their praise. "As in all her gardening books," Eudora Welty wrote, "Elizabeth Lawrence writes here from her own experience and personal records and out of relish and delight. This is richly rewarding. She has remained an original. Those of us who treasured her friendship as well as her writing and her own beautiful garden will find Elizabeth here. She's written with the intimacy that comes of full knowledge, true and patient love, and a grower's sense of continuity in the natural world, and a lyricist's lifetime practice of praise." Eleanor Perényi, author of *Green Thoughts: A Writer in the Garden,* recognized Lawrence's "memorial to the horticultural folkways of the rural South." "To have a posthumously published book of [Lawrence's] now is the sort of bonus that makes one think the world is not so bad after all," wrote Henry Mitchell, garden columnist for *The Washington Post* and author of *The Essential Earthman*. He praised the "warmth and openness" that flowed between Lawrence and her correspondents and that constituted "a kind of love-tangle," as well as her "clear and unhackneyed prose" and her "profound understanding of her subject." British gardener and garden writer Rosemary Verey wrote that she had learned the expression "dirt gardeners" when she had visited Raleigh, North Carolina (long after Lawrence had moved to Charlotte), and praised the knowledge that comes only to those "who know the feel of the soil and the character of plants."[6]

All of this praise would have been music to the ears of Elizabeth Lawrence, but perhaps a review in the *New York Times* by Stanley Kunitz would have given her the deepest satisfaction. Kunitz, a fine poet and gardener, began by recognizing the place gardening held in Lawrence's life—"a form of total expression, a supremely human enterprise." *Gardening for Love* was "an enchanting work, unlike any other gardening book in existence." He praised Allen Lacy's editing of the materials Lawrence had left behind as "something of a miracle," and he concluded his long review with an observation perhaps even more relevant today than it was in 1987, when he made it: "In this deeply troubled period of our national life it is a refreshment of the heart to read about that other America . . . people of modest means, but honest, forthcoming, trusting."[7]

Gardening for Love *and* A Rock Garden in the South

In Lawrence's box of papers, Joanne Ferguson made another discovery—a manuscript about rock gardens in the South. Hunt had told her that she might find it, although Hannah Withers, one of Elizabeth's closest friends, had not known that Elizabeth was working on that, too.[8] The rock garden manuscript also had an uncertain history.

Soon after the publication of *Gardens in Winter* in the spring of 1961, Lawrence was encouraged to think again about finding a publisher for a rock garden manuscript that she had been working on for years. The immediate impetus for her renewal of interest was a telephone call from Ben Morrison of Pass Christian, Mississippi, congratulating her on her last book. Elizabeth and Ben were now on a first-name basis, after having been corresponding for years on every imaginable subject, and he urged her not to give up. Soon afterward, she wrote him that she had "got the kitchen stool immediately, and searched the top of the cupboard for the rock garden manuscript. Glancing through it I was relieved to find it comparatively free of poetry, but what a good time Mr. McAdoo [her editor at Harper] would have running his blue-pencil through all those names! Perhaps he is right, and that it is too personal to be of interest to anyone but me. Rereading what I had written nearly twenty years ago about people I am fond of was like reading my diary."[9]

Over three decades Lawrence's writing style had evolved from presenting scientific information in a straightforward manner, as she had done when she first began publishing articles about rock gardens, mostly in the *Bulletin of the American Rock Garden Society*.[10] As her publications built up a following, readers came to expect quotations from poems and letters and testimonies of successes and failures (her own and those of some of her correspondents) mixed in with descriptions of plants. But this approach was often a problem for editors, and Lawrence had to remind herself that her delight was in the garden, not in publications. Over the years, of course, her energy for getting her work published waned, and by the time the rock garden manuscript got filed away in a box of other unfinished and unpublished manuscripts, she was disappointed, but not embittered.

Lawrence may have first become interested in growing rock garden plants as a child, when her family moved to a house in Raleigh that already had an established rock garden. Later, she was to say that it had been designed by a "famous garden designer," whose name she had forgotten but whom she had read about in one of her mother's garden magazines. (No evidence has turned up about who that might have been.) This existing rock garden may have been the basis for one that Lawrence described as her own in the rock garden manuscript: it followed along a curving path from the driveway at one end to a wall fountain at the other. "From the garden proper," she explained, "it is entered through an ivy-covered arch in the hedge." She described the careful process by which she and "Page" (a man who helped her in the garden and in the house) made stone garden steps. "He went about it with the deftness and intuition that he put into making his perfect soufflés," she observed.[11]

In 1941 Lawrence talked with W. T. Couch, the director of University of North Carolina Press, about her interest in writing a book about rock gardens, and although he encouraged her to do so, apparently she was not ready to submit a manuscript. Soon afterwards, apparently, she completed some thirty pages, which she entitled "A Southern Bouquet of Saxatile Plants for Gardens for the Carolinas and California." This unpublished manuscript contains parts that later were included in *A Rock Garden in the South,* which was published after her death. There are quotations from poems and from her correspondents in the "Bouquet" manuscript that appeared in the later book, suggesting that the earlier version may have been one that the Harper editor read. The "Bouquet" manuscript also contains a chapter about Mr. Krippendorf, called "The First Flower," which she took out and used as the first chapter in *The Little Bulbs,* published in 1957. This incomplete history of just one manuscript shows the way in which Lawrence was always moving chapters around, until she found a publisher for them.[12] Ellen Flood felt confident that a major publishing house would want the manuscript, and in 1949 she asked Elizabeth to send it to her so that she could take it around. Flood was successful in having *Rock Garden* read at Charles

Scribner's Sons, but she received a letter just after Christmas saying that the audience for such a book was too small for them to undertake its publication. Three years later, Lawrence submitted a manuscript to the University of Oklahoma Press with the title *Rock Gardens from Coast to Coast*. The response this time was encouraging, and an editor wrote to Lawrence to say that publication looked feasible. A copy of the report from a reader for the Press noted how few rock garden books were still in print, and none, in fact, dealt with rock gardening in the South. Admiring Lawrence's wide knowledge of plants and horticulture, as well as her informal style, the reader went on to suggest that some revisions should be required in order to eliminate the impression of sometimes hasty or careless work. Lawrence was especially urged to put more of her personal opinions and experiences into the revised manuscript. The reader recommended publication.[13]

It was a very encouraging report, one that Lawrence had every reason to believe would lead to publication. A month later, the editor wrote again to say that he hoped that Lawrence would be able to make the necessary revisions as proposed in the reader's report and submit a final manuscript so that it could be published at the University of Oklahoma Press. But the book, in fact, was not published, and Lawrence's files do not indicate why she did not respond to the editor's letter. The winter of 1952, when the offer was received, was a relatively good time in her life: her mother's health was still generally good, they had moved into their new house, and Elizabeth had put in a new garden. It is hard to find anything that was going on in her life that made revising the manuscript impossible. And yet she must have declined to do so. What we must assume is that the task of revising the manuscript according to a set of instructions, which Lawrence seems not to have understood, was too daunting. Apparently, she did not resubmit the manuscript, but instead put it back in its folder, where it remained. She seems not to have discussed it in the way she always talked about her unpublished market bulletin book. Perhaps she chose to concentrate her energies elsewhere, but meanwhile, she published three more articles in the *Bulletin of the American Rock Garden Society*. In the fall of 1984, having sold her house in Charlotte and moved to Maryland to be near her niece, Lawrence was unable to revise further chapters that she had submitted to the editor of the Bulletin, and the manuscript had to be returned.[14]

When Joanne Ferguson found the rock garden manuscript, she again involved Allen Lacy in discussions about publication, and a second notable gardener, Nancy Goodwin, agreed to help. Goodwin was operating a nursery at Montrose, the estate where she lives with her husband near Hillsborough, North Carolina. As an admirer of Lawrence's, she was well qualified to assist in the project; also she had the same intense passion for plants and the same curiosity to learn more about them that would be required in order to expand the encyclopedia of plants that made up the bulk of Lawrence's manuscript. Working with Lawrence's typed chapters, Goodwin saw firsthand how Lawrence had gone on learning over the years, from the handwritten corrections and insertions she had made to improve sentences, adding new information, focusing on what was important. Having learned gardening from "my parents, my grandparents, and books by Elizabeth Lawrence," Goodwin found herself face to face with the intelligence, the honesty, and the curiosity that had drawn her to Elizabeth's earlier work.[15] In addition to the material Goodwin added to the dictionary of rock garden plants, a section on dwarf conifers and woody plants was added to the manuscript by Paul Jones, a horticulturist at The Sarah P. Duke Gardens in Durham. Several years passed before the book was finally finished, but in 1990, *A Rock Garden in the South* was published posthumously. Duke University Press had been purposeful in moving the long-deferred project along, and when the book appeared, the dust jacket exhibited an impressive array of good opinions about Lawrence from her admirers—Elisabeth Woodburn, Eudora Welty, and Katharine White. With praise from an unnamed reviewer at *Southern Living,* however, Lawrence was introduced to millions of readers: "A few garden writers offer prose that goes beyond the spade and spray to convey the experience and pleasures of gardening. The late Elizabeth Lawrence was such a writer."

Lawrence's descriptions of rock garden plants begin with a sprightly introduction. "All rock gardeners are snobs," she observes, "without fear of offending, for no one will take it to himself." There is a good reason for it, however, she continues, because the cultivation of rock plants is "the highest form of the art of gardening." She describes rock gardeners as "individualists, each with his specialty, his own dear delight." Noting that rock garden plants are grown "for themselves alone" and not for "show," she writes as simple an explanation for a subject often burdened with technical information as one might find.

All gardeners become rock gardeners, Lawrence says, if they garden long enough.

> They may not mean to, or even desire it, but it is natural to one long familiar with plants to single out certain individuals too newly come from wood or waterside to accommodate themselves to the perennial border and to put them where stones can protect their flowers from the weather and keep their roots cool and moist. One by one, special corners are singled out for special treasures, until they become so numerous that they must be drawn together. In this way the rock garden is created, and for this reason it is the most personal of all forms of horticulture.

One example illustrates how Elizabeth Lawrence's plant list was always something more.

> *Sempervivum* The houseleeks cannot be too dry. I first saw them used as outdoor plants in Violet Walker's garden in Virginia. They flowed over the terraces like water and presented no problem. But when I brought home large clumps of all of the kinds she grew, they promptly died. I felt cheated by such behavior for houseleeks are invariably recommended to the beginner as "kindly, plain-living, and indestructible." Even the name, ever-living, holds a deeper meaning than life-forever. I planted collection after collection, only to see the smug rosettes that looked so immovable when they were planted in their crannies in the fall, and which came through winter with undiminished ranks, disappear almost overnight in the rainy season. I found a place at last where they have taken hold and seem to be on the increase. It is the top of a rock wall that is overhung by a pink Cherokee rose and where the soil is poor and dry as a bone. It is dry even in the wettest weather. This confirms me in my belief that we could grow many more rock plants in these parts if we could devise ways to keep them dry in summer.[16]

Although a half-century has passed since Elizabeth Lawrence first began writing about rock gardens, her voice remains fresh and informing. Among her admirers is Bobby J. Ward, president of the North American Rock Garden Society, who can explain in scientific terms why Southern rock garden plants can die of "fatigue" if nighttime temperatures don't drop ("they wear themselves out at night trying to keep up with the high respiration and trying to supply oxygen to the cells"). Lawrence, he says, "knew this in her own way—but perhaps not the technical details."[17]

"In her own way" accurately describes Elizabeth Lawrence's art of living and gardening.

CHAPTER TWENTY-THREE

Closing the Garden Gate 1984

A house is a companion.

AFTER BESSIE'S DEATH in 1964, Elizabeth's life was both easier and harder. She was relieved of the physical and emotional burden of her mother's care, but she was alone for the first time in her life. She wondered if she would be able to make decisions for herself, momentarily as uncertain as her mother had felt when Nana died. But there was always something very stoic about the family, and Elizabeth drew upon that strength. She would not falter.

Elizabeth had expected to go on living on Ridgewood Avenue, but what surprised her was how much she still cared about her house. "For the first time in my life, I have everything in its place—the place *I* want it," she reported. "But I would rather have someone to annoy me. Nevertheless, I have found to my delight that a house is a companion."[1] She began ordering her groceries and planning simple meals that a housekeeper, Sadie Samuel, helped her prepare, serving her and her guests at the refectory table or in front of the fire. Her sister, Ann, came over more often for lunch, and when her nephew Chip and niece Fuzz were home from college, Elizabeth dropped everything to be with them.

Elizabeth also took advantage of her new freedom to travel. In the spring of 1965 she flew to the West Coast to visit her old St. Mary's friend Mary Wiatt and her husband, Richard Chase, in San Francisco; with her correspondent, Polly Anderson, whom she had met recently in North Carolina at a meeting of the Daffodil Society, she saw camellias and live oaks at Descanso Gardens in La Canada, near Los Angeles. After Easter in 1966, her gardening friend Mittie Wellford drove her to Botany Hill, in Polk County, west of Charlotte, to visit Catchy Tanner, who wanted them to see masses of wildflowers in bloom—bloodroot, rue-anemone, hepatica, and fragrant trillium. Some thirty years later, Tanner remembered the day vividly: "She was grand, a little sprite, not shy, just enthusiastic. . . . She sat in the front seat [of the jeep] with me, and it was rough for her. To see the wildflowers you had to lie down and roll under the fence. (Everybody wore jeans.) Elizabeth did it without hesitation."[2]

Still among Elizabeth's dearest friends were the Longs, whom she had known since her childhood in Garysburg. In 1964 the Longs' daughter, Caroline Long Tillett, her husband, Hugh Tillett, and their two boys had moved to Charlotte, and Elizabeth was delighted. After Caroline's mother died in the summer of 1965, Elizabeth took her place in Caroline's life, and the two women began having lunch together every Wednesday, a date that other friends knew was sacrosanct. But they were worried about Caroline's father, Willie Long, the family patriarch, who at seventy-four had not adjusted to living alone. Elizabeth loved him as much as everyone in his family. Members of the Long family still recall how, when Elizabeth came to Longview as a girl, she used to sit on a stool by his big chair, listening to his stories, her head tilted toward his every word.[3] Elizabeth and Willie liked to talk, and others let them. When it was safe, Elizabeth was coy and flirtatious, and everyone knew it was safe at Longview. Willie's wife Caroline and Bessie Lawrence went off to work in the kitchen with the cook, cutting up cabbage, and talking. Now both women were gone, and Elizabeth and Caroline were missing them. Elizabeth wrote to Willie to say that without young Caroline to cheer them both up, she did not know how either of them could manage. She urged him to come to see them both. And so that fall, he told his two sons to look after the place until he got back, and he went off with Caroline to Charlotte.

A day or so after he was settled in, Caroline dropped him off for a visit with Elizabeth. Caroline describes the scene when she returned. "They were talking, and when I entered the room, the conversation stopped." No amount of coaxing then could persuade either of them to continue the conversation, and naturally, she was curious. Nothing more was said until after the visit was over, and Caroline quizzed each of them separately. Finally, Elizabeth told her what had happened, and her father confirmed it: Willie had asked Elizabeth to marry him, and she had refused.[4]

Elizabeth was sixty-one years old, and if she had ever discussed with anyone whether or not she would marry, she left no traces. It is unlikely that love letters (like those written late in life between Emily Dickinson and her father's friend, Judge Otis Lord) will turn up. Elizabeth and Willie wrote about poison ivy remedies and hound dogs.[5] But if Elizabeth had wanted to marry, Willie Long, despite the differences in their ages, was someone even Nana and Bessie might have approved of. His family would have welcomed her. So why did she turn him down? According to what she reported to Caroline, she had told him that she was not capable of being a good wife to him and "mistress" of Longview, and she loved him too much to want to fail him. As her family and friends knew, she had never left her own home and garden, nor would she for Longview.

After Elizabeth had declined to marry Willie, their relationship continued as affectionately as ever. Neither wanted the other to be "mad," and each wrote at once to say come anytime, and bring anyone you want with you. For his part, Willie had not been discouraged about finding a wife. A few months later, he took an interest in a distant relative, the twice-married Westray Boyce Battle, who had been head of the WACS during World War II and was now a retired colonel. He proposed marriage, and she accepted. As soon as Elizabeth heard the news, she wrote him, "Caroline came to lunch with me, and told me that Westree (I have no idea how to spell it) is coming to Longview. I am so relieved, as I worry about you all the time. Please tell her I love her, and both of you come to see me."[6]

Elizabeth explained to a friend that though she had hurt Willie Long "when I couldn't help it" she knew he would never hurt her. "That is because he loves me as he loved my father & knows I love him the same."[7] In this statement she may have also remembered her romantic relationship with Peter Burnaugh and the hurt they had inflicted upon one another. Her feelings for Willie were clearly of a different kind, and she seems to have felt no reason to tell anyone that she had had a proposal of marriage. No evidence in letters or interviews has suggested that Elizabeth Lawrence ever felt—or was made to feel—that not having married was a failure.

In 1967 harder times descended on Elizabeth. Her mother's death had long been expected, but she was not prepared for her next loss: Ann Bridgers had terminal cancer. On several occasions after Elizabeth had moved from Raleigh in 1948, she had gone back to spend weekends with the Bridgers family; when she returned, Hannah Withers observed, she always seemed "refreshed."[8] The news about Ann was devastating. Elizabeth was also anxious because Chip was serving in the Civil Engineer Corps in Viet Nam. Just before Thanksgiving, Elizabeth fell and cracked her kneecap, though she was able to make a joke of her accident, pointing out that the fall had occurred while she was coming out of the liquor store, and she had not dropped the bourbon. In April of 1967, when she was visiting Ellen Flood in New York City, her long-anticipated meeting with Katharine White was a disappointment to both of them. When Ann died in May and Emily died the next year, Elizabeth lost the best "editors" she had ever had, and two of her best friends. Apparently, Elizabeth did not share her grief with anyone.[9] Perhaps it was too deep for tears.

In the summer of 1967, Elizabeth desperately needed a distraction. Help came again from the Longs. In Bertie County, in the eastern part of North Carolina, Margaret Long Tyler and her husband, John "Jack" Tyler, were helping other volunteer preservationists to restore Hope Plantation's early nineteenth-century house and garden so that it could be opened as a historic site. When Margaret had been a student at St. Mary's, she had lived with the Lawrences, and Elizabeth had never forgotten how much Margaret had meant to her father. After college, Margaret and Jack Tyler had married and moved to his historic family home in Roxobel, which was not far from Hope Plantation. When he thought about what should be done in the garden at Hope, he wrote to Elizabeth to ask her to come down to have a look around. Elizabeth agreed to come, and Caroline Tillett was happy to drive her, glad for a chance to be with Elizabeth and to see her cousin Margaret.

In the early summer of 1967, when Elizabeth and Caroline turned off a country road into the entrance to Hope Plantation, they saw mostly a barren landscape, farmed almost up to the front steps of the large mansion. The house itself, built around 1803, had fallen into sad neglect and was being restored to its earlier grandeur. The land had been acquired through a grant in the 1720s from the Lords Proprietors of the Carolina colony, and had then included more than one thousand acres. When ownership passed to thirty-three-year-old David Stone, Hope acquired a man who had the ambition, money, and slave labor to make it prosper. Stone directed the building of the mansion and the operation of a large plantation. His early career—as attorney, judge, and North Carolina legislator—was already distinguished; he was later to be elected to both houses of the United States Congress, and, in 1808, he became Governor of North Carolina. The mansion reflected Stone's scholarly interests: his second-floor library contained some fourteen hundred volumes. Looking out from the portico or from the widow's walk, Stone could show visitors his great plantation—as far as the eye could see. More than 150 years after the carpenters had completed a balustrade around the widow's walk and the house was ready for the family's occupancy, Elizabeth and Caroline accompanied Jack Tyler up the narrow, winding stairs for a view. The estate was much smaller in size (now only eighteen acres, later to be increased to forty-five), but the silent rural landscape was still impressive.

Elizabeth, best known for her selection of plant materials, always began her discussions of garden design by asking her clients to consider the overall effect of what they hoped to achieve. The considerable expense of restoring Hope Plantation expressed the preservationists' desire to feature the house itself, and so she first focused Tyler's attention on preserving its dominance by the placement of the road, fences, parking lots, and secondary structures. They talked and walked, and at the end of a very pleasant day, Elizabeth and Caroline drove home still talking about the possibilities. The familiar landscape that came to mind was the long avenue leading to Longview and the vista of surrounding fields. Back home, Elizabeth consulted Bill Hunt about characteristic flora of the coastal plain that might have been used before 1800. Then several days later when Caroline was reading Charlotte Bronte's *Jane Eyre,* she called to tell Elizabeth that one scene in particular had reminded her of Hope. When Elizabeth found the passage in which Jane Eyre looks over Thornfield, she agreed that it was inspirational. "I followed still, up a very narrow staircase to the attic, and thence by a ladder and through a trap-door to the roof of the hall.... Leaning over the battlements and looking far down, I surveyed the grounds laid out like a map.... No feature in the scene was extraordinary, but all was pleasing."

Elizabeth knew the basic principle she thought should be stressed at Hope Plantation. "It seems to me that the best thing is to keep it as simple as possible," she wrote to Tyler.[10]

The wisdom of Elizabeth's advice is reflected today at Hope, where her suggested plantings of crepe myrtles, boxwoods, cedar, and magnolias draw the eye toward the handsomely restored house, "just enough planting to tie it down," she advised, so that the house itself stands up "in that stark way above everything else." In her recommendation of naturalized drifts of thousands of bulbs, an echo of Mr. Krippendorf's Lob's Wood was in her dreams. The vegetable gardens that someone thought to add later required too much maintenance and disappeared, and fruit trees that had been added were neglected. Viewed from the top of the widow's walk, the flat, unadorned landscape speaks for itself, as quiet as the afternoon when Elizabeth Lawrence stood and looked about, and could think of very little to improve upon it. When she returned to make her recommendations at Hope Plantation, they agreed with her plans. "She was," Jack Tyler remembered, "the most sensitive person I ever met. And under that shyness, there was a great deal of determination."[11]

Work at Hope Plantation had given Elizabeth a real boost of energy, and in May of 1968 she agreed to go with her Charlotte friend Hannah Withers on a National Trust tour of Castles and Gardens in Ireland, Wales, Scotland, and England. It was a cruise tour on the Bergen Line, and they both loved traveling that way because it allowed them to rest in their cabin when other passengers disembarked to see other sites. After the tour was over, they hired a driver in London to take them to gardens that Elizabeth had longed to see for years. First on their list was Gertrude Jekyll's garden at Munstead Wood. Although Jekyll's garden had ceased to exist when the property was sold in 1949 and divided into lots, Elizabeth and Hannah had read most of Jekyll's books, and Elizabeth felt that she knew her garden as well as she did her own. In doing research in 1963 for her introduction to a Jekyll anthology she had corresponded with Jekyll's nephew, Francis Jekyll, who was living in the "Hut," where his aunt had lived while the house was being built.[12] He had warned Elizabeth that there was nothing of his aunt's garden left. But Mr. Rivers, their driver, assured Miss Lawrence and Mrs. Withers that he would show them at least something of what they had come to see. While he was speaking with someone about the possibility of some American guests seeing the property, Hannah and Elizabeth scrambled out of the car and went searching for Jekyll's "Thunder House," a triangular tower at the end of her garden, where Jekyll could stand or sit and watch approaching storms. Elizabeth found it at once—it looked just as she had imagined."[13] In Vita Sackville-West's garden at Sissinghurst, Elizabeth—an enthusiastic reader of Sackville-West's collected garden articles, which had first appeared in London's *Observer* —was also on familiar ground. "I felt her presence still, as if I might come upon her any moment," Lawrence described the experience for her own readers. "In the garden of the South Cottage, I did come upon the head gardeners, Pamela Schwerdt and Sibylle Kreutzberger, whom she trained just before she died. They stopped their work to explain the use of the scuffle hoe, and give advice as to the breadth of the blade."[14] Before she left England, Lawrence purchased a scuffle hoe (used for weeding), and when she was not allowed to take it on the airplane because of the size, she dismantled it, taking the blade and leaving the handle behind. When Hugh and Anne Boyer, garden clients in Hickory, heard her story, Hugh discovered that one of Lawrence's classmates at North Carolina State College, Clinton Cilley, who owned and operated a foundry in Hickory, could help. Cilley put a handle on Lawrence's blade, and finally she had a hoe like the one she had seen at Sissinghurst.[15]

Without Ann Bridgers, Elizabeth turned more often to another close friend, Ellen Flood, but in 1970, Ellen had a stroke, followed by depression. When Ellen and a nurse companion were able to make one last trip to Charlotte, Elizabeth was grateful. In 1977 when Elizabeth saw her for the last time, Ellen was living in a Catholic nursing home, near her son and his family in Richmond, Kentucky. Elizabeth was moved by how much her old friend sometimes still seemed like the brilliant girl she had loved. When Ellen died the next year, Elizabeth lost the last of her closest friends.

With the loss of old friends, and on her own to renew old acquaintances, Elizabeth's interest in young people intensified. She especially loved hearing about her niece's experiences as a student at St. Mary's and her nephew's adventures at North Carolina State, which she had attended herself. Fuzz had Ann's sense of humor and made "Aunt" laugh; Chip, who was studying engineering, reminded Elizabeth of her father. In January 1967 Fuzz graduated from the University of North Carolina in Chapel Hill, and in March she and Walton Rogers married at St. Peter's Episcopal Church. Elizabeth entertained the wedding party and their guests at her house. When Fuzz and her husband had two daughters—Blair and Ann—Elizabeth entertained another generation of children in her garden. In 1972 Chip's marriage to Fran Heisler of Richmond, and later the births of their daughter, Evelyn, and their son, Bobby, enlarged the family circle. Elizabeth's letters in the 1960s and 70s are filled with references to Ann's grandchildren in the same way that she had written about Chip and Fuzz—as if they were her own. "I have three little girls in my pool," she wrote to Ruth Long Williams. With writer Burke Davis, who had taken Katharine White's place among her correspondents, she discussed children's books—*The Secret Garden* and the Babar books were especial favorites.[16]

In the spring of 1972 Lawrence was given an award at a meeting, in Canandaigua, New York, of the American Rock Garden Society, which she had joined in 1939, when there were very few Southern rock gardeners. Her host was Bernard Harkness, a founding member of the Society, who had had a distinguished career as a taxonomist with the Rochester, New York, Bureau of Parks. He had been to see Lawrence's garden in Charlotte, and he was eager for her to see his. After the meetings were over, he and his wife, Mabel Harkness, invited the Society's members to their home out in the country, south of Geneva, near Penn Yan. The large old cobblestone house, with a greenhouse, a gazebo, gardens of vegetables, perennial beds, herbs, and Harkness's specialty—more than two thousand alliums—as well as apple orchards, and Seneca Lake in the distance, was a memorable setting. There was a plant sale in the garage and a picnic in the garden. Almost thirty years later, Mabel Harkness remembered that day when they watched the sun setting over a large flowering chestnut tree. "Elizabeth had a very distinguished appearance—she was small, her white hair cut short—and although she was quiet, she was anything but shy. Everybody talked gardens. She was a very well-known person, and she and my husband belonged to a real hierarchy of gardening."[17]

In 1976 when a young West Coast gardener, Betsy Clebsch, and her husband were living in Chapel Hill, Clebsch drove to Charlotte to tell Lawrence how much she loved *The Little Bulbs*. The two women started talking about plants at once, and Clebsch felt that Elizabeth had lost none of her sharpness: "A tulip wasn't just a tulip for Elizabeth," she observed. "She thought about things quite philosophically." Clebsch was also charmed by Elizabeth's arrangement of small glass containers with flowers she had cut from her garden—little cyclamen, snowdrops of different kinds, twigs of wintersweet, violets, and "at least six other things I had never seen before." Elizabeth took her into the garden—it was a balmy, sunny day. They chatted "on and on—she wanted to know about California, and we had a lot of territory to cover. . . . In the South it used to be that people didn't pass around a favorite recipe. If [Elizabeth] had interesting information about how to grow iris she would tell you. She didn't keep it a secret." Elizabeth was always as much interested in people as in plants. "She really, really liked my husband (he was very nice-looking)," Clebsch remembered. "I could tell it. She was coy; she had the body language of a young girl."[18]

Elizabeth loved visitors. "Almost every day someone calls to me that he is in town," she reported, "and I dash out & collect something for lunch or supper. Yesterday, I had Tom, who is twenty-four but still in college, as he drops out from time to time, & works for awhile. I wanted to discuss Plato. He & his mother came at twelve and left at three—at four, a young man who is connected with a memory course, and at 6:30 a friend from Atlanta, who is the most brilliant horticulturist I know arrived. We had drinks & dug up plants, & he got out his notebook & asked about endless plants."[19]

In Charlotte, the distinguished horticulturist Dr. Herbert Hechenbleikner was a close friend of Elizabeth's. A faculty member at Charlotte College (the present-day University of North Carolina at Charlotte), he was also director of campus landscape, and Elizabeth was especially interested in the naturalness of some of his plantings, especially of rhododendrons. He took her to see the campus, and she often invited him and his wife, Martha, over for drinks and to have a "look around in the garden." Hechenbleikner remembered, "There were plants on top of plants, and she was still ordering and planting more and more. And she really knew plants, she knew them very well. She was a keen observer." He especially admired three of her plants that were quite unusual for her day—a twenty-five-foot eucalyptus tree by the front door, an enormous tea plant "that was quite a thing in its day," and a holly fern, which is common in Florida but generally doesn't survive a Charlotte winter. "Hers was the only one I'd seen that had attained any size."[20]

One of the most memorable afternoons for Elizabeth came when Herbert's wife, Martha Hechenbleikner, drove her to the mountains near Banner Elk, North Carolina, to meet Rosa Hicks, one of the women who sold their plants through the market bulletin. Hechenbleikner understood the attraction for Elizabeth—she had a "bonding with people who scrabbled in the dirt and who shared her love of plants." Elizabeth and Rosa had corresponded for many years, and Elizabeth had suggested to other friends that they order from her. Now she was meeting her for the first time, the only one of her market bulletin correspondents that she was ever to meet. Years later, after Elizabeth had died, Rosa Hicks still remembered her as a close friend. "I wish she had lived next door," Hicks explained. "We would be good neighbors."[21]

The Hechenbleikners sometimes took Elizabeth to meetings of the North Carolina Wildflower Preservation Society. On one occasion, they drove Elizabeth and one of her good gardening friends, Dr. Walter Brem Mayer, to South Carolina to see the big pines on the edge of the Congaree Swamp. Dr. Hechenbleikner caught a six-foot black snake, which he brought home, wrapped around his arm. "She didn't like it, but she got used to it," he remembered, "but not without a good deal of protest."

"She had a wild streak in her," Hechenbleikner observed. "She seemed demure, but she was feisty." Sometimes they discussed politics, and when he suggested that she was such a "dyed-in-the wool Democrat" that she would vote for a Democrat even "if he had horns, hook, and tail," she allowed as how she probably would. Elizabeth did not like to back down; while seemingly frail, she was, Hannah Withers remembered, "tough as whit leather." Her unwillingness to let anyone walk over her led to the general sense in the neighborhood that she could defend herself anytime anyone presumed to threaten her domain. One person who discovered that quality in her was a young college student who came to work for her.

It was Dr. Hechenbleikner who sent one of his students, Jamie Stemple, to help Elizabeth in the garden. Jamie began working for Miss Lawrence in the fall of 1972 to make some money to pay off a traffic ticket.

But when he showed up, he remembered, "I fell in love with the place and with her, immediately. I saw a lady educated far ahead of women of her time." He liked her so much that he stayed seven years. Stemple observed, "I was Catholic and from a working class background. I was somebody different in her life. I think she had a great curiosity about everything. I've never seen anything like her house, before or since. It was a thinking type house where you gathered friends in this big living room and when you wanted to write, you'd go off to your study."[22]

An instance of the "feisty" quality that Hechenbleikner and others saw in Elizabeth is illustrated in Stemple's memory. "She was straight and above-board, and she was possessive of me. She got mad when I told her I had been unloading some wood for a lady down the street. And once I was trimming the front hedge, and this lady came by and talked to me about helping her, and Miss Lawrence saw us and banged on the window and called me inside, and asked what she wanted, and I told her. She said I belonged to her and I couldn't work for anyone else, and she wouldn't let me back outside to talk to the lady." But she never complained about his work. "She helped me learn—she did a lot of shifting of plants, taught me how to plant bulbs. I did a lot of pruning. I could saw. Once I cut something very short, and she said, 'Oh, that's a little short.' That was a favorite thing of mine to do." He filled her hollowed-out coconut shell with seeds for the birds and cleaned out the garden pool. They exchanged presents—she gave him autographed copies of her books, and he gave her a wooden lantern, which she loved and took into the garden to light at night. And once he spent more than he could easily afford to buy her a print of flowers in little thimbles. "That was Miss Lawrence," he said. "That's her." He hung it for her by the kitchen door, on a counter where she put her little jars with flowers.

When Elizabeth sat down to write Carol Wells, her archivist at Northwestern State University of Louisiana, she reported on what she and Jamie had been doing: "Jamie and I were rained out in the garden, so we spent the afternoon, putting my shelves in order. . . . He is very much interested in the contents of the cupboard, & very efficient at sorting. He was amused by my St. Mary's botany book where 'Polly' was written 50 times on the fly leaf, and asked Who was Polly? and a stray letter fell out of a book—"Who called you 'Libba'?" He said, "I'd like to write your biography.' "[23]

In 1971 just after returning from a second trip to England with Hannah Withers, Elizabeth received the shocking news from her editor at the Charlotte *Observer* that the newspaper would no longer carry her column. She was, she admitted, "heartbroken" because writing a column every week gave her a chance to research many different subjects, to write a short piece, and to see it published on Sunday. Perhaps she was, as Herbert Hechenbleikner said, "way over the heads of the general public." The news came at a time when she was still trying to find publishers for two manuscripts—the one on rock gardens and her market bulletin book. There was nothing she had written that she had enjoyed more than the column. Her readers rose up in righteous indignation, some of them writing letters to the editor, but their protests were to no avail. No longer being allowed to write her garden column perhaps hurt her more than any other disappointment in her career. Ironically, Lawrence had helped to "popularize" gardening, and as it became more interesting to more people, she was made to feel "old-fashioned."

At the time that her column was canceled, Lawrence had not published a major book in more than ten years. Editors had turned down her unfinished manuscripts, and she was feeling as if time was passing her by. Then someone appeared on the scene unexpectedly to give her a boost. In the fall of 1977, Pamela Harper, a rising star in the gardening lecture world, wrote admiringly of Elizabeth's books in *Pacific Horticulture,* a magazine edited by a mutual friend, George Waters. Elizabeth wrote back to thank Harper. Harper and Lawrence recognized immediately that they liked the same kinds of things, and they continued to write to each other for the next five or six years. Harper felt as if she already knew Lawrence just from reading her books. Although Lawrence apparently had not read Harper's first book, *The Story of a Garden,* published in Great Britain in 1972, she recognized in Harper's approach a gardener very much like herself: someone who learned about plants by trying to grow as many different kinds as she could. As garden book publishing became a commercial field, Harper understood that Lawrence was part of the last generation of garden writers who wrote for each other, and she treasured knowing her. "We were on the same wavelength."[24]

In April 1978 the two gardeners had a chance to meet when Harper, who was in Charlotte to give a lecture, was invited to Lawrence's house. "I felt a complete welcome," Harper remembers. "The conversation just flowed." The two women spent quite a while in the garden. Each had a list of questions for the other. Harper spent the night, and the next morning, Lawrence took her to meet Helen and Walter Mayer, who gave Harper plants from their garden. When she arrived back in Virginia, she sat down at once to type a letter to Elizabeth, saying, "Gardens (real ones) are so few, it was a thrill to see yours."[25]

The exchange of information between Pamela and Elizabeth had only begun, and for the next several years, letters went back and forth. Plants from Lawrence's garden "settled in well" in Harper's—Iris japonica had an "exquisite" bloom, but was "travelling all over the place on this light sandy soil, and I'm going to have to restrain it." The plant from Lawrence's garden that gave Harper the greatest pleasure was the creamy *Ranunculus ficaria.* ("It has woven itself in and out of *Omphalodes verra,* and the combination is exquisite.") Harper's *Hamamelis* × *intermedia* 'Jelena' (a witch hazel Lawrence did not know—"an unusual occurrence") found a home in Lawrence's garden. Pamela and Elizabeth loved many of the same plants—*Nandina domestica, Viburnum farreri, Polygonatum odoratum* 'Variegatum,' and *Zephyranthes candida.* Harper ordered *Oxalis bowiei* on Lawrence's recommendation. She, in turn, was able to identify a plant for Lawrence as *Salvia greggii.*

Lawrence's lecturing days were over, but Harper was traveling coast to coast, speaking, seeing friends, and touring gardens. In some of her lectures she showed slides of Elizabeth and her garden that she had taken during her first visit—among them, one of Elizabeth, and another of "the tiny, tiny violet tucked into the step." When Pamela wrote Eliz-

In the last decade of her life, Elizabeth wore her hair in a pixie style and sometimes entertained friends in the garden, dressed in a casual caftan. (Courtesy of John Jamison; by permission of Warren Way and Elizabeth Rogers.)

abeth to tell her about the places she had gone and the people she had seen, Elizabeth felt less forgotten. At that stage in Lawrence's life, Harper perhaps did more than anyone to keep Lawrence's name before the public.[26]

In 1982 Harper returned to Charlotte, this time to give a lecture at Wing Haven Garden and Bird Sanctuary, which had been opened to the public as a private garden, the gift of Elizabeth and Eddie Clarkson. Harper left soon after the program in order to see Elizabeth, who she had been told was no longer receiving visitors. Pamela was sure that Elizabeth would see her, and Elizabeth did. They sat by the fire and drank sherry, and Elizabeth went down her list of plants she had wanted to discuss. Elizabeth was frail, and they did not go into the garden, where through the windows Harper could see tall weeds. Harper knew that this would probably be the last time that she saw Elizabeth, and when she got home, she wrote to say that she was sorry that she had not even "set foot in your garden." But both of them knew that the glory of the garden was past. Lawrence, however, felt more optimistic about the future of garden writing than she had in many years. She wrote to Carol Wells that she believed that Harper was part of a "renaissance."[27]

Social changes in the 1960s and 1970s were unnerving and undermining for Elizabeth Lawrence, who disliked change of any kind. Having always depended upon the sure, unvarying place of the Episcopal Church in her life, she was devastated by the changes to the 1929 Book of Common Prayer. Efforts by the church to "modernize" the liturgy by updating language now considered patriarchal and exclusive had resulted in a badly divided membership. The ordination of women to the Episcopal priesthood was another dramatic change, as was the participation of more lay readers in the services. Elizabeth and her sister and many of their friends were among those most unhappy with the changes. Elizabeth became reluctant to go to church on Sunday morning, and whenever Episcopal friends could find a service that used the familiar "Rite I" in the Book of Common Prayer, they took Elizabeth. But it was not the same: she felt turned out of her own home. In the 1930s she had reflected on the loss of meaning in the period of Lent, believing that modern-day practices were but "a pale shadow" of what the season had been intended for. Now, however, the Episcopal Church itself was a pale shadow of what it had been; it was, she believed, in the hands of those who had destroyed its beauty. Without the Church, she said that she was "lost. All the bad things that have happened to me in my life have been made bearable by feeling that the Church was always there and always the same."[28]

In 1976 the Ways and the Lawrences would need all the faith that they could muster because Ann was diagnosed with breast cancer, and the surgeon performing a mastectomy was not able to remove all of the malignancy. She lived for three more years, however, and she lived them fully. Fuzz and Walton and their two children, Blair and Ann, and Chip and his wife, Fran, and their daughter, Evelyn, came more often to see her, and Elizabeth was touched by how much they rallied Ann's spirits. Ann's husband, Warren, and their children were of course more affected than anyone, but Elizabeth was shaken by the realization that her younger sister was dying. As Elizabeth's only sibling, Ann was irreplaceable.

Ann's courage in facing death was monumental: even in bed, she went on taking an interest in everything. Warren enjoyed coming home from work to tell her about the day's events; her children came often to cheer her up with visits by her grandchildren; friends and neighbors dropped by on a daily basis. The minister from St. Peter's, the Reverend Huntington Williams, remembers Ann's fortitude and grace.[29] Elizabeth could hardly bear to talk about Ann's dying, and in most letters, she never mentioned her sister's illness. Ann died February 18, 1980, and a service was held at St. Peter's Episcopal Church.

When Carol Wells realized that Ann had died and wrote to ask if Elizabeth was finding ways to cope with her loss, Elizabeth said that there was nothing that could make any difference now. Ann's death was a "final" blow, against which she had no defense. When Warren remarried, he brought his wife, Mary Alexander Way, and her teenage son to live in his house. Warren's children accepted their father's new life and welcomed Mary and her family into the fold. Elizabeth followed suit; she had always liked Warren, she liked Mary, and she wanted to help make it as "easy" as possible for the children. But the two houses now were separated by the changes, and Elizabeth struggled to live alone. She was very frail and ate very little, but she continued to find pleasure in daytime sherry and evening bourbon, as she had done all of her life. She was also taking medications for her painful arthritis: "Darvon is my friend," she said. Her loneliness was in her voice. The year after her sister's death, Elizabeth conceded, "My main trouble is *anno domini.*"[30]

In May of 1984 Fuzz and her family came for Aunt's eightieth birthday, and she was glad to see them. She checked with Fran and Chip to make sure that they would carry out her wishes concerning her papers. She had already sent many boxes to her archivist at Northwestern State University; they were to take others there. Elizabeth also asked Chip to destroy her letters from Mr. Krippendorf; after her death, when Chip and Fran brought boxes of personal letters home, they found Carl Krippendorf's letters and did as Aunt had instructed. Of course, one wonders why Elizabeth allowed all the other letters to be kept, and left instructions for these to be destroyed, but there is no evidence at all that their relationship was anything other than that of two old friends who loved one another (which Carl's wife and granddaughter knew). Perhaps Elizabeth was afraid that someone reading Mr. Krippendorf's letters might make false assumptions about a "romantic" relationship. Or perhaps Elizabeth wanted to be secretive, leaving her biographer and her readers guessing.

In late summer of 1983, Elizabeth faced up to her situation: "I have slowly & painfully come to the conclusion that I can't live in this house and garden much longer, and I must start getting it ready to sell, & looking for an apartment. I have tried very hard to make a go of it for the children's sake."[31] Her niece persuaded her to move to Annapolis, and Elizabeth agreed. She was proud of the fact that she had found a buyer for the house herself, convinced that he had bought it "for the garden."[32]

When cleaning out the last of her boxes of papers, she came upon her small notebooks of poetry. One of her poems, probably written in the 1930s, after Nana's death, must have seemed especially poignant.

> The light was fading when I closed the gate,
> And crossed the lawn and stood before the door.
> The door was open, so I did not hesitate.
> Inside the night had come. I called before
> I went into the darkness. You were there
> And heard me, and replied. Without a light
> I stumbled through the hall and found the stair.

And slowly climbed the first and second flight.
I thought: my life is in this house—how can
It be removed? And having mounted all
The steps, I turned and called your name and ran
Downstairs. There I found the now well-lighted hall
Already unfamiliar; I heard
Strange voices, and came into a new
Arrangement of the rooms. My eyes still blurred
With undried tears, I searched the house for you.

The Annapolis region had family connections: Nana had married a Baltimore man, Frank Bradenbaugh, and Bessie (and her brother Frank) had been born there. Elizabeth looked forward to seeing an old friend, Louise Wilson, who had known the Atterburys. Fuzz tried various means of helping Aunt to live on her own—first with her family, then in her own apartment. Sometimes Fuzz would take a picnic lunch and they would go out to the small country church, St. James Episcopal, in nearby Lothian, and eat sitting on the steps near the cemetery. But Lawrence continued to fail, and the doctor recommended that she be moved into a nursing home. She died on St. Barnabas Day, June 11, 1985, a few weeks after her eighty-first birthday, and less than a year after she had closed the garden gate in North Carolina. She had wanted to be buried in the cemetery at St. James's, and on a rainy afternoon, Fuzz and Walton stood there alone with the minister to participate in the service from the Book of Common Prayer. The Burial of the Dead service had sounded beautiful to Elizabeth when she heard it read for her father and her mother and sister, and it had not changed. For her the words "Earth to earth" had always had a personal meaning.

Epilogue ❧

IN THE LAST YEAR of her life, Elizabeth wrote in a shaky hand these notes:

> Time does not pass in one continuous movement, but in a series of spurts. Like the minute hand of an electric clock, it stands still for awhile, before moving ahead. Then, in one terrifying moment, it rushes past. It rushed past me one morning in Church. It was the first Sunday after Chip went to the Virginia Episcopal School. I looked up from my hymnal to see the cross being carried by a boy, as small as Chip was the first time he had served as Crucifer. Until that moment time had stood still while the children were children, as in one moment, all those years, from the time Chip first carried the cross.[1]

She continued to look back, more certain that the happiness of "the children" had been the right reason to move to Charlotte. They had felt blessed. Fuzz remembered, "Aunt's house was a haven and a refuge from the outside world."[2]

As of this writing, members of the Garden Conservancy and the Southern Garden History Society are working with the present owner of the Lawrence home, Lindie Wilson, and friends of the project to develop a plan to preserve the Elizabeth Lawrence house and garden. If successful, they may ensure the survival of one small haven and refuge in a new century so far dominated by technology and wars. The dream of the secret garden continues.

Notes

Dates given in brackets have been assigned by the author.

Abbreviations

AL	Ann Lawrence
APB	Ann Preston Bridgers
APBP Duke	Ann Preston Bridgers Papers, Rare Book, Manuscript, and Special Collections Library, Duke University, Durham, NC
CD	Caroline Dormon
DC NSUL	Dormon Collection, Northwestern State University of Louisiana, Cammie G. Henry Research Center
EL	Elizabeth Lawrence
EW	Eudora Welty
EWC	Eudora Welty Collection, Mississippi Department of Archives and History
LFP	Lawrence Family Papers (privately held)
LWC NSUL	Lawrence and Way Collections, Northwestern State University of Louisiana, Cammie G. Henry Research Center
RD	Ruth Dormon

Chapter One

1. Elizabeth Lawrence, *A Southern Garden* (Chapel Hill: University of North Carolina Press, 1942), 137.

2. Details about the Lawrence family are based on hundreds of letters, journals, histories, and newspaper articles, which are cited in endnotes. For background I have also done extensive research in an effort to establish authenticity. For example, records show that it did rain on Lawrence's Barnard commencement, that temperatures in New York City were in the sixties, and that it was a day in the eighties when she arrived home to North Carolina; Lawrence's garden notes include bloom dates.

3. To help readers keep up with who these people are, here is a brief guide to some of the principals. Lawrence's mother is Elizabeth Bradenbaugh Lawrence, called "Bessie." Her maternal grandmother is Ann Beard Neal Bradenbaugh, called "Nannie" by family and friends, and "Nana" by her grandchildren. Her maternal great-grandmother is Elizabeth Lewis Neal, called "Grandma." Her great-grandfather is Joseph B. Neal, called "Grandpa." On her father's side, Lawrence's grandfather, Rob-

ert de Treville Lawrence, is called "Grandpa-pa." Her paternal grandmother is Eliza Atkinson Lawrence, called "Grandma-ma." Lawrence's maternal relatives lived in Parkersburg, West Virginia; her father's family in Marietta, Georgia.

4. I am indebted to historian Philip Wayne Sturm, Ohio Valley College, for information about the James Neal family.

5. Henry Peden, a Maryland genealogist, traced for me the Bradenbaugh line.

6. Nannie Bradenbaugh's letters to her children (August 1 and August 14,1887), LFP.

7. EL to APB (1934), APBP Duke.

8. EL to Dannye Romine (Powell), private letter (June 14, 1976).

9. Interview with Elizabeth Sammel Lutz.

10. EL to Carol Wells (January 7, 1980), LWC NSUL.

11. Elizabeth Lawrence to Eudora Welty (November 16, 1942), EWC.

12. Articles from the *Atlanta Constitution* in the Lawrence Collection, Sturgis Library, Kennesaw State University.

13. The name Kennesaw may be a corruption of the word Canasoga, dating from DeSoto's travels, and pronounced "Gansagi" by the Cherokees, who were living in northern Georgia when the Spanish explorer came up from Florida in 1540. Sarah Blackwell Gober Temple, *The First Hundred Years: A Short History of Cobb County, in Georgia* (Cobb County, GA: Cobb Landmarks and Historical Society, 1997), 2–3.

14. Helen Lawrence Vander Horst was at the time of my interview living in her grandparents' house on Whitlock Avenue in Marietta, where I met her. She gave me a vivid sense of family life, and she told me that her Uncle Sam Lawrence had met Bessie Bradenbaugh and her mother at a party at a local hotel. I used her memories, those of other family members, research in the Marietta History Museum, and hundreds of letters from Bradenbaugh to Lawrence to create these scenes in Marietta.

15. In this chapter I have made extensive use of courtship letters from Elizabeth "Bessie" Bradenbaugh to Samuel Lawrence, written between 1897 and 1903. I have read several hundred letters that she wrote to him, and one that he wrote to her (the only one I discovered), which are in the Lawrence Family Papers. The letters I quote from in this chapter are in that collection.

Chapter Two

1. These occasions are reported in contemporary newspaper articles in Parkersburg and Marietta, which I read in the Lawrence Family Papers.

2. My understanding of Hamlet, North Carolina, is based on a locally published history, *More Than A Memory* (Hamlet, NC, 1997), which I read on loan from the Hamlet Public Library.

3. EL to APB [ca. 1935?], APBP Duke.

4. W. R. "Rocky" Bonsal of Southern Pines, NC, has been helpful in sharing what he knows about his grandfather's and his father's friendship and business relations with Sam Lawrence.

5. EL to APB [ca. 1935?], APBP Duke.

6. Interview with Dixon "Dick" Riddle, Garysburg, NC.

7. Frances Roye of Jackson, Northampton County, NC, made it possible for me to meet people and identify sites both in my visit to Garysburg and in many exchanges of e-mails.

8. EL to Burke Davis [ca. 1980?], LWC NSUL.

9. Interview with Willie Long Jr., Roanoke Rapids, NC.

10. Roy Strong included this poem in *A Celebration of Gardens* (Portland, OR: Sagapress/Timber Press, 1991), 183. It is identified as "Quoted by Elizabeth Lawrence in *A Southern Garden*."

11. EL to Caroline Dormon (October 15, 1957), DC NSUL.

12. EL recorded all of these activities in her journal, which many years later she gave to Willie Long's son, William G. Long, who placed it in the library at Longview.

13. Belgium was invaded by the Germans at the beginning of World War I, and there was widespread sympathy in America for the Belgian people.

14. Catherine Robinson of Garysburg, NC, showed me her collection of playbills, commencement programs, ladies' club booklets, and other memorabilia. T. G. "Sonny Boy" Joyner and Dixon Riddle knew the Lawrences and helped identify names and places for me.

15. Elizabeth Lawrence, "Elizabeth Lawrence—An Autobiography," in *A Garden of One's Own: Writings of Elizabeth Lawrence,* eds. Barbara Scott and Bobby J. Ward (Chapel Hill: UNC Press, 1997). 3. Reprinted from *Herbertia* (September 1943).

Chapter Three

1. Lawrence's company was called "Sand and Gravel" and "Stone and Gravel" at different times in its history.

2. Margaret Supplee Smith and Emily Herring Wilson, *North Carolina Women: Making History* (Chapel Hill: UNC Press, 1999), 251.

3. *History of the Raleigh Woman's Club*, NC State Library.

4. Frances Ranney Bottum to EL (January 17, 1956), LWC NSUL.

5. Martha Stoops, *The Heritage: The Education of Women at St. Mary's College, Raleigh, North Carolina, 1842–1982* (Raleigh, NC: St. Mary's College, 1984), 88.

6. Smith and Wilson, *North Carolina Women*, 94. The authors observe that the painting "provides strong visual evidence for the merging of Christian piety and feminine compliance as part of the North Carolina female school experience."

7. EL to Carol Wells, LWC NSUL.

8. Uncatalogued papers, LWC NSUL.

9. Stoops, *The Heritage,* 185.

10. Frances Bottum to Elizabeth Lawrence, LWC NSUL.

11. Interview with Laura Chase McDermott. Her mother, Mary Wiatt Yarborough Chase, died in 1995 at age ninety-one.

12. "Crushes" and "smashes" have been written about extensively as part of the culture in girls' schools and women's colleges in the late nineteenth and early twentieth centuries. The work that has become a standard in the field is *Disorderly Conduct: Visions of Gender in Victorian America*, by Carroll Smith-Rosenberg (New York: Knopf, 1985). More recently, Lois W. Banner has described the practices of same-sex relationships at Vassar and Barnard in her biography *Intertwined Lives: Margaret Mead, Ruth Benedict, and Their Circle* (New York: Knopf, 2003).

13. Glenda Elizabeth Gilmore, *Gender & Jim Crow: Women and the Politics of White Supremacy in North Carolina, 1896–1920* (Chapel Hill: UNC Press, 1996), 205.

14. Smith and Wilson, *North Carolina Women*, 218.

15. Stoop, *The Heritage*, 231.

16. Elizabeth Lawrence, " 'Cullud Folks,' " *St. Mary's School Bulletin* (1926), 22–34.

17. Lawrence once said that when she got to college, she thought that she could tell the stories she had heard as if they were her own. When she began writing for publication, however, she became overly sensitive about using even a phrase that she had acquired from someone else.

18. The Dean of Women of Columbia University had spoken at St. Mary's during Lawrence's junior year, when perhaps St. John talked with her about changes at Barnard.

19. EL unpublished essay [1979], LFP.

Chapter Four

1. EL unpublished essay [1979], LFP.

2. Nancy Milford's biography, *Savage Beauty* (New York: Random House, 2001), details the life and times of Edna St. Vincent Millay.

3. Ibid, 89.

4. Frederick Lewis Allen, *Only Yesterday: An Informal History of the Nineteen-Twenties* (New York: Harper, 1931), 17.

5. EL to APB [late 1930s?], APBP Duke. "Afternoon on a Hill" first appeared in 1917 in *Poetry* magazine.

6. Untitled typescript (n.d.), LFP.

7. In addition to reading college publications in the Barnard College archives, I have read books about Barnard College that include Virginia Gildersleeve, *Many A Good Crusade* (New York: Macmillan, 1954); Amy Loveman, Frederica Barach and Marjorie M. Mayer, *Varied Harvest: A Miscellany of Writing by Barnard College Women* (New York: Putnam, 1953); Annie Nathan Meyer, *It's Been Fun* (New York: Henry Schuman, 1951); Marian Churchill White, *A History of Barnard College* (New York: Columbia University Press, 1954); and Lois W. Banner, *Intertwined Lives: Margaret Mead, Ruth Benedict, and Their Circle* (New York: Knopf, 2003). Height's rejection by Barnard appears in Height's *Open Wide the Freedom Gates: A Memoir* (New York: Public Affairs, 2003).

8. The letters to EL from Grace St. John (September 12, 1922) and Samuel Lawrence (September 25, 1922) are in the Lawrence Family Papers.

9. Sam Lawrence to EL (fall, 1922), LFP.

10. My interview with Elizabeth Lazer Hormon took place in her New York City apartment.

11. For my understanding of student activities at Barnard, I consulted materials housed in the Barnard Archives, including programs of the Greek Games, student publications, memoirs, scrapbooks, and photographs. I was especially helped in this research by Jane Lowenthal and Donald Glassman, Barnard archivists. Of special interest is *Greek Games: An Organization for Festivals*, compiled by Mary P. O'Donnell and Lelia Marion Finan (New York: Barnes, 1932).

12. EL to APB (1949), APBP Duke.

13. Untitled typed transcript, LFP.

14. EL to Carol Wells (n.d.), LWC NSUL.

15. Both Elizabeth and Ann Lawrence, who lived for a time in New York City, got to know Mr. Bracelen, who liked them both.

16. Elizabeth Lazer Hormon interview.

17. Sam Lawrence to EL, LFP.

18. Lawrence's contemporaries would probably have recognized this quote from Rose Fyleman's popular "There Are Fairies at the Bottom of Our Garden." The little girl steals away to become the Queen of the Fairies at night.

Chapter Five

1. "Love itself shall slumber on" is a manuscript I discovered among the papers of Ann Preston Bridgers in the Rare Book, Manuscript and Special Collections Library of Duke University. The scene at the Kit-Kat Ball is as she described it in "Love itself."

2. This letter has not turned up in any of Lawrence's papers.

3. EL to APB (May 30, 1939), APBP Duke.

Chapter Six

1. EL's autobiographical statement appeared in *Herbertia* (1943). Reprinted in Barbara Scott and Bobby J. Ward, eds., *A Garden of One's Own: Writings of Elizabeth Lawrence* (Chapel Hill: UNC Press, 1997), 3–4.

2. Readers may wonder how I came by my weather and bloom information: weather charts (by time and place) can be ordered over the Internet from the U.S. government; Lawrence's bloom dates for the Raleigh garden are listed in the back of *A Southern Garden.*

3. "desolate": Frances Ranney Bottum to EL (January 17, 1956), LWC NSUL.

4. Sam Lawrence to EL (1922), LFP.

5. Interview with Marion Turner Hubbard.

6. EL to APB (1930s), APBP Duke.

7. EL to Burke Davis [ca. 1979?], LWC NSUL.

8. "I've dreamt in my life dreams that have stayed with me ever after, and changed my ideas; they've gone through and through me, like wine through water, and altered the colour of my mind." Emily Bronte, *Wuthering Heights,* chapter 9.

9. Nana Bradenbaugh to EL (1926), LFP.

10. It is possible that EL placed this paper in her journal in later years, but if she did, I think the placement would also suggest that she connected Peter Burnaugh with her trip abroad.

11. EL's travel journal and letters home are part of the privately held Lawrence Family Papers. Because they are mostly undated and are unavailable to researchers, I will not take up space with notes each time I refer to them in the text.

12. Described in her garden column (Charlotte *Observer,* November 5, 1967).

Chapter Seven

1. Elizabeth Lawrence, *Gardens in Winter* (New York: Harper and Brothers, 1961).

2. Untitled typed transcript, LFP.

3. Zetta Lowery to EL (January 3, 1932), LFP.

4. Elizabeth Lawrence, *Through the Garden Gate,* ed. Bill Neal (Chapel Hill: UNC Press, 1990), 119.

5. APB to Emily Bridgers (March 21, 1928), APBP Duke.

6. Interviews with Elizabeth Daniels Squire and C. B. Squire.

7. APB to EL [1942?], LFP.

8. EL to APB (1946), APBP Duke.

9. APB to EL [1942?], LFP.

Chapter Eight

1. EL to APB (1934), APBP Duke. I discovered "Piper, pipe a song" while looking through a folder marked "Anonymous," filed there because the manuscript does not contain the author's name—but without question, it is the work of Elizabeth Lawrence. All quotations and paraphrases from "Piper, pipe a song" are taken from this manuscript.

2. EL's article about a historic garden in Columbia, South Carolina. Charlotte *Observer,* April 2, 1967.

Chapter Nine

1. "Elizabeth Remembers Malbone," unpublished manuscript, LFP.

2. Harriet Lawrence Huston was published in *Poetry* in 1923 and won awards from the Poetry Society of Georgia. *Looking up the Stairwell,* with illustrations by the author, was privately printed in 1968 by The Ashantilly Press in Darien, Georgia. I am indebted to her sons, Alexander Cann and Samuel Cann of Savannah, Georgia, for talking with me about their mother.

3. Lawrence's poetry notebooks belong to the Lawrence Family Papers.

4. Additional notes, LWC NSUL. In the note that began, "Why I write," Elizabeth Lawrence scribbled these sentences, which are very difficult to read but nevertheless worth considering as a fragment of her thoughts: "It is as if the pleasure to me were found whole & instant, like new chicks, and need only to be put side by side to make

a literate [?] pattern. Sometimes a shell is missing because I can't find it. Then emotion [?] must be put in its place, that is sad but it cannot be helped. I always continue the research, and presumably, if ever, years after, the missing piece is found." It is not clear, at least not to me, whether she is talking about the pleasure of writing poetry or of doing research for her garden writing.

5. The texts of Lawrence's poems come from her poetry collections in the Lawrence Family Papers.

Chapter Ten

1. J. P. Pillsbury, "Landscape Architecture and Professional Training in North Carolina," unpublished history, 1938. North Carolina State University Library.

2. Introduction by Allen Lacy in EL, *Gardening for Love* (Durham, NC: Duke University Press, 1987), 18.

3. In a biographical survey of 255 women who contributed to the development of landscape architecture in the United States, there is not a single entry for a Southern woman. Catherine R. Brown, *Women and the Land: A Biographical Survey of Women Who Have Contributed to the Development of Landscape Architecture in the United States* (Baltimore: Morgan State University Built Environment Studies, 1979).

4. For a history of the Cambridge School see Dorothy May Anderson, *Women, Design, and the Cambridge School* (West Lafayette, IN: PDA Publishers, 1980). The Lowthorpe School merged with the Rhode Island School of Design in 1945, becoming a department within the Division of Planning. Some of the school's records are housed in the RISD archives. Each of these two schools has a rather complicated history, involving name changes and alliances with other institutions, and the records of alumnae, while impressive, appear incomplete.

5. Jane Brown, *Beatrix: The Gardening Life of Beatrix Jones Farrand 1872–1959* (New York: Viking, 1995), 1. Brown's books on eminent British gardeners have earned her the reputation as the best garden biographer.

6. The U.S. Department of the Interior has undertaken to document the names and contributions of landscape architects in *Pioneers of American Landscape Design: An Encyclopedia.* Volume II is now being prepared. In seeking to recognize leaders in the field who have been little known beyond their own locales, the editors are finding more women than have been included in any other reference work.

7. *Beatrix,* 143.

8. Ibid., 189.

9. EL to APB [1935?], APBP Duke.

10. Judith B. Tankard, *The Gardens of Ellen Biddle Shipman* (New York: Sagapress, 1996), 5. Sponsored by the Library of American Landscape History, the project to document as much as possible of Shipman's career was well served by Tankard's careful research and interpretation.

11. Ibid., 4.

12. The Dewitt and Ralph Hanes house and garden were given to Wake Forest Uni-

versity, where the residence is used as the president's house. In 1997, the garden was restored by the current occupants, Laura and Tom Hearn, in memory of her parents.

13. Searches have not turned up any business records that would indicate what Lawrence was paid for her work, either as Busbee's assistant or on her own. It seems likely that some commissions included modest fees, and that other work, such as landscaping the grounds for the Little Theatre, was done for no pay.

14. EL to APB (August 10, 1934), APB Duke.

Chapter Eleven

1. Much of this information comes from Virginia Tuttle Clayton, *The Once & Future Gardener: Gardening Writing from the Golden Age of Magazines 1900–1940* (Boston: David R. Godine, 2000).

2. This overview of magazines comes from 1932 issues of *Better Homes and Gardens;* the image of the happy housewife becomes even more popularized in the years after World War II.

3. EL to APB (November 16, 1939), APBP Duke.

4. EL to APB (July 23, 1937), APBP Duke.

5. Barbara Scott and Bobby J. Ward have tracked down Lawrence's articles in garden bulletins and magazines and have edited them in *A Garden of One's Own* (Chapel Hill: UNC Press, 1997).

6. EL to APB (1962), APBP Duke.

7. Today's gardeners searching the Internet can find more than three thousand sources of information on torenias, including a "Torenia Membership Page," where one of the favorite topics—discussed from coast to coast—is harvesting torenia seeds.

Chapter Twelve

1. Several months after the publication of *A Southern Garden,* Lawrence received a letter from the Authors Guild inviting her to become a member. "Now, as we are in a war," the letter explained, "the usual formalities required by our Membership Committee are being temporarily waived." The need for authors to have the services of such an organization and for the Guild to have new members was "particularly acute" (June 30, 1942), LFP.

2. Joseph Mitchell to EL (July 1, 1955), LFP.

3. Charlotte Hilton Green, "Elizabeth Lawrence and Her Southern Garden" (Raleigh, NC: *News & Observer,* May 3, 1942).

4. EL to APB (July 23, 1937), APBP Duke.

5. University of North Carolina Press Papers, Southern Historical Collection, Wilson Library, University of North Carolina, Chapel Hill, NC.

6. Ibid.

7. Letters between EL and UNC Press, LFP.

8. January 22, 1946, LFP.

9. LWC NSUL, 1949.

10. Lifetime sales of *A Southern Garden* are estimated at about thirty thousand by David Perry, current editor in chief at UNC Press.

11. *Herbertia,* vol. 9, 1942.

12. Lester Rowntree, undated review in *Golden Gardens,* LFP.

Chapter Thirteen

1. EL's letter to APB included lines from Shakespeare's sonnet 66, which begins, "Tir'd with all these, for restful death I cry: As, to behold desert a beggar born." It is about the need to tend those who are in want, and ends, "Tir'd with all these, from these would I be gone/Save that, to die, I leave my love alone."

2. Interview with Nell Joslin Styron.

Chapter Fourteen

1. AL to EL (August 30, 1926), LFP.

2. Ann Lawrence's letters to her family are in the Lawrence Family Papers.

3. EL to APB [1934?], APBP Duke.

4. Lawrence, *Gardens in Winter,* 158.

5. EL to Emily Bridgers (September 28, 1945), APBP Duke.

6. EL to APB (1940s), APBP Duke.

Chapter Fifteen

1. Interview with Mary Ellen Flood Reese.

2. EL describes all of these scenes in letters to APB, written in the 1930s and 1940s. APBP Duke.

3. EL to APB (1948), APBP Duke.

4. Lawrence, *Through the Garden Gate,* unnumbered page 1.

5. Interviews with Hannah Withers and Hannah Withers Craighill.

6. EL to Carol Wells (August 1980), LWC NSUL.

7. Isabelle Bowen Henderson to EL (1950), LFP.

8. Lawrence, *Through the Garden Gate,* unnumbered page 1.

9. Unpublished notes, "Additions" to LWC NSUL.

10. "Whispery" is a word that several friends agreed described Elizabeth's voice. The "hush before she spoke" was remembered by Mr. Krippendorf's granddaughter, Mary Clark Stambaugh.

11. EL to CD (August 19, 1954), DC NSUL.

12. EL to APB (early 1960s), APBP Duke.

13. Interview with the Reverend John Harris.

Chapter Sixteen

1. Rosan Adams to EL [1957], LWC NSUL.

2. Interview with Mary Clark Stambaugh.

3. Lawrence, *The Little Bulbs* (Durham, NC: Duke University Press, 1986), 2. All

quotations from the Lawrence-Krippendorf letters are from this edition of *The Little Bulbs*.

4. Carol H. Woodward to EL (October 10, 1955), LWC NSUL.

5. APB to EL (1955), LFP.

6. Records of sales of *The Little Bulbs* are incomplete at best. Lawrence during her lifetime never had a satisfactory record herself. In a letter to Lawrence (dated January 16, 1963), Ruth E. Buchan of The American Garden Guild Book Club said that the Guild itself sold 17,000 copies of *The Little Bulbs* as an alternate selection. Lawrence's royalties from this and other sales were modest, according to her letters. She instigated litigation against the publisher, who had not given her an accurate count of books published and sold, and although she won the suit, her award was only about a thousand dollars. LFP.

7. Anna Sheets to EL (September 18, 1957), LWC NSUL.

8. Miscellaneous letter, LFP.

9. The Cincinnati Nature Center in Milford, Ohio, sponsors a large number of programs. The lodge where the Krippendorfs lived is open to the public, as well as the nature trails and an education center.

10. Lawrence, *Lob's Wood,* 5.

11. Sydney Eddison has written about her gardening friendship with Mary Stambaugh in *A Patchwork Garden* (New York: Henry Holt, 1990).

12. Interview with Mary Clark Stambaugh.

13. Emily Herring Wilson, ed., *Two Gardeners: Katharine S. White and Elizabeth Lawrence—A Friendship in Letters* (Boston: Beacon Press, 2002), 210–211.

14. Elizabeth Lawrence, *Through the Garden Gate,* ed. Bill Neal (Chapel Hill: UNC Press, 1990), 235.

15. Allen Lacy, "Introduction," in EL, *The Little Bulbs* (Durham, NC: Duke University Press, 1986), xii.

16. Pamela Harper, dust-jacket copy for EL, *The Little Bulbs* (Durham, NC: Duke University Press, 1986).

Chapter Seventeen

1. The reasons that she was let go *are* obscure. I spoke with a man who had worked on the newspaper at the time, but he said that he had no memory of Elizabeth Lawrence. Lawrence was considered a freelance writer rather than a full-time employee of the newspaper, which makes finding an "official" record very unlikely. Nevertheless, among old-timers in Charlotte, the feeling persists that Lawrence was the best garden writer the newspaper would ever have.

2. *Silent Spring* is considered to be one of a handful of books that changed the course of history, and the creation of public and private agencies to protect the environment is a testament to its importance. The most comprehensive account of Carson's personal achievement is in Linda Lear's definitive biography, *Rachel Carson: Witness for Nature* (Boston: Henry Holt and Co., 1997). Carson never married, lived with her mother, and

wrote at home. In these and other ways, Carson and Lawrence had parallel lives, though Carson's fame is unmatched.

3. Vita Sackville-West, *In Your Garden Again* (London: Michael Joseph, 1953), 21.

Chapter Eighteen

1. Bobby J. Ward to Emily Herring Wilson (October 20, 2003).

2. Lawrence's "Rock Gardens in Winter" appears in that indispensable collection of her garden articles, *A Garden of One's Own*, edited by Barbara Scott and Bobby J. Ward.

3. See Karen Cole, "A Chapter in Southern Garden Writing: The Correspondence of Elizabeth Lawrence and Caroline Dormon," *Journal of the New England Garden Society*, vol. 9 (Fall 2001), 45–54.

4. Staci Catron-Sullivan, director of the Cherokee Garden Library, has made a list of more than 350 plants that Lawrence named in *Gardens in Winter*.

5. EL to CD [1959?], DC NSUL.

6. EL to CD (1961), DC NSUL.

7. Ibid.

8. Carol H. Woodward, "New Garden Book Crop," *New York Times* (April 23, 1961).

9. EL to CD (n.d.), DC NSUL.

10. EL to B. Y. Morrison, DC NSUL.

11. Katharine S. White, *Onward and Upward in the Garden* (Boston: Beacon Press, 2002), 134–135.

12. Lawrence and Dormon sometimes made critical remarks about particular people in their field, and Dormon especially cautioned Lawrence to destroy such letters of hers.

Chapter Nineteen

1. Edith R. Eddleman, "Foreword," in EL, *A Southern Garden* (Chapel Hill, NC: UNC Press, 1991), xix; "A Friendly Society," *Gardening for Love* (Durham, NC: Duke University Press, 1987), 23; Carl Starker quoted in EL, *Gardens in Winter*, 21.

2. *The Little Bulbs* (Durham, NC: Duke University Press, 1986), 3, 5.

3. RD to EL [first letter, 1942], LWC NSUL.

4. EL to RD (postmarked November 25, 1943), DC NSUL.

5. RD to EL [first letter, 1942], LWC NSUL.

6. RD to EL (April 6, 1943), LWC NSUL.

7. RD to EL (October 30, 1942), LWC NSUL.

8. Bobby Ward points out that this is the spider brake fern from eastern Asia, not native to the U.S. "But it has escaped and naturalized, and it's interesting that Ruth knew that fact. Such knowledge!"

9. RD to EL [1943], LWC NSUL.

10. RD to EL (April 6, 1943), LWC NSUL.

11. RD to EL (September 17, 1944), LWC NSUL.

12. RD to EL (October 24, 1943), LWC NSUL.

13. RD to EL (April 6, 1943), LWC NSUL.

14. EL to APB (October 1944), APBP Duke.

15. RD to EL (November 8, 1944), LWC NSUL.

16. EL to CD (postmarked March 12, 1947), DC NSUL.

17. LWC NSUL. I have read several hundred letters between Lawrence and Dormon, which are in their archives at NSUL, as well as letters to Lawrence from Inez Conger of Arcadia, Louisiana. My strongest impressions of Caroline Dormon, however, were formed in the two visits I made to Briarwood, near Saline, Louisiana, where Richard and Jessie Johnson were incomparable hosts. Before she died, Dormon chose Richard to continue her work, and he and his wife are in residence at Briarwood, which is now open to the public as the Caroline Dormon Nature Preserve.

18. EL to Carol Wells [1977], LWC NSUL.

19. Fran Holman, *"The Gift of the Wild Things": The Life of Caroline Dormon* (Lafayette, LA: University of Southwestern Louisiana, 1990), 12.

20. Marcia Myers Bonta, *American Women Afield: Writings by Pioneering Women Naturalists* (College Station: Texas A&M University Press, 1995), 216.

21. David Snell, "The Green World of Carrie Dormon," *Smithsonian* (February 1972), 28–33.

22. CD to EL (March 8, 1960), LWC NSUL.

23. CD to EL [1960], LWC NSUL.

24. CD to EL (March 8, 1960), DC NSUL.

25. CD to EL (September 1, 1960), LWC NSUL.

26. CD to EL (June 5, 1962), LWC NSUL.

27. CD to EL (August 15, 1962), LWC NSUL.

28. EL to CD [1961], DC NSUL.

29. CD to EL (February 15, 1959), DC NSUL.

30. EL to CD (October 15, 1957), DC NSUL.

31. EL to Carol Wells (1977), LWC NSUL.

32. EL to CD (1959), DC NSUL.

33. EL to APB (postmarked July 23, 1937), APBP Duke.

34. Being a Fellow of the Royal Horticultural Society meant no more than applying for membership and paying dues, but nevertheless, Hunt and Lawrence were proud to belong.

35. William Lanier Hunt to EL (September 19, 1955), LWC NSUL.

36. Interview with Ken Moore.

37. William Lanier Hunt, "Introduction," in EL, *A Southern Garden* (Chapel Hill: UNC Press, 1967), xxii.

38. EL to Beverly Seaton [June 1978], courtesy of Beverly Seaton.

39. Flora Ann Bynum, one of the founders of the Southern Garden History Society, paid tribute to William Lanier Hunt in the Fall 1996 issue of *Magnolia,* the bulletin of the Southern Garden History Society. Bynum, who also knew Elizabeth Lawrence, is

perhaps Hunt's successor in helping to sustain garden organizations. Bynum lives and gardens in Old Salem in Winston-Salem, North Carolina.

40. Some of the information about Lamm comes from Bobby J. Ward, "A Garden of One's Own: Letters from Elizabeth Lawrence to a Friend," *The Trillium*, vol. 2, no. 4, September 1992. *The Trillium* is the newsletter of the Piedmont Chapter of the American Rock Garden Society. I also read many of the letters Ward refers to in his article when I visited Lamm's daughter, Linda Lamm Lawson, in Wilmington, North Carolina.

41. Ibid.

42. Mary Kratt, *A Bird in the House* (Charlotte, NC: Wing Haven Foundation, 1991).

43. Interview with Cama Merritt.

44. Interview with John Jamison.

Chapter Twenty

1. All quotations from the letters are from *Two Gardeners: Katharine S. White and Elizabeth Lawrence—A Friendship in Letters,* ed. Emily Herring Wilson (Boston: Beacon Press, 2002).

2. Interview with Elizabeth Way Rogers.

3. *The New York Times* (June 2, 2002).

Chapter Twenty-one

1. "History of The Jackson Garden Club January 15, 1931, to June 1, 1952," by Mrs. C. W. Welty, unpublished, EWC.

2. Susan Haltom, "'Where Wonder Expresses Itself': Flowers in Eudora Welty's Garden and Prose," *The Influence of Women on the Southern Landscape* (Winston-Salem, NC: Old Salem, Inc., 1997), 133. Haltom, who is the project director for the restoration of the Welty garden, interviewed Eudora Welty in the late 1980s. The garden was opened to the public in April, 2004. The Welty House is also undergoing a restoration, and both house and garden are under the supervision of the Museum Division of the Mississippi Department of Archives and History. Both Haltom and Mary Alice White, director of the Welty House, were welcoming when I visited the properties in the summer of 2003.

3. Chestina A. Welty to EL (June 22, 1942), LFP.

4. *A Southern Garden*, 98.

5. EL to APB (1944), LFP.

6. EL to EW (postmarked December 1, 1944), EWC. Reprinted with permission of Elizabeth Welty Thompson and Mary Alice Welty White.

7. EL to Emmy and Bill Maxwell (December 21, 1987), William Maxwell Collection, Rare Book & Special Collections Library, University of Illinois at Urbana-Champaign. Reprinted with permission of Elizabeth Welty Thompson and Mary

Alice Welty White. The visit may have occurred early in 1953, when Eudora Welty was away for an extended period, and Elizabeth Lawrence's own mother was well enough for her to feel freer to travel. It could have occurred as late as the spring of 1962, however, when Lawrence was lecturing in Oxford, Mississippi, and Welty was teaching for a semester at Smith College. Eudora Welty told Susan Haltom that Lawrence had "accepted Chestina's hospitality and ended up staying six weeks." (Haltom, 134–135). Haltom and I agree, however, that after thirty or forty years had passed, Welty's memory of the visit was probably unclear, and it most likely was of a much shorter duration.

8. EW to EL (February 18, 1954), LFP.

9. EL to EW (postmarked February 24, 1954), EWC.

10. EW to Lodwick Hartley (November 18, 1954), Lodwick Hartley Papers, Southern Historical Collection, University of North Carolina at Chapel Hill.

11. Unpublished notes, LWC NSUL.

12. Eudora Welty, "A Note on Jane Austen," *Shenandoah* (Spring 1969), vol. XX, no. 3, 4.

13. Eudora Welty, *One Writer's Beginnings* (Cambridge, MA: Harvard University Press, 1984), 20.

14. EL to APB [1963], APBP Duke.

15. EW to EL (February 18, 1954), LFP.

16. EL to EW (postmarked November 16, 1942), EWC.

17. EW to EL [1942?], LFP.

18. Ibid.

19. EW to EL [1943], APBP Duke.

20. Lawrence, *Gardening for Love,* 65–66.

21. EW to EL [1943], APBP Duke.

22. EW to EL [1942], LFP.

23. EL to EW (postmarked November 16, 1942), EWC.

24. EL to EW [1943], APBP Duke.

25. EL to EW [September 11, 1944], APBP Duke.

26. Lawrence, *Gardening for Love,* 35.

27. *Gardening for Love,* 36–37; "The Wanderers" first appeared in Welty's collection of stories *The Golden Apples,* published in 1949.

28. EW to EL [1973], LFP.

29. EW to EL [1942], EWC.

30. EL to EW (postmarked November 16, 1942), EWC.

31. Suzanne Marrs, *One Writer's Imagination* (Baton Rouge, LA: Louisiana State University Press, 2002), 86–88.

32. EL to EW (postmarked May 27, 1946), EWC.

33. EL to EW (postmarked April 16, 1969), EWC.

34. EL to APB [April 14, 1963], APBP Duke.

35. Ibid.

36. EW to EL (April 5, 1982), LFP.

Chapter Twenty-two

1. Elizabeth Lawrence, *Gardening for Love: The Market Bulletins,* ed. Allen Lacy (Durham: Duke University Press, 1987), 15–16, 24. All subsequent quotations, unless otherwise noted, are from this book.

2. "Friends in Oregon," *Pacific Horticulture* (Summer, 1977); "Letters from the West," *Pacific Horticulture* (Spring, 1978); "Brothers of the Spade," *Pacific Horticulture* (Winter, 1981).

3. Burke Davis to EL [1981?], LWC NSUL. In 1997 Davis was one of the first people I talked with about Lawrence, and his personal respect and affection for her, his knowledge of gardening, and his intellect and wit have brightened my research.

4. Interview with Joanne Ferguson. Ferguson's memories and her files concerning her contact with Lawrence have been essential to my understanding of the history of the market bulletin book.

5. Lacy describes his work with the manuscript in his introduction to *Gardening for Love.*

6. Welty's and Perenyi's praise appears on the back dust jacket of *Gardening for Love*; Henry Mitchell's review, "Cultivating Love-Tangle and Bouncing Bet," in the "Bookworld" section of *The Washington Post* (April 26, 1987); Rosemary Verey's review in *Hortus: A Gardening Journal* (Autumn 1987, no. 3); and Stanley Kunitz's "Friendly Strangers Bearing Flowers" in *The New York Times Book Review* (October 11, 1987).

7. Stanley Kunitz, "Friendly Strangers Bearing Flowers," *The New York Times Book Review* (October 11, 1987).

8. Interview with Hannah Withers.

9. EL to B. Y. Morrison, LWC NSUL.

10. The American Rock Garden Society (ARGS) was founded in 1934, and in 1994 the name was changed to the North American Rock Garden Society (NARGS). There are thirty-five NARGS chapters, including five in Canada. Programs, exhibitions, and plant exchanges are promoted through national and regional meetings, and the *Bulletin of the ARGS* is a valuable source of information. An early "Bible" of rock gardeners is said to be *The English Rock Garden,* by Reginald Farrer, published in 1919. The "American Bible of Rock Gardening" is considered to be H. Lincoln Foster's *Rock Gardening: A Guide to Growing Alpines and Other Wildflowers in the American Garden,* published by Houghton Mifflin in 1968.

11. Elizabeth Lawrence, *A Rock Garden in the South* (Durham: Duke University, 1990), 9–10. This section on designing a rock garden first appeared in the unpublished manuscript "A Southern Bouquet," which Lawrence sent to Emily Bridgers and Ann Preston Bridgers. It is included in the Ann Preston Bridgers Collection, Special Collections, Perkins Library, Duke University.

12. Unpublished notes, LWC NSUL.

13. The letters from Scribner's and the University of Oklahoma Press are in LWC NSUL.

14. Laura Louise Foster, editor, *Bulletin of the ARGS,* to EL (November 26, 1984), LWC NSUL.

15. Interview with Nancy Goodwin.

16. *A Rock Garden in the South,* 120.

17. Once again, Bobby J. Ward has explained another aspect of Lawrence's gardening knowledge.

Chapter Twenty-three

1. EL to APB (1964), APBP Duke.

2. Interview with Catchy Tanner.

3. Interview with Ruth Long Williams.

4. Interview with Caroline Long Tillett.

5. Caroline Long Tillett has a small collection of letters between her father and Elizabeth Lawrence. Lawrence also left copies of a few of her letters to Willie in her archives.

6. EL to Willie Long (December 3, 1965), LWC NSUL.

7. EL to an unnamed correspondent. I discovered this comment about Willie Long in an undated, unmailed letter in the Lawrence Family Papers. It may have been written to Rose Wharton, a friend of Linda Lamm's in Wilson, North Carolina, and a frequent correspondent. They often discussed poetry, which was the subject of this letter that alludes to Long.

8. EL to APB (1960s), APBP Duke.

9. Except for a letter to Katharine White, which I have cited, I have found no mention of Ann Bridgers' death in Lawrence's letters, nor did anyone I interviewed remember Lawrence's having told them.

10. EL to John Tyler (1967), LWC NSUL.

11. Interviews with John "Jack" Tyler at Hope Plantation, and with Caroline Long Tillett at Longview.

12. Gertrude Jekyll, *On Gardening* (New York: Charles Scribner's Sons, 1964). Reissued as *The Gardener's Essential Gertrude Jekyll* (Boston: David R. Godine Publisher, 1986).

13. Interview with Hannah Withers. EL described the iris and Foxtail lilies and the weald in a letter to Linda Lamm, reprinted in "A Garden of One's Own," by Bobby J. Ward, *The Trillium* (September 1992), vol. 2, no. 4.

14. "Very English, Very Kentish," Charlotte *Observer,* May 4, 1969.

15. Interview with Anne and Hugh Boyer.

16. EL to Ruth Long Williams (postmarked September 11, 1978). The Lawrence-Davis correspondence is in LWC NSUL.

17. I visited Mabel Harkness in Penn Yan, New York, in the summer of 2002, when this interview took place, over a delightful lunch and a tour of the gardens with Mrs. Harkness's gardener, Jill Byington. Mrs. Harkness was especially pleased to show me

the guest book that Elizabeth Lawrence had signed on May 13, 1972. Mr. Harkness had died in 1980.

18. Interview with Betsy Clebsch. Clebsch is the author of books on salvias, published by Timber Press. Her clump of *Iris unguicularis,* which Lawrence gave her in the 1970s, still blooms in her garden in La Honda, California.

19. EL to Carol Wells (1979), LWC NSUL.

20. Interview with Dr. Herbert Hechenbleikner.

21. Interview with Rosa Hicks. Curry and John Jamison and I visited with Rosa Hicks and her husband and sons in their mountain home near Banner Elk, North Carolina, and returned with plants she had freshly dug for our gardens.

22. Interview with Jamie Stemple.

23. EL to Carol Wells [1979], LWC NSUL.

24. Interview with Pamela Harper.

25. Pamela Harper to EL (April 6, 1978), LWC NSUL. Thanks to Pam Harper for sending me copies of Lawrence's letters to her.

26. A seminar in honor of Elizabeth Lawrence was held September 25–27, 1991, at the North Carolina State University Arboretum (the present-day J. C. Raulston Arboretum) in Raleigh. Harper gave the opening address, "Elizabeth and Her Garden." Others on the program were Nancy Goodwin, Edith Eddleman, William Lanier Hunt, Douglas Ruhren, J. C. Raulston, and Allen Lacy.

27. EL to Carol Wells [1979], LWC NSUL.

28. EL to "Mr. Aldrich" [1983], LWC NSUL.

29. Interview with Huntington Williams.

30. EL to Carol Wells (1982), LWC NSUL.

31. Ibid.

32. This proved not to be the case, and the garden fell into neglect, before it was bought by Lindie Wilson in 1986. A master gardener, Wilson estimates that the garden still contains about 60 percent of Lawrence's plant materials.

Epilogue

1. Unpublished notes, LWC NSUL.

2. Interview with Elizabeth Way Rogers.

Acknowledgments

When I began research for this biography more than a decade ago, I wrote on a card two things Elizabeth Lawrence had said, and stuck the card above my computer screen. The first was advice to gardeners: "Never let yourself be deceived about the work." The other was something she said about herself: "I want to be surrounded by loving friends, and still be left all to myself." Both of her statements have helped me to complete this biography.

In endnotes to this manuscript I have mentioned some individuals for their particular help, and I would like to name here others who contributed to my understanding. I begin by thanking three of Lawrence's family members—her niece, Elizabeth Way Rogers; her nephew, Warren Way III; and his wife, Fran. They have talked with me many times over many years, and they gave me complete access to family papers that are still in their possession. I also thank Blair, Ann, and Evelyn for sharing their memories of "Aunt." Although we had never met before I called them up and told them that I wanted to write about their aunt, they accepted me with amazing generosity and understanding, and they never put any restraints upon my freedom to write the biography as I thought it should be written. Elizabeth and Warren have also been accepting of my need to refer to them in the manuscript as their aunt did— "Fuzz" and "Chip"—despite the choice they made when they went off to college that they were to be called by their adult names. Among other family members, I am especially indebted to Robert de Treville Lawrence and his wife, Howard. Treville deposited books and papers in a Lawrence family archive at Kennesaw State University in Marietta, Georgia, which I have used extensively. In addition, I have been treated to wonderful Southern hospitality by Howard and Treville, first in Atlanta, and later in Marietta, where they both grew up.

One of the first people to encourage me was Dannye Romine Powell of Charlotte, North Carolina, whom I have known as a poet and whom Lawrence knew as a friend. It was Dannye who, listening to me and LeAnne Howe talk, observed that LeAnne had an intuitive sense of my undertaking to write about a private life. Burke Davis and his wife, Judy, who live in Greensboro, gave me many hours of conversation about Lawrence, whom they met in the late 1970s.

As a writer, gardener, and correspondent, Davis meant a great deal to Lawrence in the last four or five years of her life.

Several gardeners have been my guardian angels. Pamela Harper has been a source of information and inspiration. Bobby J. Ward has quickly answered many e-mails, read chapters, and tried to teach me something about botanical nomenclature. Lindie Wilson, who now owns the Charlotte house and garden that belonged to Lawrence, is another gifted gardener, and a gracious hostess. Mr. Krippendorf's granddaughter, Mary Clark Stambaugh, met me at the Cincinnati Nature Center to show me around her grandparents' former estate. As I am writing this, snowdrops from her grandfather's woods are blooming in mine. I don't know how many insights I claim as my own that probably rightly belong to John Jamison. He has been generous in sharing his understanding of Elizabeth Lawrence, whom he met in 1976 and claims as his gardening mentor, and he drove me to meet Rosa Hicks near Banner Elk, one of Lawrence's favorite market bulletin correspondents. I will never forget my visits with John and his wife, Curry, in their beautiful mountaintop house and garden in Asheville.

In Parkersburg, West Virginia, Dr. Robert Sams invited me and Fran Way to spend the night in his house, which once belonged to Lawrence's maternal great-grandparents. Kathleen Ziff not only helped make arrangements for our visit to Parkersburg but remains, we hope, a new friend. Caroline Long Tillett's taking me to see Longview plantation and Garysburg, North Carolina, and my conversations with her and her brothers contributed greatly to my understanding of the importance of the Long family in Lawrence's life.

Librarians and archivists have also been essential. In Natchitoches, Louisiana, at Northwestern State University of Louisiana, Lawrence's large archive is well maintained by Mary Linn Wernet and her staff. Many of Lawrence's papers are there because an alert archivist working at the time, Carol Wells, began a correspondence with Elizabeth Lawrence. Virginia Daley, a Duke librarian, told me that I would find letters from Elizabeth Lawrence in the Ann Bridgers Papers in Duke's Special Collections. It is a great cache of letters, and I have made extensive use of them. I again thank the staff at Wake Forest University, especially Elen Knott; Robert Anthony at the North Carolina Collection, and the staff at the Southern Historical Collection at the University of North Carolina at Chapel Hill; Janie Morris at the Rare Book, Manuscript, and Special Collections Library at Duke University; the alumnae office and librarians at St. Mary's School in Raleigh, North Carolina; Liz Triplett at the Richmond (Virginia) Public Library; the staff of the Parkersburg and Wood

County (West Virginia) Public Library; the Hamlet (North Carolina) Public Library; Dr. Ray Swick, at the Blennerhassett Island Historical State Park near Parkersburg, West Virginia; the staff at the Enoch Pratt Free Library in Baltimore, Maryland; the staff at the Kennesaw State University Library and the Marietta (Georgia) History Museum; and the late Jane Lowenthal, archivist at Barnard College, and the current Barnard archivist, Donald Glassman. Garden Web site searches have yielded information in a timely fashion, and I have enjoyed corresponding via e-mail with gardeners, especially Barbara van Achterberg.

Thanks to Michael Campion, Parish Register, St. James Episcopal Church, Marietta, Georgia; the staff of St. Peter's Episcopal Church, Parkersburg, West Virginia; office volunteers at Christ Episcopal Church, Raleigh, North Carolina; for research assistance—Frances Roye, who helped in Halifax and Northampton Counties; Bobby Moser in Hamlet, North Carolina, and Beth Paschal, Zoe Webster, Sis Cheshire, Ruth Long Williams, and Jim Clark in Raleigh, North Carolina; gardeners who shared their understanding of Lawrence—Genie White, Elizabeth Pringle, Mary Francis Chapman, Ann Armstrong, Lucille McKee, Loyce McKenzie, and Frances Inglis; Dr. John G. Seeley; Beverly Seaton; Susan Haltom, Suzanne Marrs, and Mary Alice Welty White, whom I met at the Welty House in Jackson, Mississippi; for discussions of Lawrence's garden designs—Lisa Briley at Historic Hope Foundation, and Hugh and Ann Boyer in Morganton, North Carolina; Dia Steiger at Wing Haven Garden and Bird Sanctuary in Charlotte; the late Betty Leighton, my first reader; Yvonne Rush and her staff; and the incomparable Sunny Wu, who understands me and my computer.

On my longest days what encouraged me was the comments by an anonymous panelist who read my unsuccessful 1998–99 N.E.H. Fellowship application and found my proposal to write a biography of Elizabeth Lawrence "refreshing."

Thanks to "loving friends": Heather Ross Miller, Doris Betts, Linda Lear, Paula Duggan, LeAnne Howe, Mary Dalton, Susan Faust, Dudley Shearburn, Florence Gatten, Gail McNeill, Phyllis Ammons, Vida Cox, Phil Archer, Penny Niven, Isabel Zuber, Elizabeth Phillips, Eva Rodtwitt, Laura Hearn, and the members of St. Anne's Episcopal Church.

Without my sister and brother-in-law, Janis Herring Eberhardt and her husband, Glynn Eberhardt, who have looked after our mother since our father died, I would not have been able to remain in North Carolina to work on this book. I also thank Mama, Sarah Allen Herring, for teaching us to love to read and to write. My family at home has always encouraged me, and I thank them all—Ed, Eddie, Laurie, Sally, Carolyn, and Julie. Just as I was finishing the manuscript, Eddie's and Laurie's baby, "Buddy," was born, happily diverting my attention from the book and the garden.

Authors and manuscripts depend upon the kindness and capabilities of editors, publicists, and publishers, and I have been especially fortunate to have the best: thanks to Joanne Wyckoff, Brian Halley, Kathy Daneman, and Lisa Sacks at Beacon Press. Before sending the manuscript off to Beacon, I could not have had a better reader than Catherine Bishir in Raleigh, North Carolina, who lives not far from Elizabeth Lawrence's old neighborhood.

Finally, I would like to especially thank the members of my writing group, "Bio Brio": Michele Gillespie, Anna Rubino, and Margaret "Peggy" Supplee Smith, whose good cheer and critical reading around my kitchen table saw me through. Now, it's on to your manuscripts.

This book is dedicated to Jane "Tita" Hatcher, the friend of my life. We began playing basketball together in the eighth grade, and now we garden.

Index

"EL" in the index refers to Elizabeth Lawrence.

Index

Index